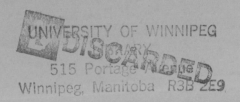

O WONDROUS SINGER!

Other books by Barbara Marinacci: LEADING LADIES

THEY CAME FROM ITALY

O WONDROUS SINGER!

An Introduction to Walt Whitman

BARBARA MARINACCI

ILLUSTRATED

DODD, MEAD & COMPANY

NEW YORK

Grateful acknowledgment is made for permission to quote:

From "Ode to Walt Whitman" from BURNING CITY by Stephen Vincent Benét. Copyright 1935 by Stephen Vincent Benét. Copyright renewed © 1963 by Thomas C. Benét, Stephanie B. Mahin and Rachel Benét Lewis. Reprinted by permission of Brandt & Brandt.

From "A Pact" by Ezra Pound from PERSONAE. Copyright 1926 by Ezra Pound. Reprinted by permission of New Directions Publishing Corporation.

Library of Congress Catalog Card Number: 77-105292

Printed in the United States of America
by The Cornwall Press, Inc., Cornwall, N.Y.

For my mother . . .

In the swamp in secluded recesses,
A shy and hidden bird is warbling a song.

Solitary the thrush,
The hermit withdrawn to himself, avoiding the settlements,
Sings by himself a song.

Song of the bleeding throat,
Death's outlet song of life, (for well dear brother I know,
If thou wast not granted to sing thou would'st surely die.)

          •   •   •

Sing on, sing on you gray-brown bird,
Sing from the swamps, the recesses, pour your chant from the bushes,
Limitless out of the dusk, out of the cedars and pines.

Sing on dearest brother, warble your reedy song,
Loud human song, with voice of uttermost woe.

O liquid and free and tender!
O wild and loose to my soul—O wondrous singer!

        —from *"When Lilacs Last in the Dooryard Bloom'd"*

CONTENTS

ILLUSTRATIONS

Following page 116

The poet's parents
Walt Whitman's birthplace
Walter Whitman, Jr., in the early 1840s
"The Carpenter" portrait of Whitman
Manuscript page from the first edition of *Leaves of Grass*
"Christ Picture" of Whitman
Whitman as "The Laborer"
Author's revisions on a page in *Leaves of Grass*
Whitman during the Civil War
Edwin Forbes' drawing of Whitman at mess call
Anne Gilchrist
Whitman in 1872
Walt's first letter to Anne Gilchrist
Whitman in the late 1860s or early 1870s
Caricature of Whitman by Max Beerbohm
"Butterfly Portrait" of Whitman
Drawing of the poet's home in Camden, New Jersey
Whitman in his mid-sixties
Painting of Whitman by John W. Alexander
Two interior views of the home in Camden

Allons! whoever you are come travel with me!
Traveling with me you find what never tires.

I

WHOEVER YOU ARE COME TRAVEL
WITH ME!

(A Prologue)

This is the story of a man and a book of poems. The man is Walt Whitman; his book is *Leaves of Grass.*

For thirty-five years, like a slow-growing embryo, the book developed within its creator. The first edition of *Leaves of Grass* was published in 1855, and in the nearly forty ensuing years Whitman was to change his book many times. As his own life unfolded, he added new poems while altering and rearranging the others. Altogether, *Leaves of Grass* appeared in nine different versions.

Walt Whitman thought of his book as the offspring of both his soul and his body. Indeed, he and his *Leaves* are so intertwined that they cannot readily be separated. Into his poems the poet put his childhood, his manhood, and his old age. And he told not only of himself as he was, but of what he wished to be, as a self-styled prototype of the new American nationality. He recorded experiences and dreams, loves and loathings, urges and pleasures, convictions and doubts, fears and exaltations—all the while extolling the rich and dramatic history of the United States, describing its vibrant and varied present, and boldly prophesying its

1

future. Many of Whitman's poems also voiced his lifelong concern over mortality; through his poetry he achieved both resolution and the immortality he desired.

It was a busy and paradoxical age, this nineteenth-century America. Idealism countered materialism; science had begun to supersede traditional religious faith; humanitarian goals were ever-threatened by selfish motives. All men, it was argued, should be free and equal—but in reality some enjoyed special advantages, either inherited or seized. Regional interests fought angrily against each other and against national solidarity, while the nation itself battled to expand its dominion. Within the American character gross crudity and outlandish prudery coexisted uneasily, and citizens of the new republic expressed both a chauvinistic bravado and a cultural inferiority complex. Walt Whitman's *Leaves of Grass* reflected the many conflicts within people and their society.

In their own time, both the man and his book ostensibly failed. Whitman was ignored, or ridiculed and even reviled because of the poems he wrote and published. *Leaves of Grass* had few admirers—or buyers. Yet today, a century later, Walt Whitman is probably America's most famous poet: certainly the most pervasively influential. And *Leaves of Grass*, the lifework to which he was doggedly devoted, now takes a proud place among the great classics of world literature.

Whitman is often called "the Poet of Democracy." His was the first authentically American voice to celebrate in poetry the average or common man, the equal man, engendered by the Declaration of Independence and the Revolutionary War.

In his characteristically democratic way, Walt Whitman welcomed every reader to join him in his own journey upon life's open road, which stretched from birth to death and then beyond—across the nation, over the entire face of the earth, and deep into the human heart.

> Allons! whoever you are come travel with me!
> Traveling with me you find what never tires.

"Whoever you are": it is a phrase that recurs throughout *Leaves of Grass*. Whoever you are, Walt Whitman wrote his book especially for you. And whoever you are, whatever interests your mind and arouses your feelings, you will probably find many things in Whitman's poetry to intrigue, delight, and move you—particularly if you are patient and diligent, and know how and where to look for them.

No other American literary work has offered such an astonishingly colorful and detailed panorama of scenery and people. Here are the geographies of all regions, states, and territories. A great cast of hundreds includes poets and presidents, doctors and draymen, slaves and stevedores, lawyers and lunatics, ministers and mothers, blacksmiths and beggars, soldiers and sopranos, Indians and immigrants, farmers and fishermen, merchants and miners, trappers and trollops, captains and carpenters, clerks and corpses.

In *Leaves of Grass* too there are many nonhuman characters which convey the poet's meanings: birds—some that sing and some that soar; flowers—lilacs blooming at the backdoor in the springtime and wild irises growing shyly in the woods; stars in the night sky beaming down messages; the deep ocean ever churning, ever tossing waves upon the shore; and the grass—always the grass—covering the earth with its immortal and renewing green.

Usually readers first encounter a few selections from Whitman's poetry in anthologies. They may never pursue Whitman further into *Leaves of Grass* itself, where one gains a far better appreciation of the breadth and complexity of his literary visions and actual accomplishments. Indeed, when Whitman's poetry is read in isolated snatches, the private man and his public significance can scarcely begin to be grasped. Moreover, many readers need to accustom themselves through prolonged exposure to Whitman's special phraseology and to his unique "free verse" style—an unprecedented and startling innovation in his own era—in order to appreciate him and his works.

Some of Walt Whitman's poems are easily understood at a first reading; others take longer, needing the properly receptive mood or the reader's familiarity with aspects of Whitman's personal life or of the time in which he lived. Still other poems, or parts of poems, may prove tantalizingly elusive after many readings, even to Whitman experts.

Those who think of Whitman only as a poet may be surprised to learn of his frequent ventures into prose: prefaces to new editions of his book, essays about democracy, literary criticism, journalistic articles, mood pieces, and reminiscences. Much of this prose has bearing, directly or indirectly, on *Leaves of Grass* as a whole or in part.

There are enough poems—some four hundred—in Whitman's volume to provide material to interest many different kinds of people. *Leaves of Grass* is for the young and the old—and anyone in between. It is for both man and woman, youthful student and learned scholar, patriot and revolutionist, American and non-American, ascetic and sensualist, naturalist and city-lover, idealist and realist. It is for those who cherish the past, for those who grasp and relish each fleeting moment of the present hour, and for those who anticipate and build toward the future.

Not every poem in *Leaves of Grass* will please. Some poems are obviously superior to others; also, a poem that fascinates and stirs one reader may fail entirely to interest or affect another. But as one reads along, aided by a basic knowledge of the poet and his period, almost every Whitman poem will make a particular contribution, large or small, to the multicolored, many-textured fabric of the book—and increase one's understanding of its author.

Is the effort of reading *Leaves of Grass* worthwhile? It has proven so to many people during the past hundred years. Now and then, too, some highly sensitive reader responds to Whitman's artistic sorcery by experiencing a revelation of the human condition that truly transforms his life. Robert Louis Stevenson said that his world was tumbled upside down when as a young man he first read *Leaves of Grass*.

Each new generation after Whitman has been able to find its own special concerns in *Leaves of Grass,* making it perennially appealing to young Americans—much as Walt Whitman had predicted.

> See, projected through time,
> For me an audience interminable.
>
> With firm and regular step they wend, they never stop,

Successions of men, Americanos, a hundred millions,
One generation playing its part and passing on,
Another generation playing its part and passing on in its turn,
With faces turn'd sideways or backward towards me to listen,
With eyes retrospective towards me.

Here, then, is an introduction to Walt Whitman and his master-work, *Leaves of Grass*.

There was a child went forth every day,
And the first object he look'd upon,
that object he became,
And that object became part of him for
the day or a certain part of the day,
Or for many years or stretching cycles of years.

II

A CHILD WENT FORTH

(1819-1833)

Poets cannot choose their birth times or birthplaces. Like every-one else, they are born when and where they are born. The genesis of a poet begins in his childhood, which is his introduction to the world. What he early sees and hears, smells, tastes, and touches—and the things he feels inside along with his thoughts about them —newly and sharply experienced, make deep and lasting impres-sions. In a poet's youth the patterns and directions of his thinking and feeling are set, and he gathers in the vital images which eventually will emerge in his poetry.

If Walt Whitman had been able to select the time and place of his own origin, he would surely have chosen the very sites of his early upbringing. They provided the perfect combination of elements to suit him: the countryside, that pristine realm of na-ture; the city, domain of civilized man; and the United States in the early nineteenth century, when the young American democ-racy was growing into a vigorous maturity.

Walter Whitman, Jr. was born on May 31, 1819, in the farming community of West Hills on New York's Long Island. West Hills, now part of Huntington township, lay some thirty miles east of

New York City. But so different in appearance and spirit was it from that fast-growing, crowded metropolis that it could almost have been separated by a thousand miles or a hundred years.

Most West Hills people, like the Whitmans, still earned their livings from the soil, though some families were attached to the sea, as sailors or fishermen, while others pursued the useful rural or small-town trades of shopkeeping, blacksmithing, and cobbling. Their farms and villages were not yet joined by railway to the nearby big city. When adventuresome Long Islanders, out of need or curiosity, went to New York, they set out by horse and wagon and then crossed the East River by ferryboat to Manhattan Island.

First and basically, Walt Whitman was a child of nature. His earliest years had a simple, natural, and untainted aspect which was almost aboriginal. No wonder Walt later called Long Island "Paumanok," using its Indian name.

The island, over a hundred miles long, provided many contrasts in scenery. From a hilltop in West Hills, close to the north shore, one could see in all directions. Eastward were the dense woods of pine and scrub oak where Indians had dwelled long ago, lush meadows where sheep and cattle grazed, and out on the island's far tip, rocky ledges where sea birds camped. To the north was the Sound, and from its snug harbors fishing boats set out daily, their white sails catching wind and sunlight. The seacoast lay southward, facing the Atlantic Ocean but in many places protected from its pounding surf by long sand bars; on its beaches a small barefoot boy could happily wander, smelling the briny air and picking up treasures from the ocean's depths cast upon the shore. Far to the west, on the very rim of Long Island, was the town of Brooklyn; across the river were the brown and gray streets and buildings of New York.

The Whitman family lived in a sturdy farmhouse built by Walt's father, Walter Whitman, Sr., an experienced carpenter now working at farming. Jesse was the first child born to him and his wife, Louisa; Walter, Jr.—always called "Walt"—was the second; then came Mary.

Those who knew Walt in those years probably never expected him to amount to much in the world. Large for his age, slow-moving, slow-talking, he had an air of dreamy indolence. He said little, preferring to listen; even while he gazed at the storyteller, there was an abstracted look in his blue-gray, heavy-lidded eyes. Instructions, reminders, and sermonizing were usually lost on him. Was he forgetful or dull-witted or downright lazy? Perhaps he thought that the world's plain daily business would take care of itself.

Walt liked to wander outdoors by himself. In the springtime the pungently sweet scent from his mother's lilac bush lured him down the back steps and out into nature. There a boy would be a brash intruder unless he walked quietly, reverently sending his spirit to join the secret fellowship of all existences, living and non-living.

To know, to understand, some object or creature he saw, Walt seemed to envelop and inhabit it, to "become" it, for a while—as if his spirit temporarily left his body to invade something not himself, absorbing its very essence, then carrying back some sensation or wisdom that would stay forever in a recess of his mind, for future usage. Like an ever-porous sponge, Walt took in a million sensory details of nature experienced on farm, in woods, in meadowland, and at the shore line. Much later, in the autobiographical poem "There Was a Child Went Forth," Whitman would recall and describe this absorptive phenomenon in his childhood:

> There was a child went forth every day,
> And the first object he look'd upon, that object he became,
> And that object became part of him for the day or a certain part of
>   the day,
> Or for many years or stretching cycles of years.
>
> The early lilacs became part of this child,
> And grass and white and red morning-glories, and white and red
>   clover, and the song of the phoebe-bird,
> And the Third-month lambs and the sow's pink-faint litter, and the
>   mare's foal and the cow's calf,
> And the noisy brood of the barnyard or by the mire of the pond-
>   side,
> And the fish suspending themselves so curiously below there, and
>   the beautiful curious liquid,

And the water-plants with their graceful flat heads, all became part of him.

Truly, the natural world which Walt was discovering held countless wonders both vast and tiny. And one by one he took them in, making storage places for each. Long after his childhood, having found a way to express this awareness of the marvels surrounding him, Whitman fashioned a famous credo in nature's behalf:

> I believe a leaf of grass is no less than the journey-work of the
> stars,
> And the pismire is equally perfect, and a grain of sand, and the
> egg of a wren,
> And the tree-toad is a chef-d'oeuvre for the highest,
> And the running blackberry would adorn the parlors of heaven,
> And the narrowest hinge in my hand puts to scorn all machinery,
> And the cow crunching with depress'd head surpasses any statue,
> And a mouse is miracle enough to stagger sextillions of infidels.

The people of Walt Whitman's childhood were just as important as nature in influencing his future poetry. He had come directly from them, so who and what they were partly determined the person Walt would become. Afterward Walt acknowledged the parental role in shaping his life, both genetically and environmentally:

> His own parents, he that had father'd him and she that had
> conceiv'd him in her womb and birth'd him,
> They gave this child more of themselves than that,
> They gave him afterward every day, they became part of him.

Walt's mother, born Louisa Van Velsor—always to be the deepest emotional attachment of his life—came from Dutch and Welsh backgrounds. Her parents lived only a few miles away at Cold Spring Harbor, so naturally Walt often visited them. His grandmother Naomi, or Amy, was a Quakeress who wore plain garments and a cap and had a gentle manner. Her use of the language traditional with the Friends—"thees," "thous," and "thys," and calling days and months by numerals instead of names—Walt later echoed in his poems.

Walt's maternal grandfather, Cornelius Van Velsor, looked thoroughly Dutch—red-faced, hearty, stockily built—although he was a native American. Besides running a farm, the "Major" kept a stableful of racehorses. Almost every week he drove a wagon all the way to Brooklyn, sometimes even ferrying over to New York, to deliver produce for sale. He often took paying passengers too, and quite probably young Walt sometimes went along to keep him company.

From his Dutch forebears Walt acquired his large, sturdy frame, a ruddy complexion, a liking for cleanliness, and an essential vigor. Walt's particular gift for language may have come from Grandmother Amy's ancestry: the Welsh love the sheer flow of euphonious words.

Walt Whitman's father contributed his full share to the making of the poet. The Long Island Whitmans derived from Zechariah Whitman, an English minister who had come to Connecticut in the seventeenth century. (He was named after the Biblical prophet.) His son Joseph prospered as an early settler on Long Island, and the roots of the clan which he established had grown down and around the island for five generations. But through the years the family's once-sizable homestead had been subdivided among descendants into smaller holdings, many of which were sold. Walter Whitman was finding it hard to support his growing family on the small income earned from what he raised on his farm.

As a young man, Walter had lived for a while in New York City, apprenticed to an uncle who was a carpenter. He had received only a rudimentary education, but he took an avid interest in books and ideas, partly because his own mother, born Hannah Brush, had been a schoolteacher. He was intensely interested in one subject: gaining full equality for the common man. In New York Walter had known and admired the writer Thomas Paine, who, despite his fame and influence during the American Revolution, was being treated as a social outcast because of his supposedly dangerous, politically radical ideas.

Walter Whitman also cherished his connection with the famous Quaker dissenter Elias Hicks, who had been his own father's friend. Hicks believed in the individual's intrinsic right to pursue his own personal yet God-directed "inner light." Although Walter Whitman never belonged to any church or creed, his religious ideas and sympathies were aligned with the Hicksite branch of Quakerism—as were his son Walt's, after him. Walter and Louisa attended Hicks' sermons whenever they could, and once they took young Walt along. The impressionable boy would never forget the hypnotic effect the old man had upon his listeners.

Reflecting upon his origins in his own old age, Walt Whitman declared that his "subterranean tenacity and central bony structure (obstinacy, wilfulness)" were due to his paternal English inheritance. Though not a wholly complimentary tribute, it did define an essential ingredient in Walt's single-minded pursuit of the poet's vocation, despite discouragements, rebuffs, neglect, and poverty. Whitman might have mentioned other possible acquisitions from his English stock: firm dedication to ideas and ideals—philosophical, political, cultural; a liberal turn of mind regarding both religion and politics; an intense interest and pride in national history.

Walt Whitman's preoccupation with education in the wider sense—instructing and inspiring others to new insights and wisdom in their conduct of life—might conceivably be traced to his grandmother Hannah, a strong figure in his boyhood. (Her husband, Jesse Whitman, had died some years before Walt's birth.) And maybe too some of Reverend Zechariah Whitman's religious "calling" passed down to his distant descendant: Walt's poetic sermons frequently concerned religion.

As for the personalities of his parents themselves, Whitman gave them brief word sketches in "There Was a Child Went Forth":

> The mother at home quietly placing the dishes on the supper-table.
> The mother with mild words, clean her cap and gown, a wholesome odor falling off her person and clothes as she walks by . . .

The mother bore an aura of maternal and womanly virtues; from her there flowed a calm, steady, reassuring love. If Walt's mother could never fully comprehend him, she nevertheless accepted him just as he was—as she did all her children, each so different from the others, with his or her own strengths and shortcomings. She seemed to expect or demand nothing from Walt, and he often sought her out, to sit quietly watching her at work or listening while she talked. (As a poet, Walt would usually utter the word "mother" in a fond yet idolizing way. Giant-sized, elemental mother symbols appeared in his poetry, variously as the ocean, death, liberty, the democratic spirit, and the American republic.)

Walt's father was not viewed in retrospect with the same respect, affection, or trust:

> The father, strong, self-sufficient, manly, mean, anger'd, unjust,
> The blow, the quick loud word, the tight bargain, the crafty lure . . .

To Walt the word "father" would never have the same positive meaning as "mother." By temperament Walter Whitman was a perfectionist; he was also moody and easily upset and irritated. His love and approval were often held in abeyance, not freely given or displayed. Frequently he spun dreams of some glory or sudden success; then when his neatly wrought schemes fell apart, perhaps because he had conceived them unrealistically, he took his frustration and disappointment out on his family. (Some biographers have claimed that he was an alcoholic or periodic drunkard.) He perplexed, dismayed, and even terrified his children— until they were old enough to see him as he really was: a single human being whose various grand aspirations had all ended in failure.

Within his childhood home Walt daily experienced opposites in the very natures of his parents, yet these contradictions somehow balanced each other. Walt would early realize that the whole universe pulsated with this same opposition or polarity of things joined in an intimate, eternal bondage: positive and negative, light and darkness, life and death, male and female. The human sphere also abounded in other dichotomies: love and hate, faith and doubt, real and ideal, good and evil, body and soul, self and society. As a poet Walt Whitman would explore and try to define the essential unity of such diametrical forces.

Young Walt especially admired his family's womenfolk: his mother and two grandmothers. He was also impressed with the durable reputation of his father's remarkable grandmother, the widow Sarah Whitman, who had smoked tobacco, cursed like a man, and ridden a horse around the farm while bossing the slaves. Healthy, resilient, physically vigorous, sensible, mothers of large broods, always courageous in adversity, these women took no interest at all in the changing feminine fashions; they had no time for idle gossiping and parlor flirtations and romantic novels. They were women of and for the earth, not "ladies." Their main concerns were their husbands' welfare and the nurturing of their children. To such women Walt Whitman would grant an importance fully equal to, even surpassing, men's. He knew that women would largely determine the quality of America's future citizenry, since it was they who gave birth to children, then looked after their health and inculcated lifetime values.

The women of Walt's childhood were expert storytellers, and some of their tales would be woven into *Leaves of Grass*. From Grandmother Hannah, Walt heard anecdotes of the Revolutionary War, in which the Brushes and the Whitmans had taken active parts. Grandmother Amy told of sea fights and tragedies which her father, a captain, had known about or had even witnessed—such as John Paul Jones' famous encounter with a British ship. Walt would later graphically recount the episode involving the plucky "little captain" in "Song of Myself."

Like all impressionable children before and after him, from this early storytelling Walt learned to admire certain human values—like courage and dedication. Heroes did not drop their weapons or surrender their ships; they bravely fought to the last for a great cause, sometimes snatching it from defeat and oblivion. Inspired by a noble ideal, facing death undaunted, a man became godlike; and though the body might perish in battle, the soul—the mysterious spirit which had propelled him—would surely live on to fight anew. To Whitman as poet, a flag or banner would symbolize this courageous, ideal-affirming propensity of the human soul:

> A spiritual woven signal for all nations, emblem of man elate above
> death,
> Token of all brave captains and all intrepid sailors and mates,
> And all that went down doing their duty . . .

Walt's own mother was barely literate, but she had a wisdom and sensitivity that often escape the sophisticated and well-educated. From her Walt heard stories that often related subtle feelings rather than dramatic deeds. She could hold his attention with a gentle, poignant story from her own girlhood—such as that of the beautiful Indian woman who visited her home one morning, which Walt would retell in "The Sleepers."

> Never before had she seen such wonderful beauty and purity,
> She made her sit on a bench by the jamb of the fireplace, she cook'd
> food for her,
> She had no work to give her, but she gave her remembrance and
> fondness . . .

And when she went away, Louisa felt bereft.

> All the week she thought of her, she watch'd for her many a month,
> She remember'd her many a winter and many a summer,
> But the red squaw never came nor was heard of there again.

From a tale such as this, Walt realized that even a transitory touch, sight, or relationship could leave a permanent memory. In his old age, he would readily acknowledge his immeasurable debt to his mother for "the reality, the simplicity, the transparency" within her very life. "*Leaves of Grass* is the flower of her temperament active in me," he said.

Walt spent only a part of his boyhood in the Long Island countryside. After he was four years old he stayed there with his relatives only on holidays, weekends, and vacations.

Hoping to make a better living as a carpenter, Walter Whitman moved his family to Brooklyn in 1823. The Whitmans already had three children and a fourth, Hannah, was on the way. In Brooklyn new homes and places of business were being built all over town; surely Walter would find plenty of work to do.

Because of its nearness to New York City, Brooklyn was swiftly growing as industries and a thriving commerce expanded. Wharves multiplied along the natural harbor; they sent out local products, took in goods from Europe, and served as exchange centers for manufactures from New England and cotton and tobacco from the South. Now Brooklyn was preparing for the great increase in shipping which would come with the opening of the Erie Canal in 1825, making midwestern America both a source for raw materials and a new market place.

Boatyards hammered out hundreds of new ships: river boats, ferries, and ocean-going vessels, some of them with the new steam engines. Factories already hummed with the newly designed machinery that stitched, wove, stapled, pressed, pounded, sliced, printed. More workers—from interior farmlands and from abroad —arrived, swelling the population and creating a need for houses. And with several ferry lines providing regular service to and from Manhattan, Brooklyn was already advertised as a fine place for a New York businessman to settle his family, away from the congestion, crime, and costly real estate of the big city.

At first the Whitmans rented a house near the waterfront—an exciting location for a boy who was naturally curious about everything. The child went forth now and absorbed the new vistas in the urban world:

> The streets themselves and the façades of houses, and goods in the
> windows,
> Vehicles, teams, the heavy-plank'd wharves, the huge crossing at
> the ferries,
> The village on the highland seen from afar at sunset, the river
> between,
> Shadows, aureola and mist, the light falling on roofs and gables of
> white or brown two miles off . . .

In West Hills Walt had known a natural environment, based on living close to the soil, into which people unobtrusively fitted, at ease with the past, contented with the present. Now, in Brooklyn and New York City, he saw humanity busily constructing a far different future, made possible by democracy and the Industrial Revolution.

In the city too Walt often encountered vivid reminders of his country's history. When he was five years old, General Lafayette, on a visit to the United States, came over to Brooklyn on the Fourth of July to lay a cornerstone for a new public library. Children flocked to the ceremony, eager for a glimpse of the old hero of the Revolutionary War, who had fought at Washington's side. Naturally Walt was among them. When men lifted the youngsters over a trench so that they could stand in front of the crowd, Lafayette himself picked Walt up and gave him a hug and a kiss when he set him down.

Whitman would later find a happy omen in this brief early contact with the past, with an actual, living "antecedent" or "precedent"—one of those people, objects, events, or beliefs that came first and therefore shaped the present and eventually the future. He must have fancied that Lafayette had instinctively selected him as a spokesman-to-be for democracy—a verbal link between the brave and idealistic men who had battled to establish the new American republic that assured the rights of the common man and those future ranks of Americans who surely would need instructions and renewed inspiration from the nation's past.

Walt was six years old when he started his formal schooling. Free public education for everyone was becoming standard in American towns and cities, now that voting rights were being granted to the working class; it was believed that educated people would make better voters.

In the Brooklyn public schools a single teacher, assisted by several older children, gave lessons in reading, writing, arithmetic, and geography to several hundred pupils at once. The learning process involved memorizing and repeating, like a catechism, the teacher's answers to set questions:

TEACHER—My dear children, the intention of this school is to teach
you to be good and useful while in this world—that you may be
happy here and in the world to come. . . . What is the intention
of this school?

CHILDREN—The intention of this school is to teach us to be good
and useful while in this world—that we may be happy here and
in the world to come.

Pupils inclined to be neither good nor "useful" received flog-
gings. Walt must have gotten his fair share—perhaps for day-
dreaming during dull sessions. His ardent pleas in after-years for
the abolition of corporal punishment in schools may well have
been based on unpleasant personal experience with the rod, though
he would have also been upset over the humiliation and pain
suffered by others.

A child with a sensitive, inquisitive, and imaginative intelligence, Walt did not take to this rigid and restrictive form of
schooling. It could hardly demonstrate his subsequent summary
of education's goal. "Its aim is not to give so much book-learning,
but to polish and invigorate the mind—to make it used to thinking
and acting for itself, and to imbue it with a love for knowledge."

Walt, to be sure, was not a precocious scholar. One of his
teachers, when told years later that this former pupil was now
a renowned poet, remembered Walter Whitman, Jr., only as a big,
clumsy, and slovenly boy. "We need never be discouraged over
anyone," he concluded fatuously. Perhaps in some small and
wholly negative way he had been responsible for the rearing of
creative genius, for Walt had been propelled by boredom and
dislike into the bustling city streets, away from the crowded,
spirit-stifling classroom.

Walt loved the open air of the city, where there was so much to
see and hear and smell—and ask about. Builders and craftsmen
paused in their labors to answer Walt's questions, flattered that a
child could be so interested in their work. In these young rambling
days Walt began his mental list of the city's occupations, noting
a thousand details of the activities going on around him, to be
enumerated someday in his "catalogue" poems:

Stone-cutting, shapely trimmings for façades or window or door-
lintels, the mallet, the tooth-chisel, the jib to
protect the thumb,
The calking-iron, the kettle of boiling vault-cement, and the fire
under the kettle,
The cotton-bale, the stevedore's hook, the saw and buck of the
sawyer, the mould of the moulder, the working
knife of the butcher, the ice-saw, and all the work
with ice,
The work and tools of the rigger, grappler, sail-maker, block-
maker . . .

Walt would find nobility in a man's doing his job well and
taking pride and pleasure in his work, whatever it might be. In
democratic America every man could be his own king. The young
nation was becoming powerful because of the energetic drive in
hundreds of thousands of plain people—"average" men who never
before in history had been allowed to govern themselves, or to
advance their fortunes.

Now as the youthful poet-in-training walked through the city
he was gathering impressions to emerge one day in the famous,
exulting chorale of working-class Americans:

I hear America singing, the varied carols I hear,
Those of mechanics, each one singing his as it should be blithe and
strong,
The carpenter singing his as he measures his plank or beam,
The mason singing his as he makes ready for work, or leaves off
work,
The boatman singing what belongs to him in his boat, the deck-
hand singing on the steamboat deck,
The shoemaker singing as he sits on his bench, the hatter singing as
he stands . . .

Already to Walt the city was more than a material structure
built of rocks, bricks, and glass, of cement, wood, and iron. The
men who had aspired, worked, lived, and died there had left
friendly ghosts to communicate with him, their messages to appear in his poems:

You doors and ascending steps! you arches!
You gray stones of interminable pavements! you trodden crossings!
From all that has touch'd you I believe you have imparted to your-
        selves, and now would impart the same secretly
        to me,
From the living and the dead you have peopled your impassive
        surfaces, and the spirits thereof would be evident
        and amicable with me.

The dockworkers made a pet of Walt, and the ferry pilots gave him many a free ride over to Manhattan Island and back. Part of the time he spent below deck, watching a team of six horses plod round and round, turning the axle of the great wheel which churned through the water to move the river ferries, in the years before steam-powered machinery. Machines—those marvelous, man-made innovations—were always to intrigue Walt Whitman.

Yet even more thrilling to him were the vistas spread on all sides of the ferry's deck: sky, water, land, buildings, and wharves. These early back-and-forth river passages began Whitman's life-long passion for ferryboats. In "Crossing Brooklyn Ferry"—one of his masterpieces—Whitman would summon up some of the sights of river and bay which he had first observed when a boy:

The sailors at work in the rigging or out astride the spars,
The round masts, the swinging motion of the hulls, the slender
        serpentine pennants,
The large and small steamers in motion, the pilots in their pilot-
        houses,
The white wake left by the passage, the quick tremulous whirl of
        the wheels,
The flags of all nations, the falling of them at sunset,
The scallop-edged waves in the twilight, the ladled cups, the frolic-
        some crests and glistening,
The stretch afar growing dimmer and dimmer, the gray walls of
        the granite storehouses by the docks,
On the river the shadowy group, the big steam-tug closely flank'd
        on each side by the barges, the hay-boat, the
        belated lighter,

> On the neighboring shore the fires from the foundry chimneys
> burning high and glaringly into the night,
> Casting their flicker of black contrasted with wild red and yellow
> light over the tops of houses, and down into the
> clefts of streets.

Brooklyn and New York provided Walt with many rewarding experiences during his childhood, but they failed to enrich his father. For all his skillful carpentry, Walter Whitman did not acquire a tidy fortune. What money he earned was swiftly spent to support his ever-increasing family. He was really more interested, anyway, in politics and democracy than in acquiring wealth and property. Living in the city at least made it easier for him to talk with like-minded people and to attend lectures and rallies —although time and energy for such activities were scanty in the life of a daily workman and paterfamilias.

Walter Whitman's radical republican opinions were now whetted by his reading of the *Free Inquirer,* a socialist newsletter published by Frances Wright and Robert Dale Owen. Through her articles and public lectures, "Fanny" Wright, a Scotswoman settled in the United States—heroine to both Walter Whitman and Walt—kept telling the American workers that they were the "wage slaves" of the new industrial barons ruling factories, commerce, and transportation. Then, in her little book, *A Few Days in Athens,* Frances Wright popularized the Epicurean philosophy of ancient Greece and Rome with its motto of *carpe diem*—"seize the day." She and other writers encouraged people to shift their religious thinking from the "world hereafter" to the world here and now. Individuals should no longer look to a nebulous afterlife as the ultimate reward or punishment for earthly conduct. All too often religion had been used by tyrants to control the populace. The established social order had usually taught that enjoying life was sinful and that the common man should not reap the fruits of his own labors in the world. But now, with the spread of democracy, the present day, the passing hour, were seized. Whitman in *Leaves of Grass* would extol this mood, this awareness of the time-present as the best time to be alive, to admire what was beautiful and good, to love and be loved:

> This minute that comes to me over the past decillions,
> There is no better than it and now.

In his father's household, through sheer contact rather than conscious tutelage, Walt picked up plenty of ideas that would serve him for a lifetime.

Although he was critical of aspects of the American republic, Walter Whitman was as patriotic and optimistic as his son would be after him. He proudly gave his second group of sons resoundingly American names: George Washington, Thomas Jefferson, and Andrew Jackson Whitman. The national election of 1828 had greatly encouraged him. Andrew Jackson, the first President truly a "man of the people," was elected to office by a whole new phalanx of voters, in a surge of the popular will. The outcome had been frightening and foreboding to those who believed that "democracy" was synonymous with "mob rule." To them, Jackson's stormy tenancy of the White House merely confirmed their fearful opinion. But the conservatives and aristocrats were declining in power and influence; increasingly, that once-scorned word "democracy" appeared in speeches and in print as ambitious politicians appealed to the mass of new voters.

"Old Hickory" Jackson was Walter Whitman's idol, and Walt in turn admired him, cherishing the boyhood memory of having glimpsed him during a visit to Brooklyn. Jackson was unpretentious, forceful to the point of roughness, tuned in to the needs of the common man; a more dedicated, determined, and dogged democrat never existed. He had dismissed ranks of government employees who considered their jobs permanent sinecures granted by birthright and social ranking, initiating the "spoils system." He also demolished the National Bank, which had helped to stabilize the nation's currency but had also used the government's money to expand the holdings of the few men of already established position and property.

In Jackson the liberal tradition stemming from Jefferson found its strongest heir. But in this new age of rapid industrialization, of swift westward expansion, of steamships and railroads, the economic, political, and living conditions were bound to be vastly different from the rural communities of free men which Jefferson had envisaged for America at the time of his presidency. Jackson possessed the third President's confidence in democracy, but he altered and expanded this vision to include the "average" Americans who worked in cities and lived on the frontier.

In the midst of nineteenth-century America's industrial progress and material prosperity, the nation underwent frequent business depressions. At such times the common people, especially the city-dwellers, suffered from unemployment and the scarcity of food. During "boom" years Walter Whitman easily got jobs, but during the economic setbacks, when few people were building anything, he often was out of work. Although his family never experienced real poverty, it sometimes dwelled at its border.

The Whitmans rarely stayed in one place for more than a year, since Walter Whitman customarily bought a house with a mortgage, fixed it up while his family lived in it, then sold it—hopefully at a profit—and moved on. But there were times when they could not meet the mortgage payments and had to leave prematurely.

This impermanence of the Whitman home during Walt's childhood may well have influenced his later philosophy of spiritual migration as expressed in "Song of the Open Road"—which also mirrored the restless movement of his epoch. Traveling, moving along the road, was the American thing:

> Allons! to that which is endless as it was beginningless,
> To undergo much, tramps of days, rests of nights,
> To merge all in the travel they tend to, and the days and nights
>   they tend to,
> Again to merge them in the start of superior journeys,
> To see nothing anywhere but what you may reach it and pass it,
> To conceive no time, however distant, but what you may reach it
>   and pass it,
> To look up or down no road but it stretches and waits for you,
>   however long but it stretches and waits for
>   you . . .

And anyone who wished to venture out upon Whitman's open road should go unencumbered by either material possessions or emotional ties:

You shall not heap up what is call'd riches,
You shall scatter with lavish hand all that you earn or achieve,
You but arrive at the city to which you were destin'd, you hardly
        settle yourself to satisfaction before you are
        call'd by an irresistible call to depart,
You shall be treated to the ironical smiles and mockings of those
        who remain behind you,
What beckonings of love you receive you shall only answer with
        passionate kisses of parting,
You shall not allow the hold of those who spread their reach'd
        hands toward you.

Perhaps another element in Walt's formative years also contributed to his "open road" philosophy: his father's occasionally obvious unhappiness over the restrictions and responsibilities which marriage and parenthood imposed upon him. The compelling need to support a large group of children—finally to number eight (a ninth child had died in infancy)—always took precedence over his philosophizing about democracy and equality and liberty, or promoting particular political programs. Although Walt's sympathies lay with his mother, who was the stable center of the family, the example of his father's frustration must have impressed him sufficiently to make him hesitant ever to marry. Walt's father probably affected Walt's life in far more ways than he ever suspected—or admitted, even to himself.

Walt's formal schooling ended when he was about eleven years old; it was time for him to start adding to the family income and learning a trade. He left school with little regret, since nothing there had ever excited or challenged his mind.

At first Walt worked as an office boy for a firm of lawyers. He sat at a desk and copied papers, or ran errands in Brooklyn or over to New York. One day in Manhattan he saw rich old John Jacob Astor arriving at his mansion, helped from his coach by servants. Swaddled in furs, ancient, decrepit, Astor looked as if life held no joys at all for him. Walt could hardly envy America's wealthiest man. One's life surely would be better spent in doing something nobler for humankind than amassing money for oneself.

By chance, Walt was led closer to his ultimate vocation. Until he worked for the lawyers, he had done little reading other than school texts, the Bible (offered at Sunday school for moral instruction, not for its drama and poetry), and various political tracts and philosophical treatises which lay around his home. No words had sung to him, no stories in books had fed his imagination, conjuring up pictures of sheer beauty or rousing action and deep emotions. He had thought that the worlds he knew outside his door—nature and the city of men—contained enough for him.

Seeing some glimmer of intelligence in Walt, his employers taught him the rudiments of putting sentences together. More important still, he was given a card to the nearby circulating library. There Walt discovered another world, in a wholly different dimension, which would quickly become just as real and vibrant and wonderful as his direct experiences in life itself. Walt's newfound world was made up only of words, but these words were strung together in a way he had never seen before or had ever supposed possible. He was partly reminded of the family storytelling which had enthralled him as a young child. Yet now the words, distilled from the life he knew or from times long ago and far away, were printed: set in type, inked, then pressed upon paper. As he read alone in his room or beneath a tree or down at the seashore, somehow words could summon up magical moods, visions of noble deeds, shimmering romances, exquisite portrayals of people and the earth's wonders.

Walt first read all the stories of *The Arabian Nights,* then moved on to Sir Walter Scott's novels and poetry, feasting his mind with literature reflecting past eras he had known nothing about. And from there, for the rest of his life, in an unceasing self-education, Walt roamed wherever he would in the inexhaustible realm of the world's books: novels and philosophy, poetry and science, drama and history—each having its special fascinations and valuable lessons. Above all writers, though, the poet seemed best able to express what people felt deepest about; by some mysterious, unerring gift the poet could choose the right words and find the melodies to describe life's pleasures and sorrows, its uncertainties and hopes, somehow blending them into designs which gave meaning to human existence.

During this crucial period in his youth when he first discovered the power of language over one's mind and feelings, Walt must have considered becoming a writer himself someday—as most young people, conscious of approaching maturity, mull over a variety of possible future vocations.

After a year or so, Walt saw enough of lawyers' work to know that he was not cut out for a legal career. He then served a brief apprenticeship with a doctor, but realized that the medical profession did not suit him either.

At the age of twelve Walt started work in the printing office of one of his father's favorite newspapers, the *Long Island Patriot* —affectionately called "the Pat." Taught by an old printer named William Hartshorne, Walt quickly took to this new trade. He learned to sort the jumble of type called "pi" and to use the composing stick. He enjoyed handling the metal type, slicing and stacking the crisp paper sheets, and smelling the ever-present printer's ink.

Thus as a "printer's devil" Walt Whitman began his lifelong intimacy with words, type, ink, and paper. By experiencing printing firsthand, he saw that books did not somehow appear miraculously complete and perfect, that newspaper articles were not composed by invisible geniuses, but that the words, formed by the writer's mind, were transcribed by hand, often laboriously, and afterwards altered before they were reproduced on printed pages. He lost some of his awe of the printed word and the published page—and gained thereby. The possibility that he himself might become a writer no longer seemed so remote, especially when the publisher of "the Pat" sometimes let him insert some of his own literary efforts—verses, little stories—in the weekly paper. Putting his thoughts and feelings into words was becoming a habit, even a compulsion, with Walt. In a while, he grew bold enough to send a few pieces to the New York *Mirror*. It made a great moment when he discovered that one was actually accepted and printed up—"on the pretty white paper, in nice type."

A craftsman who took great pride in his work and in passing his skills on to others, Hartshorne made an excellent instructor for Walt—who probably was fondly recalling him long afterwards when he wrote:

> The jour printer with gray head and gaunt jaws works at his case,
> He turns his quid of tobacco while his eyes blurr with the manu-
> script . . .

A well-known character around Brooklyn, Hartshorne always carried a cane, and he wore a wide-brimmed hat—which one day would be a part of Walt's uniform too. Walt was much impressed with the old man's background: he had been a soldier in the Revolutionary War, fighting under Washington's command. Also, as a resident of Philadelphia in earlier days, Hartshorne had seen and heard Washington and Jefferson and others among the nation's "Founding Fathers." So here at close hand was another connection with the past, and Walt took advantage of it, attentively listening while Hartshorne spun out stories of the war long ago—some of which probably entered into *Leaves of Grass*.

On Sundays Hartshorne took the apprentices to the Dutch Reformed Church, a dark, fortress-like building in which the minister expounded upon the wickedness of the world and the various sins of the people inhabiting it. In "A Child's Amaze" Walt would recollect his bafflement over the God who presided over pastor and congregation:

> Silent and amazed even when a little boy,
> I remember I heard the preacher every Sunday put God in his
> statements,
> As contending against some being or influence.

Walt had been raised with the Hicksite belief that life should be lived fully and joyously for itself and not be regarded as a painful ordeal which tested each soul's qualifications to enter heaven. No wonder Walt never became a churchgoer, for he could not accept most of the conventional definitions of God. To him God was a vast and positive force that pervaded the universe, not some petty-minded and cranky deity who fussed over human frailties and failures. Whitman took God's presence in nature and in each individual almost for granted; sometimes he would express it in a way that seemed blasphemous to readers with strictly traditional religious ideas.

> Why should I wish to see God better than this day?
> I see something of God each hour of the twenty-four, and each
> moment then,
> In the faces of men and women I see God, and in my own face in
> the glass,
> I find letters from God dropt in the street, and every one is sign'd
> by God's name,
> And I leave them where they are, for I know that wheresoe'er I go,
> Others will punctually come for ever and ever.

In about 1833 Walt's family left Brooklyn and moved back to Long Island, close to West Hills. Mrs. Whitman was in poor health, and it was hoped that the country atmosphere would improve her. Walt stayed behind, boarding with a family, secure and happy enough in his training for a career in printing, or possibly even journalism.

On frequent visits to his family, Walt renewed his early and easy acquaintance with nature. In the summertime he searched along the beach for gulls' eggs left to warm and hatch in the sun. In winter he poked holes through the thick ice on Great South Bay to spear fat eels for the supper meal.

He would wander off on his own, sometimes for whole days at a time. He liked chatting with the odd, shy, half-breed herdsmen who took charge of a village's cattle and sheep. He also went out to sea on fishing boats. With the fishermen, Walt became a fisherman too. From him there was no condescension, no drawing away from the sights and smells of their work. He wanted to know everything about them, and he asked about their homes and families while working along with them. Later, when considering the tasks and delights of various occupations in "A Song of Joys," Whitman's vivid imaginings of a fisherman's life came basically from his own past experiences.

O the sweetness of the Fifth-month morning upon the water as I
    row just before sunrise toward the buoys,
I pull the wicker pots up slantingly, the dark green lobsters are
    desperate with their claws as I take them out,
    I insert wooden pegs in the joints of their pincers,
I go to all the places one after another, and then row back to
    the shore,
There in a huge kettle of boiling water the lobsters shall be
    boil'd till their color becomes scarlet.

.   .   .

Another time trailing for blue-fish off Paumanok, I stand with
    braced body,
My left foot is on the gunwale, my right arm throws far out the
    coils of slender rope,
In sight around me the quick veering and darting of fifty skiffs,
    my companions.

Walt already greatly admired men who worked outdoors,
whether at sea or in the country or within the city. They often did
rugged and hazardous work; but the sky was their rooftop, their
only real master, and wide vistas spread before their eyes. Though
their thinking was plain and direct, their actions and speech
rough, they were honest, unaffected, and essentially wise. He
would always seek out and enjoy their company.

I am enamour'd of growing out-doors,
Of men that live among cattle or taste of the ocean or woods,
Of the builders and steerers of ships and the wielders of axes and
    mauls, and the drivers of horses,
I can eat and sleep with them week in and week out.

But above all, out on Paumanok, Walt explored the world of
nature around him, often pausing to let its lessons and wonders
flow through him. In the forest, he listened to birds calling to each
other as they sought mates or built nests or prepared to take
flight to other trees in other woods. They seemed to have their
own language, which he tried to learn. How many lands and

rivers or oceans, what different towns and peoples, had they passed over on their airy journeys? Closing his eyes for a moment, Walt imagined that he too had wings for free-soaring travels, to go wherever he wished.

Lying down in a pasture, Walt studied the far-stretching carpet of green grass. Each plant, and each blade of each plant, resembled all the others. There were thousands, even millions of them; yet each was a separate and perfect thing by itself. What was the grass? Did it have some hidden meaning which he might discover someday? Why did it die down in the winter, then reappear in the springtime in a magical resurrection? "All flesh is grass," the Bible said. And were people really like grass—each blade coming from a plant, which was the family, dwelling among a multitude of plants; living and then dying, then living anew, generation following generation, as long ago as when time began, and as far ahead as time could ever go?

Watching the newly born lambs and calves frolic in the meadows, Walt marveled at the way that all creatures renewed their own kind so simply yet miraculously. Surely birth, and the way to birth, was beautifully designed by something or somebody divine—so why should people regard sex as shameful or ugly?

From a lookout knoll Walt's eyes followed a schooner's outward bound passage until its masts disappeared at the watery rim of the visible world. Although he saw it no longer, Walt knew that the ship still existed, still sailed on. Perhaps after the body's death a human soul could be like this now-unseen ship, voyaging over a fathomless ocean to an unknown, distant port.

After supper, Walt might sit outside on the back steps by himself, to gaze up at the night sky. The same bright blue dome he had seen in the daytime was now an overarching black canopy where the stars, as twinkling bright as summer fireflies, slowly spun above his head. Beacons of unearthly, intangible existences, they tantalized Walt. They were uncountable, for there were stars beyond stars, and stars beyond them, burning and whirling, spreading forever into the infinite. Oh, to be able to move among those stars that shone eternities away! How wonderful it would be, when death came to man and animal and plant, if the spirit were released from the bonds of earth to soar out into the vast universe and float among those perfect stars.

And at night, when Walt lay very still in his bed, he could sometimes hear far in the distance the pounding of the ocean's waves against the shore, one after the other, as if seeking something. At times they came in fast and furiously, at other times slowly and gently, never with exactly the same sound or measure, but always coming, then falling like a giant maternal pulse or heartbeat upon the body of the land. To Walt the sea was both comforting and disturbing, enduring yet ever-changing, like life itself. Fluid, measureless, mysterious, all-encompassing, it held, he suspected, answers to all the riddles of the world.

In the long years ahead, Walt Whitman would search for the right shapes—sounds, words, meanings—to convey his wonderment at being alive in a world that was harmonious and beautiful and full of secret messages. For him, poetry became a gratefully given repayment for the gift of life itself. Often when he sang out, whether joyously or in anguish, he would use elemental images so familiar to him during his Paumanok boyhood wanderings: birds, flowers, trees, animals, earth, sun, sky, stars, ocean, sailing ships—and leaves of grass.

On the evidence of his poems, Walt Whitman was a mystic: one who achieves through deep and quiet contemplation a feeling of rapport with the entire universe, as if implicitly comprehending its purposes, connections, intricacies, and beauties. His particular brand of mysticism, on display throughout *Leaves of Grass*, had its beginnings in his impressionable, highly sensitized youth. Sometime during his childhood or early adolescence Walt may have experienced a preliminary mystical revelation or insight, which indicated his predestination as a poet and led eventually to what religious thinkers call a "spiritual awakening" or "second birth."

"Out of the Cradle Endlessly Rocking," a Whitman masterpiece written in his fortieth year, tells of just such an experience. It cannot be read as exact autobiography, for doubtless it was derived not from a sequence of real incidents, but combined of wholly separate happenings and feelings occurring or imagined in Walt's childhood and early manhood—later to be recalled and elaborated and unified by the poet as a "reminiscence" of his childhood.

The long poem reveals the "birth" of the poet, "chanter of pains and joys, uniter of here and hereafter." It distills the essence of Whitman's boyhood: his acute sensitivity to nature and his early preoccupation with the universal human themes of love, loss, death, and dedication. Just as the joys of life were magnified within him, so were its poignancies and sorrows. Some early personal encounter with death—perhaps his grandmother Hannah's when he was fourteen—may have aroused in the adolescent Walt a whole set of emotions and questions relating to mortality itself and to the correlative emotional losses.

Already stirring in Walt was a remarkable ability to sense things which other people did not see or hear, know or feel. As a youth he must have been aware of his difference from others—grownups and children both—which caused feelings of oddness, loneliness, and dislocation. ("The time of my boyhood was a very restless and unhappy one: I did not know what to do," Whitman once told a young friend. This contradicted the generally idyllic mood-pictures of his childhood portrayed in his poetry and prose.) Ultimately what Walt knew and felt would have to be expressed somehow, through some outlet, lest the heart and mind break apart from holding so much.

The poem tells of two mockingbirds who built their nest in a secluded brier patch on Paumanok's shore. The poet, then a boy, discovered the birds' sanctuary. Having a keen appreciation for all nature's creatures, he would often come close and sit quietly, to listen while the male bird, standing sentry above his mate as she warmed her four green eggs, sang out his happy songs:

Shine! shine! shine!
Pour down your warmth, great sun!
While we bask, we two together.

Two together!
Winds blow south, or winds blow north,
Day come white, or night come black,

Home, or rivers and mountains from home,
Singing all time, minding no time,
While we two keep together.

Then one day the female bird disappeared. Her forlorn mate, faithful in his vigil, called out for her unceasingly:

Blow! blow! blow!
Blow up sea-winds along Paumanok's shore;
I wait and I wait till you blow my mate to me.

Just as faithfully, the boy returned again and again to the nesting place, hearing throughout the summer the cries of that melancholy bird who had become his soul's companion—a spiritual brother to him. And though grown now, the poet recollected the long-past time with a vivid immediacy:

Recalling now the obscure shapes, the echoes, the sounds and
      sights after their sorts,
The white arms out in the breakers tirelessly tossing,
I, with bare feet, a child, the wind wafting my hair,
Listen'd long and long.

Listen'd to keep, to sing, now translating the notes,
Following you my brother.

The bird refused to believe that his mate was dead and would never again return to him.

O madly the sea pushes upon the land,
With love, with love.

O night! do I not see my love fluttering out among the breakers?
What is that little black thing I see there in the white?

Loud! loud! loud!
Loud I call to you, my love!

High and clear I shoot my voice over the waves,
Surely you must know who is here, is here,
You must know who I am, my love.

But whether the mockingbird called across the land, into the sky, or over the sea, his mate failed to come back. And when the autumnal half-moon hung low and yellow in the night sky, the bird at last admitted his loss and voiced his despair.

O throat! O throbbing heart!
And I singing uselessly, uselessly all the night.

O past! O happy life! O songs of joy!
In the air, in the woods, over fields,
Loved! loved! loved! loved! loved!
But my mate no more, no more with me!
We two together no more.

As the bird's sorrowful aria concluded, the boy heard the echoing notes, the wind's blowing, and the ocean's moans. Suddenly he felt a strange ecstasy. "The love in the heart long pent" burst forth in tears, and the boy's spirit cried out to the lonely mockingbird:

Demon or bird! (said the boy's soul,)
Is it indeed toward your mate you sing? or is it really to me?
For I, that was a child, my tongue's use sleeping, now I have heard you,
And already a thousand singers, a thousand songs, clearer, louder and more sorrowful than yours,
A thousand warbling echoes have started to life within me, never to die.

Summoned by the bereft mockingbird, the fledgling poet-spirit now struggled for recognition inside the boy, who sensed the connection between himself and the singing bird.

O you singer solitary, singing by yourself, projecting me,
O solitary me listening, never more shall I cease perpetuating you,
Never more shall I escape, never more the reverberations,
Never more the cries of unsatisfied love be absent from me,
Never again leave me to be the peaceful child I was before what there in the night,
By the sea under the yellow and sagging moon,

The messenger there arous'd, the fire, the sweet hell within,
The unknown want, the destiny of me.

The boy, that "outsetting bard," knew already that this role of interpreter and translator for the myriad voices of the world would be lonely and often painful for him. He did not shirk his fate, but he did ask the ocean, "the fierce old mother" who rocked the earth's cradle, to supply a word—"final, superior to all"—which would serve as a "clew" in his lifelong search into the profound mysteries of human existence. And throughout that night and into the dawn, the sea obligingly whispered it to him:

Hissing melodious, neither like the bird nor like my arous'd
    child's heart,
But edging near as privately for me rustling at my feet,
Creeping thence steadily up to my ears and laving me softly all
    over,
Death, death, death, death, death.

It was strange and shocking, this "word of the sweetest song and all songs"—really more riddle than clue. But the boy accepted it and fused it with the sad song that the bird, his "dusky demon and brother," had sung to him in the moonlight on the beach.

Throughout his years of singing his own songs, over and over the boy-become-poet would examine the meaning of death, that "clew" word given to him by the sea, for it was the key for understanding the life which he knew and loved.

What are you doing young man?
Are you so earnest, so given up to literature,
science, art, amours?
These ostensible realities, politics, points?
Your ambition or business whatever it may be?

III

WHAT ARE YOU DOING YOUNG MAN?

(1833-1842)

From his early training in the printing trade at the office of the
Long Island Patriot, Walt Whitman moved on to an apprenticeship at the *Long Island Star.* Although far more conservative in
its politics, this rival newspaper offered Walt a better opportunity.

The weekly publication's proprietor, Alden Spooner, was a leading citizen of Brooklyn. He used his paper as an effective platform for propounding his many ideas for civic improvements,
such as maintaining night watches and installing street lamps to
reduce crime, paving the streets for safety's sake and keeping
them clean for health's, and limiting the number of taverns. His
campaign to get Brooklyn village incorporated as a city, by com-
bining various smaller communities nearby and then establishing
a strong municipal authority for the larger population, finally
succeeded in 1834, when the New York state legislature awarded
a city charter to Brooklyn.

A public-spirited man who knew how to make words work for the
good of the citizens by arousing them to positive action, Spooner
probably made a big impression on Walt, who now clearly saw a
newspaper's ability to influence the populace. As literacy increased
along with the number of voters, newspapers proliferated in urban

areas, most adhering to particular political groups or parties, and some receiving financial support from them.

Oratory was also becoming popular; it too could alter or expand people's feelings and thinking. During his *Star* apprenticeship Walt joined a debating society—the start of his lifetime fascination with public speaking. He admired the rare power possessed by the great orators of his day. In "A Song of Joys" he would describe their spellbinding effect on the nation:

> O the orator's joys!
> To inflate the chest, to roll the thunder of the voice out from the
> ribs and throat,
> To make the people rage, weep, hate, desire, with yourself,
> To lead America—to quell America with a great tongue.

Walt continued to read books, especially the current romantic novels, like those by the American writer James Fenimore Cooper. Now, however, he also cultivated a new-found enthusiasm: the theater.

Through the *Star* office, Walt often got free passes to see dramas performed over in New York. He particularly loved to attend the Bowery Theater, which offered some of the best performers of the age, English and American, in many Shakespearean plays as well as the popular melodramas and contemporary comedies. At the Bowery Walt first saw Junius Brutus Booth—the father of Edwin and John Wilkes—as *Richard III*. The actor made such a tremendous impact upon Walt that both he and the play remained ever high in his favor. Walt now read all of Shakespeare's plays and memorized his favorite passages, which he would then declaim aloud to himself, experimenting with the endless variations of cadences and emphases to gain effects or to alter meanings. It was preparation for his own writing.

Walt preferred to do his theater-going alone, the better to take in the language and to study the nuances of the actors. He noticed the drama's ability to sway an entire audience all at once, working through the imagination, rather than by making a direct appeal to the emotions and the intellect as both journalism and oratory did.

Theater-going gave Walt the exciting sensation of being part of a large, cohesive group which was genuinely and positively American. In later years Whitman fondly recalled the spirit present at the Bowery on a good night, when it was "pack'd from ceiling to pit with its audience mainly of alert, well-dress'd, full-blooded young and middle-aged men, the best average of American-born mechanics." This assembled mass, stirred by the drama and its actors, was "as much a part of the show as any—bursting forth in one of those long-kept-up tempests of hand-clapping peculiar to the Bowery—no dainty kid-glove business, but electric force and muscle from perhaps 2000 full-sinew'd men." (A similar emotional response—powerful, masculine, and unified—Whitman would encounter among soldiers in a time of war, when they themselves were actors in a real-life drama.)

Intrigued with actors, Walt studied their techniques of portraying roles, of temporarily becoming people other than themselves. He found the old-fashioned, "hammy" style of acting "boisterous, stormy, physical, and repugnant to truth and taste." He much preferred the modern-style "mental" actor, who worked "from within to the outward, instead of being altogether outward." In a later essay Whitman remarked that the best way to represent strong emotions was actually to feel them and then project them into both words and actions. "This is a rare art," he said; "but no man or woman can be really great on the stage who has it not. The strange and subtle sympathy which runs like an electrical charge through human hearts collected together, responds only to the touch of the true fire."

Walt may have wondered whether in life itself a person might actually become what he at first pretended to be. During Whitman's entire manhood he seemed to be portraying a succession of roles, interrelated yet distinct in their phases. And in both Whitman and the poetry he wrote there is an interesting similarity between his suggestions for actors depicting characters on stage and his own ultimate assumption of a special "Personality"—a self-designed, self-imposed role intended to impress others with its "magnetism." In "To a Pupil" he would offer reasons for such a character-transformation:

> Is reform needed? is it through you?
> The greater the reform needed, the greater the Personality you
> need to accomplish it.
>
> •   •   •
>
> Do you not see how it would serve to have such a body and soul
> that when you enter the crowd an atmosphere of
> desire and command enters with you, and every
> one is impress'd with your Personality?
>
> •   •   •
>
> Go, dear friend, if need be give up all else, and commence to-day
> to inure yourself to pluck, reality, self-esteem,
> definiteness, elevatedness,
> Rest not till you rivet and publish yourself of your own Personality.

In his youth, Walt was not yet prepared to accomplish reforms by acquiring and projecting a new personality. The possibility, however, would lie dormant within him for some years.

In 1835, when Walt was seventeen years old, he moved to New York City. After several years of apprenticeship on the *Star* he qualified as a journeyman printer. Always attracted to Manhattan, Walt found a job in the print shop of a newspaper and took a room in a nearby roominghouse. No longer did he ride the ferry regularly across the river to spend just a few hours at the theater or in sightseeing; now he was able to absorb the full daily and nightly life of the city.

New York, with a population of 300,000, had nearly doubled its size in the decade since Walt had first known it. The expansion of commercial enterprises, the success of the Erie Canal, and the start of railroad connections with other parts of the nation had made the city a booming combination of manufacturing location, trading center, and port. From now on New York would be America's heart-city of business and culture. Its pulse—weak, strong, fluctuating, turbulent—would accurately indicate the condition of the country's health and wealth.

For Walt, living in New York allowed him to experience first-hand this excitement in constant growth, as he would later record in "Song of the Broad-Axe":

> The shapes arise!
> Shapes of factories, arsenals, foundries, markets,
> Shapes of the two-threaded tracks of railroads,
> Shapes of the sleepers of bridges, vast frameworks, girders, arches,
> Shapes of the fleets of barges, tows, lake and canal craft, river craft,
> Ship-yards and dry-docks ...

But Walt observed other things besides constructive activities. In the city he also saw drunkards and prodigal sons, gamblers and adulterers, prisoners and dead men, crazed women and starving children, thieves and murderers. Because of its many industries and entertainments, New York attracted all sorts of people. The city was rapidly expanding, but it could not provide enough work or decent lodgings for everyone who came there hopefully: shy lads from farms and small towns, bewildered immigrant families, Negro freedmen. But for the greedy, the politically crafty, and the criminals, the city offered a thousand lures and schemes for dubious gain.

Although New York hardly made a safe residence for a very young man on his own, Walt did not seem to worry. Already imbued with a lofty and ebullient vision of a democracy that would eventually convert all people into useful citizens, he walked wherever he liked, regarding everybody with a friendly if curious eye. His countenance never darkened with fear, revulsion, or dislike as he sauntered the city pavements, encountering a motley array of "Faces":

> Faces of friendship, precision, caution, suavity, ideality,
> The spiritual-prescient face, the always welcome common benevolent face,
> The face of the singing of music, the grand faces of natural lawyers and judges broad at the back-top,
> The faces of hunters and fishers bulged at the brows, the shaved blanch'd faces of orthodox citizens,

> The pure, extravagant, yearning, questioning artist's face,
> The ugly face of some beautiful soul, the handsome detested or
> despised face,
> The sacred faces of infants, the illuminated face of the mother of
> many children ...

All the faces, whether mean or superb, reminded Walt that men were basically equal—and equally divine. Each human life, intrinsically as worthy as any other, should be treated in a wholly democratic way. And thus he would outline his attitude in "I Sing the Body Electric":

> The man's body is sacred and the woman's body is sacred,
> No matter who it is, it is sacred—is it the meanest one in the
> laborers' gang?
> Is it one of the dull-faced immigrants just landed on the wharf?
> Each belongs here or anywhere just as much as the well-off, just as
> much as you,
> Each has his or her place in the procession.

Amiably and contentedly then, young Walt Whitman strode through "his" city, enjoying its myriad sounds and spectacles, taking them in for a future recounting in "Song of Myself":

> The blab of the pave, tires of carts, sluff of boot-soles, talk of the
> promenaders,
> The heavy omnibus, the driver with his interrogating thumb, the
> clank of the shod horses on the granite floor,
> The snow-sleighs, clinking, shouted jokes, pelts of snow-balls,
> The hurrahs for popular favorites, the fury of rous'd mobs,
> The flap of the curtain'd litter, a sick man inside borne to the
> hospital,
> The meeting of enemies, the sudden oath, the blows and fall,
> The excited crowd, the policeman with his star quickly working his
> passage to the centre of the crowd,
> The impassive stones that receive and return so many echoes ...

Probably Walt was more spectator in the city than participant, but in the winter of 1835 an external happening affected him personally. A terrible conflagration destroyed much of the business district of New York, including many buildings which housed printing offices. Walt must have been on hand to watch the fire-fighting; he would describe a scene like it later in "Song of the Broad-Axe."

> The arriving engines, the hoarse shouts, the nimble stepping and
>   daring,
> The strong command through the fire-trumpets, the falling in line,
>   the rise and fall of the arms forcing the water,
> The slender, spasmic, blue-white jets, the bringing to bear of the
>   hooks and ladders and their execution,
> The crash and cut away of connecting wood-work, or through
>   floors if the fire smoulders under them,
> The crowd with their lit faces watching, the glare and dense
>   shadows...

The disastrous fire combined with a general uneasiness in the national economy to cause a serious financial crisis in New York. Many people believed that the business depression was started by President Jackson's destruction of the National Bank. State banks had begun to issue all sorts of paper currency, which fluctuated in real value and therefore proved worthless because they were not adequately funded. Then Jackson had declared that land in the West could only be purchased "in specie"—with hard cash.

For a few months Walt kept his job, while thousands of people around him were unemployed. And in May of 1836, when he too joined the ranks of the jobless, he at least had somewhere to go. Declining to beg for food or sleep in the streets, he returned to his family on Long Island.

In June, Walt took up a new profession: teaching. His first assignment was at a small country school at Norwich, close to Cold Spring Harbor. Most Long Island towns kept their schools open for only a single season during the year, so the teachers traveled from one place to another.

Since the schoolmaster traditionally "boarded round" among his pupils' families, Walt got to know all sorts of people living in the rural setting. Apparently he relished this itinerant life, for in after-years he called it "one of my best experiences and deepest lessons in human nature behind the scenes, and in the masses."

Much of *Leaves of Grass* contains inspirational lessons from teacher to pupil or "*eleve*," from master to disciple, from spiritual "father" to his "son." Therefore Whitman's actual experiences as an instructor in schools—a tenure of some five years—have relevance to his development as a poet. Unfortunately, few details of this period in his life have been preserved. Just how well Whitman succeeded as a teacher we do not know. The recollections of several former pupils, garnered long afterwards, indicated that, like most teachers, Whitman received mixed ratings.

Even though he was barely older than some of his pupils, Walt applied himself with serious intentions to this new career. He genuinely liked children and was experienced with them, having often served as playmate or parent-substitute for his younger brothers and sisters. (During several of his teaching years his brother George, ten years Walt's junior, lived with him and attended his school.)

Like the influential French philosopher Rousseau, Walt believed that children were innately good and pure. (Infancy and childhood portrayed in Whitman's poems always have an aura of pristine charm, even sanctity; bad, ugly, and disagreeable children do not appear in *Leaves of Grass*. And as if by virtue of their close contact, mothers too are given halos.) Continuous exposure to an imperfect society, however, eventually turned most children into flawed adults. Whitman thought that skillful parents and teachers could help to offset this harm by encouraging a child's natural flow of love, happy spirits, and a sense of wonder into creative channels.

Walt certainly must have realized that his own early experiences in an institution of learning had been grossly inadequate, and he probably often wondered what he might have learned, and even become, in a totally different school environment. Education, begun in the home and continued in school, was a significant force in shaping the individual child, and its main contours would determine the national character. Therefore, it was not a matter to be undertaken negligently or with boredom or severity.

Again and again, throughout his life, in poems and in prose, Whitman would emphasize the vital importance of education in structuring and perpetuating American democracy. During his years as a newspaper editor, Whitman had ample opportunities to lecture his readers on the subject of education. "Mighty things depend upon the young of the age," he wrote. "Each little child has an immortal soul. He has the treasure house of the human mind; and it depends upon those who ought to see to his education, whether the costly and precious beauties of that treasure house shall be locked up for ever; or brought forth to gladden the eyes of men, and prove a perpetual spring of delight to their now unconscious possessor. Fully to bring out these boundless capacities requires hard and laborious attention."

Whitman always felt challenged by the prospect of changing and directing people's emotions, thinking, and very lives, essentially aiming to give them a sense of pride and a recognition of their ability to shape their own destinies. He would never cease expounding his opinions and enthusiasms—for the edification of others. His various careers all reflect a compulsion to educate those around him.

As a new teacher, Walt began to put into practice some ideas which came naturally to his particular temperament. Although probably unaware of it, he used some of the unconventional teaching methods which others of this period had been trying out, especially in New England: notably, Bronson Alcott at the controversial Temple School in Boston, then at his experimental colony at Fruitlands; young Henry David Thoreau and his brother at Concord; and the Peabody sisters in Boston. At the same time Horace Mann was starting his campaign in Massachusetts to organize and improve public education, eventually to set the plan for the entire nation.

Whitman instructed his students in the standard "Three R's" of his day, yet did not stop there. He did not want them to learn by rote, as he had had to do, but to understand the meaning and relevance of what they were learning. Frequently he read poems and asked his children to memorize them; sometimes they were his own compositions, but more often those by his favorite English and American poets. Breaking down the rigid system which kept the teacher as a severe, remote, and final authority, Walt often held informal discussions with his pupils. He knew instinctively that one learned far more in the exchange of interests and ideas than in being assigned a list of facts to memorize.

He declined to use the usual corporal punishment. Instead of whipping recalcitrant pupils, he tried to change their attitudes and behavior by gentler methods: patience, reasoning, reward, and providing good examples. And respecting each child for what he was, he did not expect them all to be copies from a single mold. What he ideally wished to achieve as an actual teacher must have been similar to the effect he later hoped to have upon would-be readers of his poetry:

> Stop this day and night with me and you shall possess the origin of all poems,
> You shall possess the good of the earth and sun, (there are millions of suns left,)
> You shall no longer take things at second or third hand, nor look through the eyes of the dead, nor feed on the spectres in books,
> You shall not look through my eyes either, nor take things from me,
> You shall listen to all sides and filter them from your self.

He often took his charges out for walks in the open air—down country roads and along paths through nearby woods and fields, where a teacher could show to far better effect than merely to tell. Under the sky, upon the earth among living things, one absorbed and knew the world directly through the senses, learning what was not revealed in lectures or textbooks in the confined classroom. Even books and poems changed and deepened their influence when taken outdoors to read, Walt found. He later insisted that his own poems could not be really understood or fully appreciated if read indoors, especially by "indoor"-type people:

And I swear I will never translate myself at all, only to him or her
      who privately stays with me in the open air.

.   .   .

No shutter'd room or school can commune with me,
But roughs and little children better than they.

Walt wanted each child in his care to think and feel for himself and never lose—as most grownups had—his fresh sense of awe
and curiosity at beholding the world. Religious feelings should not
come just on Sundays; in every moment of life one could experience things rare and infinitely precious—as Walt would one day
demonstrate in "Miracles."

Why, who makes much of a miracle?
As to me I know of nothing else but miracles,
Whether I walk the streets of Manhattan,
Or dart my sight over the roofs of houses toward the sky,
Or wade with naked feet along the beach just in the edge of the
      water,
Or stand under trees in the woods,
Or talk by day with any one I love, or sleep in the bed at night
      with any one I love,
Or sit at table at dinner with the rest,
Or look at strangers opposite me riding in the car,
Or watch honey-bees busy around the hive of a summer forenoon,
Or animals feeding in the fields,
Or birds, or the wonderfulness of insects in the air,
Or the wonderfulness of the sundown, or of stars shining so quiet
      and bright,
Or the exquisite delicate thin curve of the new moon in spring;
These with the rest, one and all, are to me miracles,
The whole referring, yet each distinct and in its place.

While teaching, Walt also composed poetry, short stories, and
essays. He had commenced a writer's apprenticeship which would
last for nearly two decades, until he found his own uniquely suitable form of self-expression. The things he first wrote—evinced in
his published efforts in the following years—were standard imita-

tions of the popular literary models of the day: sentimental, moralizing, and occasionally morbid. Nowhere to be glimpsed in them was the adventuresome poet who would eventually startle readers with his revolutionary "free verse" style, unrhymed and with irregular linear rhythms. Where was the robust personality who seemed deliberately determined to shock the civilized society by writing about matters nobody else dared to mention? Certainly not at all in these anemic soul-pourings and lectures of a late-adolescent schoolteacher.

Today, Whitman's early writings interest literary scholars only because Whitman wrote them. Giving little or no indication of a genuine talent for thinking or expression, they mark how very far Whitman was to travel before composing *Leaves of Grass*. They also often offer insights into his emotions and biographical parallels to his own life at the time.

In Whitman's first prose efforts one can frequently see his fundamental sympathy with children and with poor and neglected people. In his fledgling poems—with their lines usually rhymed and in regular meter—Walt spoke of youth's golden dreams; of despair in ever finding the perfect mate; of the dark imminence of death.

Certainly Walt Whitman was not ready yet to give his pupils about to set foot on life's open road any vigorous poetic valedictory instructions. They would have to wait for "Song of Myself," still years away.

> Long enough have you dream'd contemptible dreams,
> Now I wash the gum from your eyes,
> You must habit yourself to the dazzle of the light and of every
> moment in your life.
>
> Long have you timidly waded holding a plank by the shore,
> Now I will you to be a bold swimmer,
> To jump off in the midst of the sea, rise again, nod to me, shout,
> and laughingly dash with your hair.

Yet even in his young years, his teaching years, Walt Whitman must have put across to some of his students a portion of the values and wisdom he was already accumulating and would eventually reveal in "Song of Myself":

> I have said that the soul is not more than the body,
> And I have said that the body is not more than the soul,
> And nothing, not God, is greater than one's self is,
> And whoever walks a furlong without sympathy walks to his own funeral drest in his shroud,
> And I or you pocketless of a dime may purchase the pick of the earth,
> And to glance with an eye or show a bean in its pod confounds the learning of all times,
> And there is no trade or employment but the young man following it may become a hero,
> And there is no object so soft but it makes a hub for the wheel'd universe,
> And I say to any man or woman, Let your soul stand cool and composed before a million universes.

Twice in Walt's career as a teacher he left the schoolroom to do other things. The first time, in 1838, he started his own weekly newspaper, the *Long Islander*. Published at Huntington, Walt's birth-country, it was financed by local friends. Walt bought a small printing press in New York and launched this new project enthusiastically. He wrote all his own copy, then set it in type and printed it. He packed the finished papers into a saddlebag and rode around the countryside delivering them. Astride his horse Nina, he became a familiar figure on the landscape.

Walt also went about gleaning news bits and soliciting new subscribers. Since his own family, on both sides, were farming people, he was already familiar with the routines of farmers' lives. Living among them as a schoolmaster had further added to his acquaintance. Now as an enterprising young journalist writing for country folks and traveling among them, his liking for their way of life continued. He observed and joined in their activities, both physical and social, with a pleasure that still lingered in his memory in old age, and would be frequently recalled in passages of *Leaves of Grass*.

> To rise at peep of day and pass forth nimbly to work,
> To plough land in the fall for winter-sown crops,
> To plough land in the spring for maize,
> To train orchards, to graft the trees, to gather apples in the fall.

And for all his eventual espousal of the open road—the cutting loose from familiar ties that held one down to a single spot on earth—Whitman occasionally would give the impression that what one really should desire in life was right at close hand, from the start. The agricultural family unit probably would have best supplied the ideal human relationships.

> Will you seek far off? you surely come back at last,
> In things best known to you finding the best, or as good as the best,
> In folks nearest to you finding the sweetest, strongest, lovingest,
> Happiness, knowledge, not in another place but in this place, not
> for another hour but this hour,
> Man in the first you see or touch, always in friend, brother, nighest
> neighbor—woman in mother, sister, wife . . .

In their vital and masculine simplicity, the soil-tenders and stock-raisers whom Walt knew in those years impressed him with their force of character, which earned them bountiful harvests and the loving obedience of domesticated animals. These rural types appear throughout *Leaves of Grass*. The sophistication and amusements which the city offered its inhabitants, when contrasted with the important, earth-contacting pursuits on a farm, would afterwards strike Walt as grotesque and senseless. "Teaching a bean to wind up its pole is a more useful, though perhaps not so manly or elegant an employment, as teaching a lap dog to jump," he later sarcastically remarked when a newspaper editor—sadly observing how farmers' sons left home, eager for the glittering lights and promises of quick fortunes in the big city. Soberly he would advise them to remain at home and till the soil, to benefit themselves, their communities, and their country as a whole by growing food—instead of "preying like leeches" on the nation's vitals by abandoning honest livelihoods and flocking to the cities.

And just as he admired the farmers, who lived close to nature in a simple and unpretentious way, he liked their animals too. In a famous passage in "Song of Myself," Walt would one day express the belief that members of the animal kingdom possessed more dignity and sense than people ever realized—and perhaps were even wiser than mankind itself.

> I think I could turn and live with animals, they are so placid and
> self-contain'd,
> I stand and look at them long and long.
>
> They do not sweat and whine about their condition,
> They do not lie awake in the dark and weep for their sins,
> They do not make me sick discussing their duty to God,
> Not one is dissatisfied, not one is demented with the mania of own-
> ing things,
> Not one kneels to another, nor to his kind that lived thousands of
> years ago,
> Not one is respectable or unhappy over the whole earth.
>
> So they show their relations to me and I accept them,
> They bring me tokens of myself, they evince them plainly in their
> possession.
>
> I wonder where they get those tokens,
> Did I pass that way huge times ago and negligently drop them?

In the dawning age of evolutionary theories, Whitman seemed to feel instinctively that man had originated from other forms of life and still belonged to the animal world.

After about eight months of publishing the *Long Islander,* Walt gave up the paper—probably on the strong advice of his backers— and it was sold. Restless, dissatisfied with his limited horizons, he had grown bored with the daily routine of his work and then began neglecting it. Again he went to New York to seek a compositor's job, but the economic depression was still severe and he found no employment.

He then went to work as writer and typesetter for the *Long Island Democrat,* which had reprinted some of his essays and poems from his own little newspaper. He boarded at the editor's home in Jamaica, probably as part-payment for his work. Although James Brenton liked Walt, now twenty years old, he got perturbed when his youthful employee would sometimes fail to return after lunch to the printing office—apparently lost in reverie while he lay on his back and gazed up at the outstretched limbs and dancing green leaves of an apple tree.

Walt was just a lazy oaf, complained Mrs. Brenton. He came to dinner in his shirt-sleeves; when he sat in a chair, he stuck his long legs out for people to trip over; he had sullen moods and obviously resented her children's noisy antics.

How Brenton defended their lodger and his employee against his wife's frequent criticisms is not known. Perhaps in his way he had a fondness and sympathetic understanding for this youth who now and again had to lie beneath the apple tree and dream. Walt had not yet found the words to describe the feelings which swept over him at such moments. His very soul seemed to touch and warm him like sunlight over all his body; earthly cares and considerations were suspended by a strange, ineffable rapture that was sensuous, benign, spiritually ecstatic. In time to come he would learn how to summon such a mood and tell of it. He would compose in "Song of Myself" a renowned lyrical passage addressed to his soul—a testament to his special and inherent mysticism.

> Loafe with me on the grass, loose the stop from your throat,
> Not words, not music or rhyme I want, not custom or lecture, not
> even the best,
> Only the lull I like, the hum of your valvèd voice.
>
> I mind how once we lay such a transparent summer morning,
> How you settled your head athwart my hips and gently turn'd over
> upon me,
> And parted the shirt from my bosom-bone, and plunged your
> tongue to my bare-stript heart,
> And reach'd till you felt my beard, and reach'd till you held my
> feet.
>
> Swiftly arose and spread around me the peace and knowledge that
> pass all the argument of the earth,
> And I know that the hand of God is the promise of my own,

And I know that the spirit of God is the brother of my own,
And that all the men ever born are also my brothers, and the
women my sisters and lovers,
And that a kelson of the creation is love,
And limitless are leaves stiff or drooping in the fields,
And brown ants in the little wells beneath them,
And mossy scabs of the worm fence, heap'd stones, elder, mullein
and poke-weed.

No doubt Mrs. Brenton sighed with relief when this malingerer left her husband's employ and returned to teaching. However, Walt kept up good relations with Brenton, who in early 1840 published a group of young Whitman's essays, entitled "Sun-Down Papers from the Desk of a School-Master."

Whatever unusual thoughts and sensations he may have harbored within, Walt, on the verge of legal manhood, was thoroughly conventional in his dress, behavior, and opinions. His ideas and ambitions could still be contained in a commonplace world. In those early essays he demonstrated his dislike for smoking and drinking (habits he rarely indulged during his lifetime) and doled out other sober advice to readers. (Yet, perhaps as a sly jibe at his former hostess, he included a piece on the pleasures of loafing.)

In one article Walt naively revealed that he entertained the plan of writing someday "a wonderful and ponderous book." He even thought it might turn out to be "something very respectable." And admitting, rather coyly, that he knew very little about "a class of beings whose nature, habits, notions, and ways" lay outside his own experience, he vowed that he would not discuss womankind therein.

That "wonderful and ponderous book" still lay far away from its author's grasp. By the time he commenced writing it, he would know enough about the opposite sex at least to include her too in his volume. But when Walt Whitman offered *Leaves of Grass* to the public, few readers indeed were to find anything "wonderful" in it—let alone "respectable."

While teaching school in 1840, Walt got involved in politics. He had just turned twenty-one and was eligible to vote. Through a friend, he was made an electioneer, with the job of canvassing votes for the Democratic Party in Queens County. His years of experience in various debating societies now proved useful.

Walt thus took a small part in one of the most savagely fought presidential contests in American history. The incumbent President, Democrat Martin Van Buren—the practical, conscientious successor to Andrew Jackson—was challenged by the Whig Party's hero-candidate, William Henry Harrison. "Tippecanoe," known for his valor in battles against both Indians and British, was promoted as a prototype of the "western man." Posters depicted him living in a log cabin and swilling hard liquor; actually, he was a quiet-living gentleman-landowner. Since Jackson had enjoyed enormous popularity as a backwoods "man of the people," the Whigs were now making a similar appeal to the great mass of American voters who obviously admired rough, vigorous, and manly public projections of themselves. (Poet Walt Whitman, fifteen years later, would introduce himself to the American people in much the same vein.)

Important issues were debated during the election campaign: whether high tariffs should be imposed on European imports, and always the heated arguments over how much space in the westward-moving nation should be given to slaveholders. But the contest was really one of public popularity.

Walt, a loyal Jacksonian Democrat, worked hard for his party's cause. He did not shy away from direct confrontations with political foes. In a public debate, when his opponent accused Van Buren of an assortment of private vices—absurd but nonetheless vicious—Walt called him a liar. The dispute spilled over at once into the local papers. Walt did not cease his assertions and rebuttals until he finally had the last word.

But fighting Harrison's appeal as a noble military figure and stemming the inevitable strong current of public reaction to twelve years of Democratic administration proved futile. Moreover, Van Buren had been blamed for the economic setbacks of the last years, from which the country was only now emerging. When the Whigs won, Walt at least could be proud that his own precinct in Jamaica was one of the few places in New York State that the Democrats had captured.

In the years to come, Whitman would often be disappointed over election results, but he usually regarded them philosophically. The people, after all, had had their say, whether or not their choices might be prudent. Where else but in the United States was the great majority allowed to select their leaders and representatives? The very freedom to vote, he felt, would eventually right any temporary errors of judgment.

After the Democrats' defeat in 1840 there were certainly no political plums for Walt to pluck as a reward for his strenuous efforts. He returned to schoolteaching and to "sun-down" writing. But his recent participation in politics had roused him; he had liked expressing on platform and in print his own opinions about public issues and officials. Primed for more, he found small-town affairs not big enough now for his scope; and his classroom contained no voting-age citizens to influence.

Like most young men who have not yet discovered their true callings, Walt was trying out different occupations and interests. Later on, reflecting back on this youthful period of life—his and others'—he felt tolerant toward this dabbling with activities and enthusiasms:

> What are you doing young man?
> Are you so earnest, so given up to literature, science, art, amours?
> These ostensible realities, politics, points?
> Your ambition or business whatever it may be?
>
> It is well—against such I say not a word, I am their poet also . . .

In the spring of 1841 Walt went to New York to try his luck once again. A man now, he felt more confident of making his own way there. Jobs were easier to find, and he soon started work as a typesetter for Park Benjamin.

Publisher of the *New World*—which he brazenly advertised as the largest, cheapest, and handsomest paper in the world—Benjamin was a highly successful but often unscrupulous entrepreneur who profited from the ever-mounting sales of newspapers in the burgeoning city. He thrived in the midst of the savage feuds that went on perpetually among competitive papers, especially the "penny press" publications, which attracted readers with their low prices and sensational stories. In this era when new papers appeared or disappeared almost daily, some reputable and worthy news journals were founded, much of their initial success and perennial popularity due to the special abilities of their editors—most notably, Horace Greeley of the *Tribune* and William Cullen Bryant of the *Evening Post*. Journalism as a profession was becoming lucrative or respectable—or even both.

A few months after his arrival in New York, young Walter Whitman, Jr., delivered a speech at a Democratic rally. On the following day it was quoted in the *Post*. He had proposed that his party now battle for "great principles" and not just attempt to raise "this or that man to power." As a would-be politician in the big city, Walt had much to learn. Tammany Hall, becoming the stronghold of the city's Democratic Party, fought for power, not principles; the people it promoted generally used every means at their command to win elections and seize control over the city's administration and finances, for their party's benefit.

Whitman now became acquainted with the opportunistic—rather than idealistic—politician: the man of greed, not creed. Men of this stamp employed gangs of ruffians to bludgeon people who did not vote in the prescribed way.

Walt's enthusiasm for a political career inevitably declined after his exposure to certain politicians and their followings in New York. He spoke from some bitter personal experience when he wrote a cynical editorial in the following year. "We give leading office holders far, far more credit for superiority than one in a thousand deserves," he observed. "The mass look aloft and see the great in their holiday clothes, prepared to bear the scrutiny of all eyes, and clothed in dignity as a mantle; and they, the lookers on, are struck with admiration. . . . But to him who has an opportunity of looking behind the scenes, all present a different aspect. The glitter, and the glory, and the majesty, fade away. He sees that people of rank are nothing more than those of common grade. And he sees, too, all the manoeuvres, the tricks, the claptrap, and the wire pulling, which the spectators in front know nothing of."

Rather than trying to obtain a political sinecure, Walt began to concentrate on furthering his own ambitions as a writer. He peddled around town some of the stories and poems he had been composing during the past years. A story was accepted by the *Democratic Review*. Its editor, John O'Sullivan, had founded the magazine on the premise that Americans should take pride in the accomplishments of their own artists; he maintained that American writing should be published and promoted. He knew that the continued importation of literary material from England and the Continent encouraged a slavish worship of European culture—to the detriment of a rising native American artistry. O'Sullivan would soon launch the "Young America" movement to spread his program further. In the meantime, with the magazine as his prime showcase, he printed stories, essays, and poems by some of the best American writers: Hawthorne, Poe, Longfellow, Lowell, Bryant, and Whittier.

The youthful Walt Whitman felt justifiably proud to be welcomed into such an illustrious company. His contribution, however, hardly proved a worthly sample of his country's literary talent. Entitled "Death in the Schoolroom," it told a lachrymose tale of a teacher's brutal beating of a fatherless, undernourished schoolboy of sterling character, whose honesty he had peremptorily misjudged. Two more stories in a similarly moralizing and sentimental vein—each with boyhood virtue quashed by cruel fathers—appeared soon afterward in the *Democratic Review*. Then during the autumn Walt's employer, Park Benjamin, published two of his poems in the *New World*. And in January of 1842 *Brother Jonathan* printed a poem by Walter Whitman, Jr., with the title of "Ambition":

One day an obscure youth, a wanderer,
Known but to few, lay musing with himself
About the chances of his future life.
In that youth's heart, there dwelt the coal Ambition,
Burning and glowing; and he asked himself,
"Shall I, in time to come, be great and famed?"

Like many a young man before and after him, Walt had his dreams of glory. And though he sometimes—as his poem phrased it —had "his airy castles thus dashed down," he persisted in seeking his fortune on the main, well-traveled road. Becoming a professional writer seemed quite possible now, since several New York publishers had seen merit in his compositions.

How different, though, was this early poem from the rousing call to adventure and self-discovery which Walt Whitman would later sound in "Song of the Open Road." The latter, written at the verge of middle age, captured perfectly the spirit of youth's boundless vigor and optimism and idealism—which a much younger Walt, writing of a pallid and effete dreamer, had not even approached, whatever he may have felt deep inside.

> Afoot and light-hearted I take to the open road,
> Healthy, free, the world before me,
> The long brown path before me leading wherever I choose.
>
> Henceforth I ask not good-fortune, I myself am good-fortune,
> Henceforth I whimper no more, postpone no more, need nothing,
> Done with indoor complaints, libraries, querulous criticisms,
> Strong and content I travel the open road.

Already, though he did not know it yet, Walt had set foot upon the long brown path, with its twists and turns and forks, which stretched far ahead of him in the open air.

This is the city and I am one of the citizens,
Whatever interests the rest interests me,
politics, wars, markets, newspapers,
schools . . .

IV

THIS IS THE CITY

(1842-1848)

Walt Whitman became a staff writer on a New York morning
paper, the *Aurora,* in early 1842. Then in March, two months
before his twenty-third birthday, he was appointed its editor.
Given full charge of assembling the news and preparing it for publication, plus writing editorials and special features, Walt took on
a heavy responsibility for such a young man.

He started off by telling his readers of his determination to
"render *Aurora the* paper of the city." Furthermore, he wished
to make it "the most readable journal in the republic." Cheap
newspapers like the *Aurora,* he asserted, assisted in the development of the nation; the "penny press" was really a school for citizens. "They carry light and knowledge among those who most
need it," he explained.

Whitman stated what he hoped would be the guidepost of his
paper: "We glory in being *true Americans.* And we profess to
impress *Aurora* with the same spirit. We have taken high American ground . . . based upon a desire to possess the republic of a
proper respect for itself and its citizens, and of what is due to its
own capacities, and its own dignity." Already Walt was trumpet-

ing his clarion call of Americanism—eventually to resound through-out *Leaves of Grass*.

Walt soon became embroiled in a hot city feud. Catholic priests asked for financial aid from the city for their parochial schools, which were crowded with the children of thousands of Irish immi-grants recently settled in New York. But the city officials pointed out that the traditional and sacrosanct American separation of Church and State made such a subsidy unthinkable. The priests could not understand this distinction: after all, weren't they edu-cating future American citizens? They and the Irish immigrants continued to press their demands, and the squabble became noisy and vehement—and finally dangerous, when some politicians eager to capture Irish votes actively encouraged the gathering of mobs, who enforced their opinions with violence.

Among native New Yorkers the latent prejudice against foreign-ers was quickly stirred up. For a while Whitman seemed to parrot their disgust over the "bands of filthy wretches" who delivered a grave "insult to American Citizenship" by their behavior. And he called the priests leading the agitation "sly, false, deceitful villains."

When a correspondent criticized Whitman for his "strong lan-guage," Walt responded in the fighting spirit that would character-ize much of his poetry later on: "We never *intend* to mince mat-ters—to stop for honeyed words—to crust the wholesome dose we administer, with sugar—to be polite unto filthy vice—to stand on ceremony with a traitor—to treat a scoundrel with dainty punc-tilio."

But Walt, it turned out, wished to make it clear that he and the *Aurora* did not agree with the new Native American Party, which wanted to deprive everyone of foreign origin from United States citizenship. Neither then nor ever would Whitman's Ameri-canism be exclusive or bigoted; he promoted the democratic code, not special birthrights. "Our love is capacious enough, our arms wide enough, to encircle all men," he declared, "whether they have birth in our glorious republic, the monarchies of Europe, or the hot deserts of Africa."

In *Leaves of Grass* Walt Whitman's loving arms would stretch

out widely to enclose the whole of mankind, whether in his own
land or anywhere abroad—and whether of present, past, or future
generations. In his jubilant "Salut au Monde" he would send off
greetings to everybody:

> All you continentals of Asia, Africa, Europe, Australia, indifferent
> of place!
> All you on the numberless islands of the archipelagoes of the sea!
> And you of centuries hence when you listen to me!
> And you each and everywhere whom I specify not, but include just
> the same!
> Health to you! good will to you all, from me and America sent!

Yet despite his fond respect for foreign lands and peoples, editor
Whitman feared that America's experiment in democracy might
be corrupted by alien ideas which were "feudal" or aristocratic
in tone, or narrowly and oppressively religious. "This nation—all
vigorous in the bloom of youth, and, like youth, susceptible to a
lasting stamp from chance impressions—is in danger of being deterred from a proud and lofty path," he warned his *Aurora* readers.
Each packet and steamship arriving at the docks from abroad
carried some infectious anti-Americanism in its hold. Hopefully,
however, the republic would not be dissuaded from its work on
the "Great Problem": that of "how far Man, the masterpiece of the
cunningest omniscience, can have his nature perfected by himself,
and can be trusted to govern himself. We possess the chance of
spreading to the gaze of the world, the glorious spectacle of a
continent peopled by *freemen*."

Such, then, were a few of Whitman's thoughts in his early twenties. People astonished by the remarkable creation of *Leaves of
Grass* sometimes assume that Whitman's attitudes, like his style,
emerged suddenly full-blown, bypassing a budding stage. The
newspaper editorials which Whitman wrote in the 1840s indicate
that the trends and substance of much of his thinking hardly
changed when he evolved from journalist to poet. There was a
definite connection between the mature poet and the young editor
who welcomed foreigners to his shores yet warned them not to

force their outmoded beliefs and practices upon a new nation developing its own democratic ways.

Walt Whitman always respected many of the values from mankind's past history, but he believed that the United States must deliberately alter them, or cast them aside if necessary, when structuring a nation of "free and perfect individuals." So Whitman the poet one day would be saying:

> America, curious toward foreign characters, stands by its own at all hazards,
> Stands removed, spacious, composite, sound, initiates the true use of precedents,
> Does not repel them or the past or what they have produced under their forms,
> Takes the lesson with calmness, perceives the corpse slowly borne from the house,
> Perceives that it waits a little while in the door, that it was fittest for its days,
> That its life has descended to the stalwart and well-shaped heir who approaches,
> And that he shall be fittest for his days.
>
> Any period one nation must lead,
> One land must be the promise and reliance of the future.

Whitman's supreme confidence in the world's great need for American leadership and domination, as the best and possibly only way of spreading democracy, permeates *Leaves of Grass*. Not only fundamental to his own beliefs, it was thoroughly in harmony with the American statesmanship, whether idealistic or militant, current in his day and lingering ever afterward.

While making editorial pronouncements about America's noble destiny, Walt took time out to ramble around the city familiar to him since boyhood but changing daily as it spread uptown and grew skyward. In the midst of the hubbub of building and motion and people everywhere, he sometimes missed the quiet countryside. Walt was not the only editor ever to describe New York as "noisy, roaring, rumbling, tumbling, bustling, stormy, turbulent."

And, he asked, "Who has any, even distant, idea of the profound repose, the hushed lethargy of silence?"

Sometimes just to keep his mind in order, Walt took a day off to mosey along the seashore, appointing an assistant to see to the mechanics of his job. At Coney Island—deserted on spring days except for a few sea gulls—he inspected the tide line, splashed through the surf while loudly declaiming some passage from Homer, or sat upon a dune and read. "A quiet repose is a peculiarity of high breeding," he noted in the *Aurora*. Already he prized a simplicity of manner: "a kind of antifussiness—a stillness without being awkward—an absence of uncouth animation." The poet's demeanor in future years would fit well this early outline.

During Walt's *Aurora* tenancy, however, he was consciously cultivating the persona of a successful young man-about-town. He dressed in the height of fashion and even wore a flower in his lapel. He was tall—over six feet—and sturdy-looking. In those days, too, he despised uncut beards. "Near the City Hotel we passed a man with the face of a goat," Walt reported. "His upper lip was completely covered with black bushy hair, as were also his jaws and under the chin. People turned round in their walk to look at the creature. It is an abominable practice, this, of converting a human countenance into a locomotive map!" How amazed he would have been had he known that to the generations after him his most prominent and memorable feature would be the bountiful beard of his later years.

The impression which Walter Whitman, Jr., New York editor, wished to convey to his fellow citizens probably was summarized in his word sketch of a character in a story published not long afterward: "His countenance was intelligent, and had the air of city life and society. He was dress'd not gaudily, but in every respect fashionably; his coat being of the finest broadcloth, his linen delicate and spotless as snow, and his whole aspect that of one whose counterpart may now and then be seen upon the pave of Broadway of a fine afternoon."

And sauntering up and down Broadway—that great north-south thoroughfare on Manhattan Island—Walt had the time of his life while collecting material for, or ruminating over, next morning's columns. "We took our usual stroll down Broadway . . . What a glorious morning it was! . . . and just enough people walking on the pave to make one continued, ceaseless, devilish provoking, delicious, glorious jam!" Walt enjoyed crowds of people, and where they were he went, depicting them later in his newspaper —taking the air in Battery Park, shopping along Broadway, buying and selling in the busy wholesale markets by the East River, worshipping in churches and synagogues, or gathered to watch a burning house.

In the *Aurora* Walt also summarized some of New York's variety and contradictions, still noticeable a century and more after him: "New York is a great place—a mighty world in itself. Strangers who come here for the first time in their lives, spend week after week, and yet find that there are still hundreds of wonders and surprises, and (to them) oddities, which they have not had a chance of examining. Here are people of all classes and stages of rank—from all countries on the globe—engaged in all the varieties of avocations—of every grade, every hue of ignorance and learning, morality and vice, wealth and want, fashion and coarseness, breeding and brutality, elevation and degradation, impudence and modesty."

This teeming city set upon its own island Whitman would celebrate again and again in *Leaves of Grass*, whether just mentioning it in the midst of his eulogistic national surveys or devoting a whole poem to the subject. As with Long Island, he usually used its Indian appelation—"Mannahatta."

> I was asking for something specific and perfect for my city,
> Whereupon lo! upsprang the aboriginal name.
>
> Now I see what there is in a name, a word, liquid, sane, unruly,
> musical, self-sufficient,
> I see that the word of my city is that word from of old,
> Because I see that word nested in nests of water-bays, superb,
> Rich, hemm'd thick all around with sailships and steamships, an
> island sixteen miles long, solid-founded,
> Numberless crowded streets, high growth of iron, slender, strong,
> light, splendidly uprising toward clear skies,

Tide swift and ample, well-loved by me, toward sundown,
The flowing sea-currents, the little islands, larger adjoining islands,
        the heights, the villas,
The countless masts, the white shore-steamers, the lighters, the
        ferry-boats, the black sea-steamers well-model'd,
The down-town streets, the jobbers' houses of business, the houses
        of business of ship-merchants and money-brokers,
        the river-streets,
Immigrants arriving, fifteen or twenty thousand in a week,
The carts hauling goods, the manly race of drivers of horses, the
        brown-faced sailors,
The summer air, the bright sun shining, and the sailing clouds
        aloft,
The winter snows, the sleigh-bells, the broken ice in the river,
        passing along up or down with the flood-tide or
        ebb-tide,
The mechanics of the city, the masters, well-form'd, beautiful-
        faced, looking you straight in the eyes,
Trottoirs throng'd, vehicles, Broadway, the women, the shops and
        shows,
A million people—manners free and superb—open voices—hospital-
        ity—the most courageous and friendly young
        men,
City of hurried and sparkling waters! city of spires and masts!
City nested in bays! my city!

Whitman's editorship of the *Aurora* brought out his opinions on
a number of topical matters, which he knew would daily be read
and considered by a few thousand readers. Political problems especially concerned him.

In the 1840s the nation had two major political parties. The
Whigs, descended from the old Federalist Party, were led by
Henry Clay and Daniel Webster. They favored a strong central
government and a limited franchise. They insisted upon a high
tariff, which would aid the development of American industries
by discouraging foreign imports while adding to the federal reve-
nues. They asked the national government to subsidize "internal
improvements" like railroads, canals, highways, and bridges. In

general, the Whigs represented both the aristocratic and business-minded people in the North.

The Democrats, inheritors of Jefferson's Democratic-Republican Party, expected state and local governments to retain primary control over laws and finances; they tended to distrust the ever-enlarging scope of the federal government—although Jackson's presidency had been exercised with an unprecedented firm, even autocratic authority. The Democrats generally wanted the suffrage extended to all freeborn men; they also encouraged the naturalization of foreigners. And they favored giving out the public lands of the West in free parcels to homesteaders. Because of these programs, the Democratic Party attracted the western settlers, the newly enfranchised workingmen, and immigrant citizens—all three groups, despite their differences, embodiments of the "average" or "common" man. Liberal thinkers and social reformers were often Democrats too. All of these voters disliked the institution of slavery, either out of principle or because it posed a threat to their own livelihoods.

Yet the plantation owners, usually slaveholders, traditionally were Democrats too, because the party derived from its agrarian and equalitarian-minded founders in the South—Jefferson and Madison. Since their economic well-being depended upon an easy exchange of their raw cotton and tobacco for the necessary, inexpensive manufactures from Europe, they objected adamantly to the Whigs' demand for ever-higher tariffs. The outstanding leader of these Southern Democrats was John C. Calhoun.

The Democratic Party, then, contained strange bedfellows. Conscientious Democrats like young Walt Whitman had trouble reconciling and promoting all their various, sometimes contradictory ideas and demands. As a loyal Democrat, editor Whitman advocated free trade. Now that the Whigs were in power, he thundered out at their imposition of a protective system which he compared to England's, one which had caused such friction between American colonists and the "mother country." To Whitman, England displayed the worst features of the Industrial Revolution. "She presents a glorious picture of the benefits of high duties," he ranted. "A government swarming with bloated parasites, and pompous lordlings—her treasury wrung from the bloody sweat of her masses, and distilled through the hot crucible of poverty, with groans and curses, and howlings of torment—her thousands of greedy human leeches, fattening on legalized extortion and theft— is she not a pretty example for us to imitate?"

Whitman noted that in the tariff system the Southern farmers were penalized while the manufacturing interests of the North were benefited. "What right has one man to expect that the fostering care of the government may be given to him more than to his neighbor?" he argued.

Whitman knew what had happened a decade before. To combat tariff proposals, Senator Calhoun proclaimed any state's right to nullify an act of Congress with which it disagreed—and its ultimate privilege to secede if the national government attempted to impose its will upon it. Only President Jackson's determination to hold the Union together and a compromise introduced by Henry Clay had eased Calhoun's stand. But a precedent had been introduced, and sooner or later the dangerous double doctrines of nullification and secession were bound to reappear, either over tariffs or the growing Northern agitation against slavery.

Although Whitman firmly believed in the importance of maintaining the unity of the American states, occasionally he would display sympathy, even encouragement, for those who advocated states' rights—as he would express, almost on the eve of the Civil War, in "To the States":

> To the States or any one of them, or any city of the States, *Resist much, obey little*,
> Once unquestioning obedience, once fully enslaved,
> Once fully enslaved, no nation, state, city, of this earth, ever afterward resumes its liberty.

Walt's refusal ever to regard uncritically the people elected to office went along with his doubts about some of the laws they enacted. He asserted the individual's right to rebel, if need be. Eventually, in "Myself and Mine," he would declare his independence in thinking and action, his inclination toward civil disobedience:

> Let others promulge the laws, I will make no account of the laws,
> Let others praise eminent men and hold up peace, I hold up
>   agitation and conflict,
> I praise no eminent man, I rebuke to his face the one that was
>   thought most worthy.

Leaves of Grass contains many a passage that might delight an anarchist or a determined revolutionist. Whitman, however, was always a talker, not an activist; his polemic poems would take the place of placards. Underlying his ostensibly revolutionary urge was his belief in the worth and native intelligence of the common man, the ordinary American citizen who deserved the best possible representation and treatment. He was angered whenever he felt the voter was being misled, shortchanged, or tyrannized. And in *Leaves of Grass* he would issue frequent reminders about whom democracy was really for:

> The sum of all known reverence I add up in you whoever you are,
> The President is there in the White House for you, it is not you
>   who are here for him,
> The Secretaries act in their bureaus for you, not you here for them,
> The Congress convenes every Twelfth-month for you,
> Laws, courts, the forming of States, the charters of cities, the going
>   and coming of commerce and mails, are all for
>   you.

In the *Aurora,* Whitman urged that the franchise be extended so that eventually everyone could vote: "We hesitate not to avow ourselves among the foremost of those who desire our experiment of man's capacity for self government, carried to its extreme verge. Every year, we wish to see the doors thrown wider and wider, and the path made broader and broader. We delight in the progress of that doctrine which teaches to elevate the low, and bring down the high." He knew that "fearful men, and proud men, and selfish men" would try to halt the spread of democracy, but said that their efforts would be in vain.

Walt already believed that men could never be legislated into moral behavior; laws would not make men good. "Were communi-

ties so constructed that to prune their errors, the only thing necessary should be the passage of *laws*, the task of reform would be
no task at all," he said. "Utopia would come to pass on double
quick time." Harboring the Democratic distrust of a strong central
government, Whitman endorsed the maxim, "The best government is that which governs least."

In "Song of the Broad-Axe" Whitman would one day limn his
own picture of a utopian society, still keeping to the idealistic concepts of government by and for people as individuals and equals—
and rebels, when necessary—which he had considered long before
while the *Aurora's* editor. The greatest city was not the place
which offered the busiest commerce, the most plentiful money, the
tallest buildings, the best schools and libraries, and the most numerous population. No, the great city stood—

> Where thrift is in its place, and prudence is in its place,
> Where the men and women think lightly of the laws,
> Where the slave ceases, and the master of slaves ceases,
> Where the populace rise at once against the never-ending audacity
>   of elected persons,
> Where fierce men and women pour forth as the sea to the whistle
>   of death pours its sweeping and unript waves,
> Where outside authority enters always after the precedence of in-
>   side authority,
> Where the citizen is always the head and ideal, and the President,
>   Mayor, Governor and what not, are agents for
>   pay,
> Where children are taught to be laws to themselves, and to depend
>   on themselves . . .

As a young newspaper editor, Walt Whitman began to make his
own proposals for the furtherance of democracy—to be continued
in both *Leaves of Grass* and various prose essays for the rest of
his lifetime. He would always find that the best method of instill-
ing the democratic spirit involved educating men's souls—that
deep-dwelling and immortal part of them which contained the
individual conscience. In *Aurora* he rhapsodized on the subject of
the soul: "so grand and noble in its capacities, so thirsty for knowl-

edge, so filled with the germs of illimitable progress." Already Walt was trying to define the human soul. To this invisible entity, Whitman would later address his many inspirational and pedagogical messages in *Leaves of Grass*. But for now, the youthful editor could only cry out, "O what venturesome mariner shall launch forth, and explore it, and take a plummet in his hand and sound its depths?" He was not prepared yet to take on the arduous job himself.

For one reason or other, or a whole collection of them, Walt incurred the dislike of his employers, and in early May of 1842 he was thrust from the editorial chair at the *Aurora*. He was not unduly disturbed; apparently he had already made plans to work as an editor for the *Evening Tattler*.

After Walt's departure, an *Aurora* editorial referred to him as "a pretty pup" who had been ousted because of "indolence, incompetence, loaferism, and blackguard habits"—not the first or last time that Walt was accused of laziness. But considering the large volume of daily wordage he spun out during only several months' time, it is hard to believe that he was so laggard and irresponsible in the performance of his duties. People tended to be misled by his appearance: slow-moving, easy-going, rarely clever or quick in social repartee. Yet on occasion Walt could be surprisingly stubborn, belligerent, or excitable—presenting a sudden, shocking contrast to his usual relaxed and amiable self.

From his new position Walt published an insulting retort. He called the *Aurora*, of which he had once been so proud, "a trashy, scurrilous, and obscene daily paper," his two former bosses "as dirty fellows as ever were able by the force of brass, ignorance of their own ignorance, and a coarse manner of familiarity, to push themselves among gentlemen." Then he settled down to a newsman's workaday world.

During the years when dozens of daily city newspapers competed fiercely, an editor was unlikely to hold his job for long. In September Walt was fired again. For the next few years he worked only intermittently at regular newspaper jobs, supporting himself mainly by free-lance journalism and by selling stories to magazines.

Publisher Park Benjamin put aside any ill feeling he may have had toward Whitman for several vicious mentions in the *Aurora* ("a reptile marking his path with slime wherever he goes . . .") and commissioned him to write a temperance novel. Walt needed money. He himself disapproved of the consumption of alcoholic spirits, especially to excess. In a matter of a month or so he finished the job. (Later, ashamed of this early "hack" novel, he claimed it only took him a few days, during which he largely subsisted on gin cocktails.)

Franklin Evans, or the Inebriate was the long and woeful tale of a young man led astray in the big city by whiskey and bad company. Because of his dissipations he broke several female hearts, but at last he reformed, to become both rich and sober. This "potboiler," published by Benjamin as a supplementary offering in the *New World*, sold as many as 20,000 copies and was reprinted later. It gained a popular readership which Whitman surely would have liked to achieve with *Leaves of Grass* during his lifetime.

Walt still took an interest in political happenings. In 1844, as the editor of the *New York Democrat*, he worked for the election of James K. Polk as President and the conscientious liberal Silas Wright as state governor. It was a year for the Democrats: both men won. But Wright was disliked by the party-machine Democrats, so Whitman's enthusiastic endorsement probably cost him his job. Walter Whitman, Jr., who had once set out confidently in New York's literary market place, was now making little headway.

The Whitman family moved back to Brooklyn in 1844. Walt's mother's health was much improved, but she had to devote considerable time and patience to raising her youngest child, Eddie, born both crippled and mentally retarded. By now Jesse and Andrew were off on their own; Mary was married and lived out on Long Island.

Walt returned to Brooklyn to live with his family. After all, his food and lodging would be cheaper and more certain that way.

New York would always be right across the river, and any day or night he could visit there just by riding the ferry that he loved.

Whitman became a correspondent for the *Long Island Star*, which had employed him as an apprentice a dozen years before. His boss, a Whig, scarcely welcomed Walt's opinions on political issues, so Walt restricted his articles largely to civic and cultural affairs. For a year and a half he served the *Star* faithfully, if not with wholehearted zeal—at a salary he could scarcely brag about.

In March of 1846 Walt Whitman became the editor of the *Brooklyn Daily Eagle*. An enterprising and politically liberal newspaper, it was only five years old but already the city's most popular publication. Since the former editor, recently deceased, had been a man known and beloved by the whole community, it was a signal honor for Walt—not quite twenty-seven years old now—to be asked to take his place.

Since the paper's owners and advisors were Democrats, Walt could often venture again into political territory. He expressed the same wide-ranging impressions and opinions as he had on the *Aurora*. But now, with four years' additional experience in living, Walt's editorial voice was firmer, more mature—not quite so shrill with the intellectual pretensions and strong prejudices of his youth.

Few of Walt's basic instincts, interests, and ideas had changed—nor would they be significantly altered later. They would appear in other forms of expression, evolve into more complex shapes. The conventionally plural editorial "we" would then become the poet's singular "I," which always had behind it the forceful voice of a composite and representative American—a man of deep feeling and broad thinking who often sounded like a newspaper editor addressing his reading public.

During his stay at the *Eagle*, Walt surely aspired to be the ideal newspaper editor. Quite probably he consciously modeled himself after Bryant of the *Evening Post*—both editor *and* poet—who sometimes came over to Brooklyn just to take long walks, and have long talks, with the young editor of the *Eagle*. (After the publication of *Leaves of Grass*, however, Bryant acted as if he had never known Walt.)

In describing the great poet, in "By Blue Ontario's Shore," Walt

might also have been delineating the role of a great newspaper
editor:

> He is the arbiter of the diverse, he is the key,
> He is the equalizer of his age and land,
> He supplies what wants supplying, he checks what wants checking,
> In peace out of him speaks the spirit of peace, large, rich, thrifty,
> > building populous towns, encouraging agricul-
> > ture, arts, commerce, lighting the study of man,
> > the soul, health, immortality, government,
> In war he is the best backer of the war, he fetches artillery as good
> > as the engineer's, he can make every word he
> > speaks draw blood,
> The years straying toward infidelity he withholds by his steady
> > faith,
> He is no arguer, he is judgment . . .

And in his *Eagle* days, Walt certainly would have agreed about
the similarity. "Perhaps no other office requires a greater union
of rare qualities than that of a true editor," he wrote.

When commencing his new assignment at the *Eagle,* Walt properly showed interest in all the daily business of life—just as he
would as a poet.

> This is the city and I am one of the citizens,
> Whatever interests the rest interests me, politics, wars, markets,
> > newspapers, schools,
> The mayor and councils, banks, tariffs, steamships, factories, stocks,
> > stores, real estate and personal estate.

Quite obviously Walt relished his daily conversations with his
readers. "We really feel a desire to talk on many subjects, to *all*
the people of Brooklyn," he confessed. Then he spoke of "a curious
kind of sympathy" toward the public which was awakened within
the editor's breast. "He gets to *love* them," said he, speaking of
the communion possible between the two parties—already anticipating the bond joining poet and reader in *Leaves of Grass.*

He took his editorial responsibilities seriously, aware that
"there are numerous noble reforms that have yet to be enacted."

And Walt Whitman, ever the didactic and idealistic schoolmaster, was ready to propose them now to a classroom the size of Brooklyn—or the entire world, if it would heed him. He wanted his words to rouse people into effective personal and communal improvements, or to change or fortify their opinions and views. His method involved appealing to both reason and emotion—a joint venture later characterizing his poetry too.

The year 1846, when Whitman became editor of the Brooklyn *Eagle*, has sometimes been called "the year of decision." The United States had reached a crucial point in its development: no longer could the young nation be contained within existing boundaries. Americans kept moving westward, and many were now making their homes on the Pacific Coast. Although the land did not legally belong to them, they thought it should. They felt that they had a God-granted right to inhabit and possess this earth they found good—whether for its gold and silver ores, its vast forests full of timber and fur-bearing animals, its majestic mountains, or its rich soil warmed by a kindly sun.

More and more people noisily urged that the United States should take possession of the Northwest and Southwest portions of the continent, allowing the nation to spread from sea to shining sea. No foreign power was going to prevent the settlement by the Americans—or their eventual dominion. After all, wasn't their democracy the best possible form of government? And the Americans brought change, progress, and unlimited opportunities for the common man: these were already regarded as near-sacred processes. The republic must acquire new property in the West— if not by peaceful annexation through diplomatic negotiations, then by sheer force.

Editor Walt Whitman enthusiastically supported this doctrine of "Manifest Destiny"—a term invented by John O'Sullivan of the *Democratic Review*. "Yankee doodledom is going ahead with the resistless energy of a sixty-five-hundred-thousand horse-power steam engine!" he exclaimed. "It is carrying everything before it South and West. . . . Whether it does these things in a conventionally 'genteel' style or not, isn't the thing: but that it will tenderly regard human life, property and rights, whatever step it takes, there is no doubt."

In the Pacific Northwest the Americans wanted land that reached into British Canada. Belligerently they chanted, "Fifty-four-forty or fight!" Hardly settled in the editor's chair, Whitman bragged about America's power: "As for the vaunted ocean-sway of Great Britain, we laugh it to scorn! It can never compete with us, either in time of peace or war. . . . England is strong, but old. America is full of young blood, young impulses, and young ambition."

When the United States compromised on its demand and settled for the forty-ninth parallel, war with England was averted. After the treaty was signed, Whitman sighed with relief: "We bless God that we have shaved past the rocks so safely—though so closely." Loudly and proudly displaying determination and armed might was one thing; actively fighting was quite another. Whitman's contradictory admiration of militant courage yet evasion or dislike of actual bloodshed would reappear again, both in his life and in *Leaves of Grass.*

Then there was the matter of the Southwest—a promising domain inherited from the Spanish conquistadors now slumbering under the lazy, feudal rule of faraway Mexico, which refused to sell it to the United States. The situation enraged editor Whitman. "What has miserable, inefficient Mexico—with her superstition, her burlesque upon freedom, her actual tyranny by the few over the many—what has she to do with the great mission of peopling the New World with a noble race?" he asked rhetorically. "Be it ours, to achieve that mission! Be it ours to roll down all of the upstart leaven of old despotism, that comes our way!"

So the Americans set out to acquire these golden lands of the West, which would become the states of California, Nevada, Arizona, New Mexico, and Utah. Their cause conveniently combined with the defense of Texas, that newly annexed state which a decade earlier had become an independent republic after defying its Mexican landlords. The Mexican War struck some Americans as crudely unethical: Horace Greeley of the *Tribune* for one; Henry David Thoreau for another. Thoreau's famous, if brief, stay in the Concord jail happened when he refused to pay taxes that would help support the war—the origin of his influential tract on "Civil Disobedience."

But the Mexican War of 1846-1848 was warmly espoused by the editor of the Brooklyn *Eagle*. "We have lofty views of the scope and destiny of our American Republic," he explained. "It is for the interest of mankind that its power and territory should be extended—the farther the better. We claim those lands, thus, by a law superior to parchments and dry diplomatic rules. . . . We do not take them to be our inferiors in any respect, but to be our equals. And future generations, thousands and millions of men, appear in the dim light of coming years, to endorse our claim."

Whitman's position has been supported by actual history, if not by the standards of proper conduct among sister nations. Whitman, the future "Poet of Democracy" whose poems occasionally promoted the American hegemony of other lands for the good of their peoples, nowhere displayed more blatantly his chauvinism or "spread-eagleism" than in these *Eagle* editorials proclaiming Manifest Destiny.

Editor Whitman prophesied great things to come from the new territorial acquisitions in the West. "The boundless free West!" he exclaimed. "We love well to contemplate it, and to think of its future, and to think how widely it will minister to human happiness and national beauty." His admiration continued in *Leaves of Grass,* as when he depicted in "Song of the Redwood-Tree":

> The flashing and golden pageant of California,
> The sudden and gorgeous drama, the sunny and ample lands,
> The long and varied stretch from Puget sound to Colorado south,
> Lands bathed in sweeter, rarer, healthier air, valleys and mountain
> cliffs,
>
> .   .   .
>
> Populous cities, the latest inventions, the steamers on the rivers,
> the railroads, with many a thrifty farm, with
> machinery,
> And wool and wheat and the grape, and diggings of yellow gold.

Whitman believed that the great American of the future would come from the motley western combination of Yankee settlers,

European immigrants, and native residents. "From their loins will spring a race, nobly happy as our earlier freemen," he wrote in the *Eagle*. "For of such crude, turbulent, and unhewn energies, the grandest empires have evolved themselves." To Walt this new, idealized man of the West, and his female counterpart, would always epitomize the rough and pure spirit of American democracy itself. So when he wrote poems about the West, its citizens' character would play the grandest role:

> The new society at last, proportionate to Nature,
> In man of you, more than your mountain peaks or stalwart trees
> imperial,
> In woman more, far more, than all your gold or vines, or even vital
> air.

Walt Whitman's vision of the pioneer—that restless, westward-moving, democratic, nation-building American—always stayed with him. On his route through life, Whitman's pioneer symbolically took mankind along with him to fulfill the dreams of bygone centuries. Whitman expressed this young, hopeful, thrusting, dominating spirit effectively in his well-known poem "Pioneers! O Pioneers!":

> Come, my tan-faced children,
> Follow well in order, get your weapons ready,
> Have you your pistols? have you your sharp-edged axes?
> Pioneers! O pioneers!
>
> For we cannot tarry here,
> We must march my darlings, we must bear the brunt of danger,
> We the youthful sinewy races, all the rest on us depend,
> Pioneers! O pioneers!
>
> O you youths, Western youths,
> So impatient, full of action, full of manly pride and friendship,
> Plain I see you Western youths, see you tramping with the foremost,
> Pioneers! O pioneers!
>
> Have the elder races halted?
> Do they droop and end their lesson, wearied over there beyond the
> seas?

> We take up the task eternal, and the burden and the lesson,
> Pioneers! O pioneers!

The addition of the new territories to the Union increased the bitter intensity of the old feud of free soil versus slavery. The Southern planters, whose soil was depleted from years of overproduction and mismanagement, demanded an equal right to expand westward. They urgently needed unused lands on which to plant their cotton; naturally they expected to take their slaves with them.

Like many another "Yankee," editor Whitman decried this threatened spread of the "peculiar institution" into the West. In an article entitled "The American Workingmen, *Versus* Slavery," he declared that the new territories should not be closed to white freemen from the South who took their axes and plows into the wilderness prepared to wield them themselves. But he wanted to exclude "the *aristocracy* of the South—the men who work only with other men's hands." Slavery might benefit the rich, true; "But it is destructive to the dignity and independence of all who work, and to labor itself."

Whitman now implored all workingmen of the country "to speak in a voice whose great reverberations" would show their refusal to be put in a position of competition with slaves. With vast confidence, Whitman predicted a quick defeat of the Southern landowners in expanding their domains. Yet he did foresee the approach of an enormous nationwide torrent: "Already the roar of waters is heard; and if a few short-sighted ones seek to withstand it, the surge, terrible in its fury, will sweep them too in the ruin."

Meanwhile, this impending flood tide was being whipped into furious waves by the Abolitionists, who were obsessed by the desire to stop—forcibly if need be—the enslavement of one portion of the human race by another. Although cause-committed men like William Lloyd Garrison, Wendell Phillips, and John Brown impressed Whitman, he refused to join them in a single-minded concentration on the slavery issue. "All of them," he remarked in his old age, "thought slavery the one crying sin of the universe. I didn't—though I, too, thought it a crying sin."

As editor of the *Eagle*, Whitman called the slave trade "that most abominable of all man's schemes for making money." But as he walked the streets of Brooklyn and Manhattan and then returned to his office to write, he was much aware of many other "crying sins" in the world—and conscious too of his inability to change or cure them, as he later confessed when a poet.

> I sit and look out upon all the sorrows of the world, and upon all oppression and shame,
> . . .
> I see in low life the mother misused by her children, dying, neglected, gaunt, desperate,
> I see the wife misused by her husband, I see the treacherous seducer of young women,
> . . .
> I see the workings of battle, pestilence, tyranny, I see martyrs and prisoners,
> . . .
> I observe the slights and degradations cast by arrogant persons upon the laborers, the poor, and upon negroes, and the like;
> All these—all the meanness and agony without end I sitting look out upon,
> See, hear, and am silent.

Whitman rightly suspected that the Abolitionists' extreme agitation would harm the cause of national peace and unity. Their often fanatical methods eventually forced most Southerners—even those who opposed slavery—to join together and confront the opposition.

As for the black race, Whitman included it well within the borders of Jefferson's declaration that "all men are created equal." *Leaves of Grass* was to have many references to Negroes (with a small "n") in terms of respect or fond admiration. Whitman often portrayed them doing their work well—which was his best reason for ever praising anybody.

> The negro holds firmly the reins of his four horses, the block swags underneath on its tied-over chain,

The negro that drives the long dray of the stone-yard, steady and
tall he stands pois'd on one leg on the string-
piece,
His blue shirt exposes his ample neck and breast and loosens over
his hip-band,
His glance is calm and commanding, he tosses the slouch of his hat
away from his forehead,
The sun falls on his crispy hair and mustache, falls on the black of
his polish'd and perfect limbs.

I behold the picturesque giant and love him . . .

With his capacity for identifying himself with everyone and
everything, Walt could vividly imagine and portray the sufferings
of a captured runaway slave:

I am the hounded slave, I wince at the bite of the dogs,
Hell and despair are upon me, crack and again crack the marks-
men,
I clutch the rails of the fence, my gored ribs, thinn'd with the ooze
of my skin,
I fall on the weeds and stones,
The riders spur their unwilling horses, haul close,
Taunt my dizzy ears and beat me violently over the head with
whipstocks.

And Whitman figured what he himself might do if he lived
farther south and an escaped slave sought sanctuary at his doorstep:

The runaway slave came to my house and stopt outside,
I heard his motions crackling the twigs of the woodpile,
Through the swung half-door of the kitchen I saw him limpsy and
weak,
And went where he sat on a log and led him in and assured him,

•   •   •

He staid with me a week before he was recuperated and pass'd
north,
I had him sit next me at table, my fire-lock lean'd in the corner.

To Walt, the Negro was a man like himself, with his own free, equal, and inviolable body and soul.

In all the talk about slavery, Whitman did not forget the plight of the immigrants in America. Many foreigners suffered from social and economic deprivations and discriminations not experienced by Negro slaves, whose lives were tied into the secure—if rigid and inhumane—caste system on plantations. The arguments of the Native American Party (to be nicknamed the "Know-Nothings") grew ever more venomous, especially toward the Irish and German immigrants. Nativists demanded the denial of citizenship to all aliens; they even wanted to halt immigration itself. As the western lands were opened up for settlement, they feared that the immigrants encouraged to come over and settle there would threaten the republic far more than the existence of slavery.

Whitman had no patience with prejudiced people. "Foreigner" was a word he wanted to banish from the vocabulary of the nation's press. "How," he asked, "can any man with a heart in his breast, begrudge the coming of Europe's needy ones, to the plentiful storehouse of the New World?" And not just the hungry and homeless came, he saw; many emigrated to the United States because it was the haven of freedom and democracy. But all too often the immigrants arriving on America's shores remained in the congested port cities to make precarious and unsatisfactory livings. Whitman proposed that the government form an agency to direct them westward, where their eager capacity for work would surely be appreciated and justly rewarded.

While Walt Whitman warmly welcomed the influx of people from abroad, he warned them that the United States did not need or want their alien ways: it was constructing its own standards. He found unmistakable traces of dangerous influences in imported "culture." The English dramas and actors, which had once thrilled him, he now denigrated. Their productions were made for English not American audiences. "MISERABLE STATE OF THE STAGE.—WHY CAN'T WE HAVE SOMETHING WORTH THE NAME OF AMERICAN DRAMA!" became a headline for one of Whitman's diatribes.

The "Young America" program proposed by John O'Sullivan was resoundingly seconded by the editor of the *Eagle*. Walt formulated ambitious plans to make Manhattan the center for a revolution in the American arts. "With all our servility to foreign fashions," he said, "there is at the heart of the intelligent masses there, a lurking propensity toward what is original, and has a stamped American character of its own." And he cheered the increasing power of organizations of young patriots who were "enthusiastic, democratic, and liberal in their feelings."

In a crude form, this cultural chauvinism about drama soon broke out in the notorious Astor Place Riot, when the highly talented English actor William Charles Macready was visiting New York. Edwin Forrest, an American actor who was tremendously popular but vainglorious, fancied that Macready had slighted him when he had recently visited England, and he let his feelings be widely known. Political bosses and malcontents used this supposed "insult" as an opportunity to express Anglophobia and assert Americanism. In an ugly and frenzied support of America's "artistic supremacy," twenty-two rioters were killed and scores of others wounded.

Whitman also launched an editorial attack upon contemporary literature. Americans too long had been subservient to English taste, ready to accept whatever English products were praised by their critics (which often, to Whitman's thinking, turned out to be trash). Most American writers also imitated foreign styles rather than expressing something genuinely American in style and content. Already Whitman was seized by the notion that Americans should create their own literature. He had the utmost confidence in their ability to do so: "We forget that God has given the American mind powers of analysis and acuteness superior to those possessed by any other nation on earth."

Mightier than sword or scepter, said Whitman, was the pen: "a little crispy goose quill, which, though its point can hardly pierce your sleeve of broadcloth, is able to make gaping wounds in mighty empires—to put the power of kings in jeopardy, or even chop off their heads—to sway the energy and will of congregated masses of men. . . ." Then he made an intriguing speculation. "At this hour in some part of the earth, it may be, that the delicate scraping of a pen over paper, like the nibbling of little mice, is at work which shall show its results sooner or later in the convulsion of the social or political world. Amid penury and destitution, unknown and unnoticed, a man may be toiling on to the completion of a book destined to gain acclamations, reiterated again and again, from admiring America and astonished Europe!"

As far as we know, Walt at that time had not yet envisaged *his* revolutionary book; nor was any American involved in such pen-scrapings. But at the very time Karl Marx, in his London garret, with assistance from Friedrich Engels, was writing *The Communist Manifesto* and laying the groundwork for the monumental *Das Kapital:* two documents that would, instead of arousing widespread approval, convulse Europe and frighten America.

Music did not escape from Whitman's cultural program for America. As the critic representing his newspaper, he frequently attended concerts and operas. "Great is the power of music over a people!" he acknowledged with ardor. And then he launched one of his accustomed perorations: "As for us of America, we have long enough followed obedient and childlike in the track of the Old World. We have received her tenors and her buffos . . . listened to and applauded the songs made for a different state of society . . . and it is time that such listening and receiving should cease. The subtlest spirit of a nation is expressed through its music—and the music acts reciprocally upon the nation's very soul." (Walt would often call his poems "songs" or "chants.")

Walt Whitman also looked critically at the American people themselves, at work and at play. Their current proclivities were bound to influence the future citizenry. And although Whitman liked humankind, individually and collectively, he was not blind to faults and frailties. Much as he enjoyed ferry trips, he deplored the crowd's behavior as it swarmed and pushed on board. He interpreted this as a sign of the deadening of human sympathy caused by city living. "This rushing and raging is not inconsistent, however, with other items of the American character," he noted. "Perhaps it is a development of the 'indomitable energy' and 'chainless enterprise' which we get so much praise for. But it is a very ludicrous thing, nevertheless." He need not have worried, though, over posterity's opinion about their ancestors' behavior at the ferry landing; he did not anticipate rush hour in a subway station.

The perpetual, all-consuming pursuit of material gain was to Walt an even more disconcerting defect in the American character. "Oh, Fool! The little birds, and the sheep in the field, possess more reason than thou," he exhorted in a Biblical tone; "for when once their natural wants are satisfied, they repose and toil no more." From this money-mania Whitman traced the breakdown of religion, morality, health, and happiness. He asked his readers to guard against greed. "We work and toil, and sweat away our youth and manhood," he said, "giving up the improvement of our minds and the cultivation of our physical nature; weakly thinking that a heap of money, when we are old, can make up for these sacrifices."

Whitman would never be guilty of practicing such gross materialism, either in his own life or by praising it in *Leaves of Grass*. Often he would express pity and contempt for those who neglected the true "feast," enjoyed by those who kept a sensible balance between work and leisure. All too often heavy labors earned naught of value:

> Here and there with dimes on the eyes walking,
> To feed the greed of the belly the brains liberally spooning,
> Tickets buying, taking, selling, but in to the feast never once going,
> Many sweating, ploughing, thrashing, and then the chaff for payment receiving,
> A few idly owning, and they the wheat continually claiming.

One's innate sense of beauty should always be cultivated as food for the soul, Whitman maintained. Great works of art could benefit the character and actions of all who beheld them. Yet wonders might come from a less ambitious exposure to nature and to human artistry. Walt wished that all laboring people could have some adornment in their homes, however humble: "A print hung on the wall, a pot of flowers or even the occasional noise of an accordeon. . . ." "And if we are met with a ready rejoinder," he continued, "that 'it is hard enough for poor folks to earn the necessaries of life, let alone things which they can neither eat nor wear,' we still say that the higher appetite, the appetite for beauty and the intellectual, must be consulted too, and the bread and beef should not always be allowed to carry the day." During his forthcoming dedication to the craft of poem-making, Walt often forsook the bread and beef: he rarely gave out advice which he himself did not, or ultimately would not, heed.

There was, however, one notable exception. "Young man reader!" he commanded. "If you have good health, are over twenty-one years old, and have nothing to 'incumber' you, go and get married." On Walt's list of the world's fools were the bachelors and maidens old enough to marry but likely to "die and give no sign" of ever wanting or intending to. "There be some, doubtless, who may not be blamed, whom peculiar circumstances keep in the bands of the solitary," Whitman allowed; "but the most of both sexes can find partners meet for them. Turn, Fools, and get discretion. Buy cradles and double beds; make yourself a reality in life—and do the State some service."

Editor Whitman seemed eminently qualified for marriage, even though he helped to support his family. But whatever his excuses may have been at the time, he showed small inclination to supply his own life with new furniture. Perhaps no one had been able to measure up to Walt's idealization of his own mother as the perfect woman and mate. Or perhaps there were other "peculiar circumstances" all his own which made him delay marrying; anyway, he had never really shown much romantic interest in girls.

But most importantly, Walt may have felt that his own imagination supplied the best "cradles and double beds." He could summon them and their occupants forth whenever he wished; could alter child or woman to suit his mood; and when other concerns engrossed him, his "family" discreetly vanished—instead of intruding or crying or asking him to rush to the grocers to buy a quart of milk. Yet while they stayed, to him they were probably as real and as wonderful as any actual wife or child could be.

Whitman lived in an age when proper people avoided mentioning the parts and functions of the human body. Emphasis was upon parlor manners and a fashionable appearance, not on good health. The *Eagle*'s editor, however, took a keen, salutary interest in the matter of physical culture—"a sound mind in a sound body." He urged his readers to improve their health by bathing, good grooming, outdoor recreation, and regular exercise—for women as well as men. Whitman's preoccupation with hygiene naturally continued in *Leaves of Grass:*

> All comes by the body, only health puts you rapport with the
> universe.

In perfect physical condition, one could dwell upon every inch of the body, amply enjoying the simple, pleasurable sensations of its vital functions which led to the discovery of the soul behind them—as Whitman would express it in "I Sing the Body Electric":

> The skin, the sunburnt shade, freckles, hair,
> The curious sympathy one feels when feeling with the hand the
> naked meat of the body,
> The circling rivers the breath, and breathing it in and out,
> The beauty of the waist, and thence of the hips, and thence down-
> ward toward the knees,
> The thin red jellies within you or within me, the bones and the
> marrow in the bones,
> The exquisite realization of health;
> O I say these are not the parts and poems of the body only, but of
> the soul,
> O I say now these are the soul!

Walt took superb care of his own body. His skin and clothes were immaculately tended. He did not smoke, steered clear of drugs, and only rarely drank alcoholic beverages—these usually beer and wine. He doubtless found enough to intoxicate his senses just by feeling alive and well. He took long walks, during which he gathered material for his newspaper columns. As a matter of daily routine he went to a public bathhouse, where he exercised by swimming.

During these Brooklyn years, while striding proudly about town almost with a proprietary air, Walt was already cultivating a special pose, intended to impress all who beheld him:

> . . . The expression of a well-made man appears not only in his face,
> It is in his limbs and joints also, it is curiously in the joints of his hips and wrists,
> It is in his walk, the carriage of his neck, the flex of his waist and knees, dress does not hide him,
> The strong sweet quality he has strikes through the cotton and broadcloth,
> To see him pass conveys as much as the best poem . . .

One of Walt's jobs as editor was to agitate for civic improvements. "CLEAN THE STREETS!" Whitman ordered his subscribers in April of 1847. Apparently they paid little attention to him, because in June he went further. "Brooklyn," he said, "bids fair to be christened the ensuing summer with the name of 'the city of dirt'—and what is worse, she will richly deserve such a name." Whitman's tidy Dutch nature would not tolerate filth and garbage.

Whitman proposed turning Fort Greene into a municipal park, where on Sundays and holidays the working people could relax and enjoy some of the delights of nature within the city limits. In time the legislature granted his wish. Walt could be depended upon to compose patriotic salutes on the Fourth of July, praising the nation's heroic warriors. "The bright example, planted in the firm foundation of the nation's love, will do more good than essays from a thousand theorists," he averred.

Editor Whitman frequently admired products of man's inventive genius—whether cities, the new rotary press installed at the *Eagle*'s printing office, or the complex mechanism that propelled the Fulton Ferry. "It is an almost sublime sight," he wrote after visiting the ferryboat's engine room. "There are few more magnificent pieces of handiwork than a powerful steam-engine, swiftly at work!" He gave a detailed description of its actions, then concluded: "It makes one think that man—he who can invent such powers as this—is not such an insignificant creature after all."

The Industrial Revolution might have its drawbacks, but Whitman would always appreciate its marvels, often finding them suitable subjects for poetizing.

Many of the generative ideas of Whitman's era were expressed in current books, which Walt reviewed for the edification of his readers. Not always having time to read books completely, he picked out items that interested him, in a sort of "smorgasbord" reading which became a lifetime habit. Many literary works—even if from abroad—pleased him greatly; he especially enjoyed the philosophical novels by the Frenchwoman George Sand.

Whitman started reading the books by Thomas Carlyle, the Scottish historian and philosopher who was mentor and friend to the popular American writer and lecturer, Ralph Waldo Emerson. At first he confessed that Carlyle's "rapt, weird" style disturbed him. "No great writer achieves any thing worthy of him, by inventing merely a new *style*," Whitman remarked. "Style in writing, is much as dress in society; sensible people will conform to the prevalent mode, as it is not of infinite importance any how. . . ." Soon, however, Walt was finding things original and fascinating in Carlyle's prose—once he got used to it. By the time Whitman evolved his own peculiar style for *Leaves of Grass*, he apparently had decided that conformity to popular "dress" was inconvenient for his purpose. Sometimes an odd appearance, in either clothes or language usage, has advertised a special talent.

During these years as a Brooklyn journalist, Walt Whitman seemed to have abandoned his earlier ambition to become a creative writer. Yet now and again he revealed an underlying concern for poetry—as when he stopped by the grave of Brooklyn's "mad poet," McDonald Clarke, who had shown considerable promise but died destitute and insane, the laughingstock of the New York literati.

Whitman felt that Clarke had possessed some of the true poet's requisites: "the power, in his writings, to draw bold, startling images, and strange pictures—the power to embody in language, original and beautiful and quaint ideas." Yet he concluded, while standing over Clarke's grave, that "genius, after all, is a dangerous trait. Its fires, to be sure, sometimes enlighten and beautify, but quite often scorch, wither, and blast the soul of its possessor."

Perhaps Walt had some personal inkling of the tensions and frustrations and strange biddings within an oversensitive mind—especially when there was no satisfactory way to organize and release compelling thoughts and turbulent feelings. And concerned though he was with all the particulars of daily living—since his job involved commenting upon them—Whitman surely knew that something within him lay untouched, untapped, barely comprehended. Inevitably, at times, Walt felt almost detached from the world that was real to other people; and one day—not too distant now—he would be able to tell of it.

> Trippers and askers surround me,
> People I meet, the effect upon me of my early life or the ward and
>   city I live in, or the nation,
> The latest dates, discoveries, inventions, societies, authors old and
>   new,
> My dinner, dress, associates, looks, compliments, dues,
>
>   •   •   •
>
> These come to me days and nights and go from me again,
> But they are not the Me myself.
>
> Apart from the pulling and hauling stands what I am,
> Stands amused, complacent, compassionating, idle, unitary,
> Looks down, is erect, or bends an arm on an impalpable certain
>   rest,
> Looking with side-curved head curious what will come next,
> Both in and out of the game and watching and wondering at it.

In a little notebook Walt was soon to write: "I cannot understand the mystery, but I am always conscious of myself as two—as my soul and I: and I reckon it is the same with all men and women." In the next few years Whitman would start to explore who and what this other half of himself might be—the resident spirit that would initiate a whole new way of life.

I loafe and invite my soul,
I lean and loafe at my ease observing
a spear of summer grass.

V

I LOAFE AND INVITE MY SOUL

(1848-1855)

The now-savage rift within the Democratic Party existed in miniature in the office of the *Daily Eagle*. Its publisher, like many Northern Democrats, wanted to placate the Southerners by allowing them space in the West: only with the southern vote behind them could they hope to win the 1848 presidential election. However, editor Walt Whitman took a different stand on the question of free soil in the new American territories. More than once he must have voiced his disgust over the "Old Hunker" Democrats —so-called because they hankered or "hunkered" after political office. He felt that they cast aside their principles by compromising, and for the sake of a nebulous victory, undermined the rights of freemen of the North.

By now Walt counted himself among the "Barnburner" faction in the Democratic Party, which wished to prohibit slavery throughout the West. "Keeping the party together" didn't interest them at all; they were likened to the farmer who set fire to his barn just to get rid of rats.

In February of 1848 Walter Whitman, Jr. either resigned or was dismissed from his post at the *Eagle*. Later a rival Brooklyn newspaper friendly to him declared that he had been fired after booting downstairs an insulting "Old Hunker" politician. Not so, replied the *Eagle*'s owner, vitriolic on the subject of his former employee. "Slow, indolent, heavy, discourteous, and without steady principles, he was a clog upon our success," he said. "Whoever knows him will laugh at the idea of his *kicking any body*, much less a prominent politician. He is too indolent to kick a musketo."

Again Walt Whitman looked for a steady job. Soon, as luck had it, in a theater lobby one night he met a man who was starting a newspaper in New Orleans. Whitman immediately struck him as a good man to have on his editorial staff. In a quarter-hour a deal was made, and Walt received two hundred dollars for his traveling expenses.

Two days later Whitman left New York, taking along fourteen-year-old Jeff—always his favorite brother. Lighthearted Jeff would be a fine traveling companion, and in New Orleans he could provide a bit of family life for Walt.

Walt commenced this first long trip away from home territory with enthusiasm. By trains they sped to Baltimore, then on to Cumberland. The Allegheny Mountains were crossed by stagecoach. At Wheeling, in western Virginia, the brothers boarded a steamboat that took them down the muddy, winding Ohio River and then into the Mississippi.

Now Whitman was getting a close-up look at the "Western" man of whom he had formed great expectations. He found his table manners crude and his society surly, almost brutish. So Walt switched his attention to the amazing variety of cargoes loaded onto steamboats and flatboats and transported up or down the big river. Here before his eyes was ample evidence of his nation's enormous, energetic commerce in the products from forests, farms, mines, fisheries, and factories.

Toward the end of February—two weeks after leaving Brooklyn —Walt and Jeff Whitman arrived in New Orleans. They took a room at a hotel right across the street from the *Crescent*'s office. At once Walt went to work helping to prepare the paper's first edition on March 5. Jeff was given a job as office boy.

Walt Whitman was expected to provide the general news—usually by cutting and rewriting stories received from other sources, mainly out-of-town papers which had agreed to an exchange of news items. For an extra fee he could write "feature" articles. He soon launched a series of reports on his recent travels.

Walt put in a long workday, from nine in the morning until about eleven o'clock at night. Often as a reporter he attended social and cultural events. One night he was happy to be in the theater when General Zachary Taylor appeared, back victorious from the Mexican War and dressed in civilian clothes, ready to enjoy himself hugely. Taylor was the sort of man Walt could admire: plain-talking, fast-acting, courageous almost to a fault, and unpretentious—like Andrew Jackson, a "man of the people," and soon to become "the people's choice."

Whitman saw a show called "Model Artists," in which scantily clad performers took the poses of famous statues. Wherever the offering had been given, severe scoldings had been published in the press. Whitman, however, took a different attitude. In several editorials he stoutly defended this public exposure of the human body. "It is a sickly prudishness," he maintained, "that bars all appreciation of the divine beauty evidenced in Nature's cunningest work—the human frame, form and face." Coarseness and grossness were obviously not intended by the artists involved. "Eve in Paradise—or Adam either—would not be supposed to shock the mind," he said.

Walt's defense was thoroughly consistent with his previously expressed praises of the human body in the *Eagle*; it was to be carried further still in *Leaves of Grass*, especially in the "Children of Adam" group, in which Whitman revealed his visions of the "new" modern-day natural man and woman, as beautiful and innocent as the two Biblical progenitors had been in Eden.

> As Adam early in the morning,
> Walking forth from the bower refresh'd with sleep,
> Behold me where I pass, hear my voice, approach,
> Touch me, touch the palm of your hand to my body as I pass,
> Be not afraid of my body.

Walt readily appreciated New Orleans' many displays, from the fat mulatto woman in a street stall who sold him his morning coffee—hot, thick, bitter—to the overall atmosphere of friendly gaiety, in which French words and phrases lent an exotic charm. The city stayed fresh forever in Walt's remembrances. His fondness was extended far outside the city limits, so that always he kept a filial feeling for the whole South, portraying it in its various aspects throughout *Leaves of Grass.*

Yet Whitman often felt melancholy in this place to which he did not really belong and where he had few, if any, friends. Although Jeff kept Walt company, he was still almost a child. In leisure hours Walt wrote letters home, but for some while he received no replies—contributing to Jeff's homesickness as well as his own. Although Walt seemingly had never displayed strong sexual impulses, he was now developing a longing for close friendship: the beginning of a deep dependency upon associations with particular people—of either sex, of any age—which at times could be troubling, passionate, and overpowering.

A solitary oak tree which Walt noticed one day became etched in his mind, to be recalled when he later told of his loneliness and his need of friends:

> I saw in Louisiana a live-oak growing,
> All alone stood it and the moss hung down from the branches,
> Without any companion it grew there uttering joyous leaves of
> dark green,
> And its look, rude, unbending, lusty, made me think of myself,
> But I wonder'd how it could utter joyous leaves standing alone
> there without its friend near, for I knew I could
> not . . .

On the basis of a few newspaper sketches written at the time and a single poem, composed years afterward, some early Whitman biographers decided that his stay in New Orleans provided his first real love affair with a woman, thereby opening a door to his inner feelings, releasing his "libido," and thus enabling him to discover his hidden, creative spirit. This supposed romantic interlude—with a woman thought variously to be from a proud

Creole family or already married, who possibly conceived a child by Walt—was tragically brief: its interruption propelled Whitman into becoming a poet who could now write in a frankly impassioned and wholly unique way.

Here is the poem these biographers offered as clear evidence of Whitman's bittersweet experience:

> Once I pass'd through a populous city imprinting my brain for
> future use with its shows, architecture, customs,
> traditions,
> Yet now of all that city I remember only a woman I casually met
> there who detain'd me for love of me,
> Day by day and night by night we were together—all else has long
> been forgotten by me,
> I remember I say only that woman who passionately clung to me,
> Again we wander, we love, we separate again,
> Again she holds me by the hand, I must not go,
> I see her close beside me with silent lips sad and tremulous.

This neat explanation for the emergence of Whitman's poetic genius had to be questioned, however, when a manuscript revealed that the poem's original version gave the subject as a man, not a woman—with the attachment rough and comradely instead of traditionally romantic. Yet that earlier version (as well as the "live-oak" poem) was written during the period when Whitman was preoccupied with "manly love" or "adhesiveness"—the close and affectionate friendship between men. It is still possible that in rendering a parting incident of his past into its final form, Whitman was recapturing an actual romantic liaison with a woman in New Orleans, who assisted in his belated initiation into sexual maturity, which would play a part in the maturation of his literary gifts.

Whatever may be the real story of Whitman's "secret life" in the South, it is certain at least that his sojourn in New Orleans came to an abrupt end. Nobody knows exactly why. Perhaps Walt, seeing Jeff tired and homesick, strenuously objected to his being overworked by their employers; or his pro-Northern, antislavery opinions—much as he tried to keep them discreetly to himself—

sometimes crept out in comments or arguments; or Walt, owed extra money for his features, may have pressed for payment and hence given the paper's owners cause to find some excuse for firing him.

In any event, Walt again was out of a job; he had no reason to hang around. He and Jeff left for the North almost at once on a steamboat bound for St. Louis (one day to become Jeff's home). They took another boat up the Illinois River, then boarded a canalboat going to Chicago. On their wide swing homeward, the Whitman brothers also saw the Great Lakes and the mighty Niagara Falls.

Walt had wished to see as much of the United States as he could. Now he had viewed some of the South, taken a look at the prairies, traveled on the ingenious waterways which connected the American interior, and glimpsed thick forests where the Indians and French fur traders had once held sway. All the while he was observing the activities of the people who farmed, fished, hunted, lumbered, hauled, and built towns in the wilderness— eventually to lend many authentic details and provide broad background scenery for the "catalogues" of American life in *Leaves of Grass*.

After a train ride to Albany and a day's journey by boat down the Hudson River, Walt and Jeff were back in Brooklyn by mid-June of 1848. If the South had done anything to change Whitman radically, it was not immediately apparent. He plunged back into the political disputes which were growing hotter as the presidential election neared. At the Democratic Party's nominating convention, the antislavery "Barnburners" split off from the "Old Hunkers," then held their own caucus, which Whitman attended as a delegate. The new Free-Soil Party selected former President Martin Van Buren as its standard-bearer, to run against the two generals, Lewis Cass and Zachary Taylor, chosen by the Democrats and the Whigs.

With financial help from friends, Whitman started a weekly paper called the *Freeman* to promote Van Buren and express free-soil opinions during the election campaign. But on the day following the first issue's publication, a fire destroyed the printing office.

By the time Walt was able to publish again, the election was over. Thanks to the great popularity of Taylor and the split in the Democrats' ranks, the Whigs had easily won. Still, Walt and others saw plenty of reason to keep up their free-soil agitation— just as the Abolitionists, whose movement centered in Boston, continued their attacks upon slavery. For a year, Walt remained editor of the *Freeman*.

Forces were now at work within Walt Whitman to alter his way of life. He had recently seen for himself other regions of his great nation and watched many of its people's doings. The experience had deeply moved him and set him to wondering anew why no American writer had yet captured, or even tried to capture, the vast shape and vital spirit of the United States.

During the near-thirty years of his life Walt had absorbed so very much; and what he had not actually experienced he could hear or read about and vividly imagine. If no one else would undertake the job of putting the whole of America into a book, why not he?

The destiny as poet momentarily sensed by the boy upon a seashore at night, who had understood a lonely mockingbird's song, drew closer now. The stirring of a summons was taking place within Walt Whitman: he must begin to sing out, he must try to create a poetic idiom that would be distinctively American in spirit and scope. In "Starting from Paumanok" he would later tell something of his feeling then.

> Starting from fish-shape Paumanok where I was born,
> Well-begotten, and rais'd by a perfect mother,
> After roaming many lands, lover of populous pavements,
> Dweller in Mannahatta my city, or on southern savannas,
> Or a soldier camp'd or carrying my knapsack and gun, or a miner
>   in California,
> Or rude in my home in Dakota's woods, my diet meat, my drink
>   from the spring,
> Or withdrawn to muse and meditate in some deep recess,
> Far from the clank of crowds intervals passing rapt and happy,

Aware of the fresh free giver the flowing Missouri, aware of the
    mighty Niagara,
Aware of the buffalo herds grazing the plains, the hirsute and
    strong-breasted bull,
Of earth, rocks, Fifth-month flowers experienced, stars, rain, snow,
    my amaze,
Having studied the mocking-bird's tones and the flight of the
    mountain-hawk,
And heard at dawn the unrivall'd one, the hermit thrush from the
    swamp-cedars,
Solitary, singing in the West, I strike up for a New World.

Whitman was to serve a six-year apprenticeship in poetry-writing, from 1849 to 1855. The product of his labors, the first edition of *Leaves of Grass,* would be like no other volume of poems ever seen before. Whitman came on the literary scene with a unique, physically vigorous, spiritually exuberant poetic talent. The book's publication announced the hatching of a new species of bird—a rare bird of the human spirit that emerged from a seemingly ordinary egg. For years this spirit had lain near-dormant, encased within its conventional shell; suddenly it burst upon the world outside, to sing songs never heard before and to soar on wings which took it anywhere and everywhere.

In his later years, Walt Whitman summed up this new creative phase in his life: "After continued personal ambition and effort, as a young fellow, to enter with the rest into competition for the usual rewards, business, political, literary, &c. . . . I found myself remaining possess'd, at the age of thirty-one to thirty-three, with a special desire and conviction. Or rather, to be exact, a desire that had been flitting through my previous life . . . had steadily advanced to the front, defined itself, and finally dominated everything else. This was a feeling or ambition to articulate and faithfully express in literary or poetic form, and uncompromisingly, my own physical, emotional, moral, intellectual, and aesthetic Personality, in the midst of, and tallying, the momentous spirit and facts of its immediate days, and of current America—and to exploit that Personality, identified with place and date, in a far more candid and comprehensive sense than any hitherto poem or book."

There will never be an end to the literary scholarship that examines the genesis of *Leaves of Grass* as well as its meanings. As happens with all works of man's genius, a hundred different germinating factors have already been named, labeled, scrutinized, demonstrated. Many parallels have been drawn between other people's ideas and those propounded by Whitman. His radically different poetic style, which dropped the expected devices of rhymes and regular stanza rhythms, has also been pinned down often for thorough dissections. And line by line, word by word, his poetry has been psychoanalyzed—invariably proving that his phraseology discloses a variety of psychopathological peculiarities.

The same close attention is devoted to the transformation of the journalist-about-town Walter Whitman, Jr.—conventionally garbed, ambitious in a worldly way, a sometime-printer, school-teacher, politician, writer—into the poet Walt Whitman, a very different person indeed in appearance, mannerisms, and aims. This new "Walt"— the name which his family always called him, far more satisfactory now than Walter in its proletarian informality— kept his wide-brimmed hat at a jaunty angle; dressed in carpenter's striped work clothes, with the shirt open at the neck, exposing a red undershirt and part of a hirsute chest; let his prematurely graying hair and beard grow as they would; consorted with ferry pilots, omnibus drivers, workingmen, and artists, preferring them to the polite society gathered in parlors and literary salons; and seemed, as he strolled along the streets of Brooklyn and Manhattan, superbly confident of the friendship of the entire universe.

Yet this change in Whitman's personality was hardly as surprising as the emergence of a striking talent for self-expression; and the various ideas and feelings which spewed forth like veritable cataracts in *Leaves of Grass* were more readily traceable to their sources than Whitman's new, boldly fashioned "free verse" style.

After giving up editing the *Freeman,* Whitman did free-lance journalism for New York and Brooklyn newspapers. But he no longer seemed anxious to obtain a regular "sit" on an editorial

staff. The year 1849 marked the real beginning of Walt's metamorphosis from journalist to poet, and during it he received satisfying "proof" that nature had really intended him to take up this
new career: the shape of his own head gave the best evidence.

The nineteenth century experienced a vogue for phrenology, the
"science" of determining human character by studying an individual's skull. The human cranium had been neatly divided into
a few dozen zones, and after feeling protruberances and depressions an expert phrenologist charted his subject's attributes, defects, and other personality data.

Walt first became interested in phrenology when he reviewed
several books about it for the *Eagle,* but not until the summer of
1849 did he commence a personal investigation. He probably made
his initial visit to the Fowlers' Phrenological Cabinet in New York
as a reporter on the prowl for a story. Later he had his own "chart
of bumps" drawn up by Lorenzo Fowler himself, who either
showed an acute ability to detect character at a glance, or was
already sufficiently acquainted with Whitman to be able to render
an accurate summary. "This man has a grand physical constitution,
and power to live to a good old age," he wrote. "He is undoubtedly
descended from the soundest and hardiest stock. Size of head
large. Leading traits of character appear to be Friendship, Sympathy, Sublimity, and Self-Esteem, and markedly among his combinations the dangerous faults of Indolence, a tendency to the
pleasure of Voluptuousness and Alimentiveness and a certain reckless swing of animal will, too unmindful, probably, of the conviction of others."

But the most important item in the analysis was Fowler's assertion that Whitman possessed to a notable degree the attributes of
a poet. This may well have been the encouragement Walt needed
to propel him forward into a new career. Whitman must have
been thinking of this phrenological factor when in "Song of Myself" he said—

By my life-lumps! becoming already a creator,
Putting myself here and now to the ambush'd womb of the
    shadows.

(He would later include his phrenological analysis in an edition of *Leaves of Grass*.)

While working at becoming a poet, though, Walt had to earn a living. Staying with his family, he would be expected to pay part of the household expenses. Walt joined George and Andrew in their father's trade of carpentry. Brooklyn once again was enjoying prosperity and a building boom; there was plenty of work for skilled and enterprising carpenters. As Walter Whitman, Sr. was ailing, his work and the support of the family were increasingly taken over by his sons.

Walt built a three-story building on Brooklyn's Myrtle Avenue, and for a while he ran a small printing establishment and bookstore on the ground floor; the Whitmans lived upstairs. Walt made little money from this and other business ventures, and he sometimes supplemented his income by newspaper writing. He also tried a few real estate speculations, none of which brought in bountiful profits. But then he was not really interested in financial success: the real business of his life lay elsewhere.

As an intermittent carpenter, Walt must have enjoyed working again with his hands, as he had done as a typesetter. No doubt he often paused in his labors just to stand back and admire the precise teamwork of the other carpenters. *Leaves of Grass* would contain numerous metaphorical references to house-carpentry and knowing descriptions such as this passage from "Song of the Broad-Axe":

> The house-builder at work in cities or anywhere,
> The preparatory jointing, squaring, sawing, mortising,
> The hoist-up of beams, the push of them in their places, laying
> them regular,
> Setting the studs by their tenons in the mortises according as they
> were prepared,
> The blows of mallets and hammers, the attitudes of the men, their
> curv'd limbs,
> Bending, standing, astride the beams, driving in pins, holding on
> by posts and braces . . .

Walt found that a carpenter's worksuit was comfortable and easily cleaned; best of all, it gave him a thoroughly democratic appearance. He now wore boots too, tucking his pant-legs into them. (In a critical study, *Walt Whitman's Pose,* Esther Shephard claimed that Whitman deliberately imitated the idealistic, Christ-like poet-carpenter in a George Sand novel.)

When working as a carpenter, Walt carried books in his lunch pail, to read during time-off. His favored reading material was a volume or two of Ralph Waldo Emerson's essays.

Probably Emerson had more to do with shaping Whitman's career as a poet than anything or anybody else. Reading Emerson, one frequently encounters statements and long discourses, rendered in a style throbbing with conviction. These surely inspired Whitman, generating certain ideas and aims and confirming others. In many instances hardly coincidental, Emerson suggested and Whitman tried to fulfill. Especially important to Walt were the essays "The Poet," "Self-Reliance," "History," "The Over-Soul," "Prudence," and "Nature."

Emerson was a widely read poet, essayist, and philosopher; he was also a popular lecturer. He had resigned from the Unitarian ministry, to settle in Concord, Massachusetts, and become the center of a circle of admiring disciples and friends. The major idealistic voice of his times, as leader of the American Transcendentalists he preached nature's benevolence and beauty and the doctrine of self-reliance, which encouraged the individual to rely upon the moral and aesthetic guidance of that "gleam of light which flashes across his mind from within," disregarding what others might think or do.

The European Rationalists had elevated man's ability to reason objectively to a supreme position; their great accomplishment was the application of the scientific method to the study of a materialistic universe. Emerson countered them by maintaining that a good portion of human wisdom "transcended" facts and could only come from an intuitive or mystical contemplation of, and participation in, life. Strict reasoning could never penetrate the sphere of what Emerson called the "Over-Soul"—a pantheistic spirit that was mysterious, all-pervasive, and grandly divine. When Whitman later would mention God, his idea of deity was akin to Emerson's.

At first Whitman called Emerson "Master," the paramount discovery of his carpenter period, as though implying that without exposure to the essays he might not have become a poet. ("I was simmering, simmering, simmering; Emerson brought me to a boil.") Later Walt spoke ambiguously of Emerson's influence upon him, sometimes even denying that the Concord sage had played any part at all in his dramatic renascence as man and poet. Wanting people to think that *Leaves of Grass* had come strictly as his own inspiration, he was hardly being truthful.

Yet Walt was not a simple, ill-informed carpenter who became aware of Emerson's essays by chance and had been suddenly and miraculously altered into a poet. As a young man he had attended some of Emerson's lectures in New York; as a newspaper editor he inspected Emerson's two volumes of collected essays, published in the early 1840s. But Emerson then did not have the catalystic effect upon the journalist as he subsequently did upon the part-time carpenter who, already astir with the vague dream of becoming a national poet, rediscovered the essays and found them relevant and inspirational for his purposes.

"The Poet" was probably the most fascinating and useful of all the essays to Walt. In it Emerson deftly portrayed the ideal poet; and whatever propensities Whitman did not already possess, he considered adopting as his own. Many others besides Emerson called for a national poet; but Emerson told Whitman how to become one.

For a time, Emerson's poet might be isolated from his fellows "by truth and by his art," but his own pursuits would console him; eventually he would attract all men to him when they discovered his ability to express their own truths for them. Having new kinds of thoughts and experiences to reveal, the poet moved in the vanguard of his times. "He will tell us how it was with him," said Emerson, "and all men will be the richer in his fortune. For, the experience of each new age requires a new confession, and the world seems always waiting for its poet."

Humanity delighted in poetry, Emerson explained, because of its mind-expanding capability: "The use of symbols has a certain power of emancipation and exhilaration for all men. . . . We are like persons who come out of a cave or cellar into the open air."

He concluded that poets are "liberating gods," because through them men acquired a new sense, by which they found within their world "yet another world or nest of worlds." (Whitman's noticeable assumption, as poet, of a godlike stance may be partly due to Emerson's indirect approval.)

Like many another American artist and intellectual, Emerson regretted the absence of a contemporary and oracular poetic voice to deal with the American spirit and the nation's substance. "I look in vain for the poet whom I describe," he proclaimed in a passage which Whitman must have taken to heart, for surely, later, he was attempting to answer Emerson's quest. "We do not, with sufficient plainness, or sufficient profoundness, address ourselves to life, nor dare we chant our own times and social circumstance. . . . We have yet had no genius in America, with tyrannous eye, which knew the value of our incomparable materials . . ."

Emerson went on to enumerate possible subjects for the new American poet: "Our logrolling, our stumps and their politics, our fisheries, our Negroes, and Indians, our boats, and our repudiations, the wrath of rogues, and the pusillanimity of honest men, the northern trade, the southern planting, the western clearing, Oregon, and Texas, are yet unsung. Yet America is a poem in our eyes; its ample geography dazzles the imagination, and it will not wait long for metres."

Whitman would find that the best way for him to encompass the body and soul of his country was to make himself a part of everything and everybody:

> I am of old and young, of the foolish as much as the wise,
> Regardless of others, ever regardful of others,
> Maternal as well as paternal, a child as well as a man,
> Stuff'd with the stuff that is coarse and stuff'd with the stuff that is fine,
> One of the Nation of many nations, the smallest the same and the largest the same,
> A Southerner soon as a Northerner, a planter nonchalant and hospitable down by the Oconee I live,
> A Yankee bound my own way ready for trade, my joints the limberest joints on earth and the sternest joints on earth,

> A Kentuckian walking the vale of the Elkhorn in my deerskin leg-
> gings, a Louisianian or Georgian . . .
>
> •   •   •
>
> Of every hue and caste am I, of every rank and religion,
> A farmer, mechanic, artist, gentleman, sailor, quaker,
> Prisoner, fancy-man, rowdy, lawyer, physician, priest.

There were enough regions and people and activities in the
United States (and the world outside it) to keep Whitman busy
for a lifetime; to touch upon them all he devised for his conven-
ience the pages-long "catalogues"—for which *Leaves of Grass* is
famous, or infamous.

Emerson defined art as "the path of the creator to his work."
Finding or placing himself in a mood or situation which stimulated his imagination, the artist felt compelled to create. "He
hears a voice, he sees a beckoning," Emerson said. "Then he is
apprised, with wonder, what herds of daemons hem him in." He
rested no longer as he pursued a nebulous beauty ever ahead of
him. In solitude, the poet poured out verses, trying to capture
and cast into words a vision glimpsed.

If Walt ever became frustrated or discouraged over his inability
to express himself and his visions adequately, Emerson was there
to strengthen a faltering confidence. "Doubt not, O poet, but per-
sist," he commanded. "Say, 'It is in me, and shall out.' Stand there,
balked and dumb, stuttering and stammering, hissed and hooted,
stand and strive, until, at last, rage draw out of thee that *dream-
power* which every night shows thee is thine own." It was this
power—"transcending all limit and privacy"—that Whitman
learned to draw on, becoming, as Emerson had promised his poet,
"the conductor of the whole river of electricity. Nothing walks,
or creeps, or grows, or exists, which must not in turn arise and
walk before him as exponent of his meaning."

Yet Walt was forewarned of the road he must walk alone while
learning his craft. "The conditions are hard, but equal," said
Emerson. "Thou shalt leave the world, and know the muse only.
Thou shalt not know any longer the times, customs, graces, politics, or opinions of men, but shalt take all from the muse. . . . Thou

shalt lie close hid with nature, and canst not be afforded to the Capitol or the Exchange. The world is full of renunciations and apprenticeships, and this is thine: thou must pass for a fool and a churl for a long season." But his reward would be this: "That the ideal shall be real to thee, and the impressions of the actual world shall fall like summer rain, copious, but not troublesome, to thy invulnerable essence. Thou shalt have the whole land for thy park and manor, the sea for thy bath and navigation, without tax and without envy; the woods and the rivers thou shalt own; and thou shalt possess that wherein others are only tenants and boarders."

The poet's ability to absorb and keep whatever he admired came naturally to Whitman. In "Song of the Open Road" he would put it in his own words:

> To see no possession but you may possess it, enjoying all without labor or purchase, abstracting the feast yet not abstracting one particle of it,
> To take the best of the farmer's farm and the rich man's elegant villa, and the chaste blessings of the well-married couple, and the fruits of orchards and flowers of gardens,
> To take to your use out of the compact cities as you pass through,
> To carry buildings and streets with you afterward wherever you go,
> To gather the minds of men out of their brains as you encounter them, to gather the love out of their hearts . . .

Profoundly stirred by Emerson's proffered destiny, Whitman was willing to serve this strict apprenticeship. If he was to become the great poet whom Emerson and all America awaited, Walt would have to abandon or at least minimize mundane ambitions and concerns—whatever others, especially those in his family, might think. He would need to inform himself about the history of past ages of earth and of mankind, the geography of his own land, and the new knowledge coming from science. And as a poet-teacher he must devise a prospectus for American democracy, to insure its perpetuation and suggest needed improvements. But above all, he would have to perfect the technique of calling forth the muse or "daemon" from its deep hiding-place within, so he could write the great poetry which came, Emerson had said, when one used his innate "dream-power."

Even during his days as editor of the *Eagle*, Walt carried around little notebooks in which he jotted down ideas, impressions, instructions. "Be simple and clear.—Be not occult," was one of his first notations to himself. In these small private books he felt free to write a rhythmic, rhapsodic prose and unrhymed poems whose lines ignored the traditional poet's need to establish regular accents or meter.

In his notebooks Walt also indulged in philosophical speculations. "When I walked at night by the sea shore and looked up at the countless stars," he wrote, "I asked of my soul whether it would be filled and satisfied when it should become god enfolding all these, and open to the life and delight and knowledge of everything in them or of them; and the answer was plain to me at the breaking water on the sands at my feet; and the answer was, No, when I reach there, I shall want to go further still."

This was one of many instances in which prose material from Whitman's experiments in self-expression would eventually appear as poetry:

> This day before dawn I ascended a hill and look'd at the crowded heaven,
> And I said to my spirit *When we become the enfolders of those orbs, and the pleasure and knowledge of everything in them, shall we be fill'd and satisfied then?*
> And my spirit said *No, we but level that lift to pass and continue beyond.*

Although Whitman often wished to give the impression that his poems had flowed forth spontaneously, he made little effort to cover up the sources of many of them. Rich lodes for diligent scholars searching for the origins of particular passages in *Leaves of Grass* (especially "Song of Myself"), as well as certain Whitmanian concepts, have been these notebooks Walt kept throughout his life, the books he is known to have admired, and a disorderly, bulging "file" of random notes and miscellaneous articles clipped from magazines and newspapers, in which he often underlined statements interesting to him and then added his own commentary. He adapted ideas expressed by other writers into his own forms, sometimes even using some of their words or phrases. He also "lifted" material from historical accounts and the daily papers: stories of shipwrecks, battles, domestic tragedies.

As the design of *Leaves of Grass,* the ambitious American "prose-poem," began to take some shape, Whitman sought technical information which would fill out his wide-ranging plans. He spent many hours at New York libraries, poring over history books, anthropological lore, linguistics, descriptions of the continent's topography, religious studies and stories from many lands, and the latest scientific discoveries and theories.

Walt went often to the Egyptian Museum on Broadway, where Dr. Abbott, an ardent Egyptologist, displayed his marvelous collection of ancient artifacts and art objects. He closely questioned the proprietor about everything, the better to know that early period in civilization, features of which would appear in *Leaves of Grass,* such as this poet's tour in "Salut au Monde":

> I see Egypt and the Egyptians, I see the pyramids and obelisks,
> I look on chisell'd histories, records of conquering kings, dynasties,
>   cut in slabs of sand-stone, or on granite blocks,
> I see at Memphis mummy-pits containing mummies embalm'd,
>   swathed in linen cloth, lying there many centuries . . .

Once more Walt had made a tangible contact with "precedents" —things from the past that had structured the present and future both. The remote antiquity of Egypt stimulated new thoughts about world religions and their leaders. "Back to ten thousand years before These States," he wrote in a notebook, "all nations had, and some yet have, and perhaps always will have, traditions of coming men, great benefactors, of divine origin, capable of deeds of might, blessings, poems, enlightenment." Consciously or unconsciously, Walt was already preparing to become one of these "benefactors":

> ... myself waiting my time to be one of the supremes,
> The day getting ready for me when I shall do as much good as the best, and be as prodigious ...

Another stimulus to Whitman as poet was the World's Fair, held in the summer of 1853 near the Croton Reservoir (on the site of which is now the New York Public Library's main building). With his characteristic enthusiasm Whitman went again and again, strolling around this "Exposition of the Industry of the Nations" and viewing the products of the world's peoples exhibited within a near-duplicate of London's fabulous Crystal Palace. Walt could never see enough of the wonders achieved by man's mind and hands.

Phrenology had intrigued Whitman, confirming his long-held desire to become a poet. He now took a deeper and more sustained interest in the genuine sciences—natural, physical, and social—that were making great strides in furthering man's knowledge of the universe, the world, and himself. He believed that modern science would discover many of the truths which mankind so long had been seeking. In the past, the profound mysteries of nature had usually been explained by superstitions and religious lore. Now the elaborate workings of the entire universe—from the growth of a tiny seed to the burning of the stars—could be explored by scientists, and their answers to the riddles of existence would revolutionize man's thinking as well as the world in which he lived. Convinced that a modern poet should know nature's fundamental laws, Whitman studied science.

Probably Walt attended some of the lectures given in New York by the popular astronomer O. M. Mitchel, who had awakened public interest in the science that specialized in the heavens. Whitman would often use terms and concepts from astronomy in *Leaves of Grass:* he was fascinated with stars and space, sun and moon—but always for their possible connections with mankind. The Walt Whitman who generally found his bearings in the small

everyday miracles of life would sometimes switch his perspective
to a macrocosmic view, to give a vast and universal coherence
to his philosophy.

> I open my scuttle at night and see the far-sprinkled systems,
> And all I see multiplied as high as I can cipher edge but the rim of
> > the farther systems,
> Wider and wider they spread, expanding, always expanding,
> Outward and outward and forever outward.

> My sun has his sun and round him obediently wheels,
> He joins with his partners a group of superior circuit,
> And greater sets follow, making specks of the greatest inside them.

> •　　•　　•

> See ever so far, there is limitless space outside of that,
> Count ever so much, there is limitless time around that.

The stars were not just far-distant suns to Walt: they represented the essential order and purposeful design of the universe;
they reminded him of a great presence, a benevolent, creative and
immanent spirit "more immortal even than the stars"—so he could
not be contented with mere graphs and the recitation of facts.
The scientist preoccupied with technical investigations might not
notice the sheer wonder of the sky's display or sense the identity
of its superhuman creator. Perhaps it was at one of Dr. Mitchel's
lectures that Whitman suddenly realized, as Emerson did, that
science could never wholly understand or explain existence because its very method discounted man's emotional responses or
psychical intuitions. Dealing with facts and particulars, scientists
often forgot or obscured wholeness and beauty.

> When I heard the learn'd astronomer,
> When the proofs, the figures, were ranged in columns before me,
> When I was shown the charts and diagrams, to add, divide, and
> > measure them,
> When I was sitting heard the astronomer where he lectured with
> > much applause in the lecture-room,
> How soon unaccountable I became tired and sick,
> Till rising and gliding out I wander'd off by myself,

In the mystical moist night-air, and from time to time,
Look'd up in perfect silence at the stars.

In "Song of Myself," Whitman would cheer on the scientists in
their tasks—

Hurrah for positive science! long live exact demonstration!

Yet he would let them know that his own province lay elsewhere,
beyond their computations and measurements—though access to
it came through the realm of science:

Gentlemen, to you the first honors always!
Your facts are useful, and yet they are not my dwelling,
I but enter by them to an area of my dwelling.

In his notebook-experiments with both prose and poetry and
in his diligent study of materials eligible for his poems, Whitman
did not neglect his interest in political ideals and happenings.
During the germinal period of *Leaves of Grass* Walt associated
with a group of artists who had founded the Brooklyn Art Union.
They discussed their opinions about art, exhibited their works together, and promoted American art for Americans.

Walt fitted easily into their midst, and once he gave a lecture
to them on "Art and Artists"—a speech afterwards printed in the
Tribune. He stated his conviction that "There can be no true
Artist, without a glowing thought for freedom," then read a poem
he had written, an early version of "Europe," which showed his
disappointment over the defeats of the various attempts to further
democratic ideals in the widespread revolutions of 1848-49 in
Europe. He refused, however, to abandon hope for the ultimate
triumph of freedom and democracy.

Those corpses of young men,
Those martyrs that hang from the gibbets, those hearts pierc'd by
the gray lead,
Cold and motionless as they seem live elsewhere with unslaughter'd
vitality.

They live in other young men O kings!
They live in brothers again ready to defy you,
They were purified by death, they were taught and exalted.

Not a grave of the murder'd for freedom but grows seed for freedom, in its turn to bear seed,
Which the winds carry afar and re-sow, and the rains and the
  snows nourish.

Not a disembodied spirit can the weapons of tyrants let loose,
But it stalks invisibly over the earth, whispering, counseling,
  cautioning. . . .

Closer to home, Walt was outraged over the passage of the
Kansas-Nebraska Bill of 1854 and the repeal of the Missouri
Compromise, which had kept slavery confined to the South. He
composed "A Boston Ballad" after Boston officials yielded to the
Federal marshals who, enforcing the new Fugitive Slave Act, re-
turned Anthony Burns to his Virginia owner. The great principles
of liberty and equality for which the Revolution had been fought,
Walt felt, were being overturned.

When Walt Whitman introduced himself in *Leaves of Grass*,
he did so boisterously and brashly, claiming as his a voice that
spoke of and to all men:

  I celebrate myself,
  And what I assume you shall assume,
  For every atom belonging to me as good belongs to you.

What had brought on this self-confidence, this feeling of speaking for others? The next lines give an indication:

  I loafe and invite my soul,
  I lean and loafe at my ease . . . observing a spear of summer grass.

Walt had often been accused of loaferism—of relaxing and day-
dreaming. But now when he summoned his soul to join him as
he contemplated a blade of grass, he could describe what he felt
and thought in ways that made the images conveyed by his words

almost tactile. Whitman had virtually invented for his own usages a direct and powerfully sensory form of poetic expression. Deftly, knowingly, he blended body and spirit, the real and the dreamed, the commonplace and an inspired wisdom, the vast reaches of time and space, and a dazzling array of emotions and sensations in a wonderland contained within a single human being's all-encompassing visions. And now he wished to share these inner discoveries with others.

Emerson had suggested that a poem should assume a form natural to itself, coming from "a thought so passionate and alive, that, like the spirit of a plant or an animal, it has an architecture of its own, and adorns nature with a new thing." Poems without rhyme schemes were written now and then, but poets always established a set rhythm—measure or meter—in their lines, repeating a pattern of accented words or syllables. In his notebook poems and a few poems published in newspapers Walt had begun to ignore the traditional requirements for both rhyme and regular meter in poetry. "The poetic quality is not marshalled in rhyme or uniformity," he would later say to explain his odd new "organic" style.

The materials in many of Whitman's poems and much of his uniquely characteristic poetic form are due to his surrendering a strict and conscious control over thoughts and their expression. In this too he had been encouraged by Emerson. "Beside his privacy of power as an individual man," Emerson had said, "there is a great public power which he can draw, by unlocking, at all risks, his human doors, and suffering the ethereal tides to roll and circulate through him: then he is caught up into the life of the Universe, his speech is thunder, his thought is law, and his words are universally intelligible as the plants and animals."

Emerson's ideal poet knew he created best when speaking "somewhat wildly, or, 'with the flower of the mind.'" The intellect, "inebriated by nectar," then took its directions from "its celestial life." This mental metamorphosis, making possible the mind's flow into hidden passages, was achieved by various means. Emerson acknowledged that people often used narcotics and intoxicants "to add this extraordinary power to their normal powers."

Yet artists who originally sought "a passage out into free space" for creative purposes later yielded to pleasure and self-indulgence, ultimately gaining "emancipation not into the heavens, but into the freedom of baser places." Emerson warned that nature could not be tricked: "The spirit of the world, the great calm presence of the creator, comes not forth to the sorceries of opium or of wine. The sublime vision comes to the pure and simple soul in a clean and chaste body."

Here was surely something that the health-conscious and basically celibate Whitman could appreciate and cultivate. "All beauty comes from beautiful blood and a beautiful brain," was his own way of phrasing this natural but antiseptic environment into which the true artist should welcome his muse. Whitman did not use external and artificial means to stimulate creativity. The rest of his life would conform with Emerson's plan: "The poet's habit of living should be set on a key so low and plain, that the common influences should delight him. His cheerfulness should be the gift of the sunlight; the air should suffice for his inspiration, and he should be tipsy with water."

Probably the most important element in Emerson's influence upon Whitman in his "apprenticeship" period was this encouragement of the creative spirit resident within the unconscious recesses of the mind, and responsive to the presence of the "Over-Soul." Whitman gradually learned to release this "dream-power," trusting that its revelations would make poetry—if not traditional poetry, something that was poetry nonetheless, and quite his own. The "natural" surge of words gave an irregular cadence to Whitman's poetry: the first notable use of "free verse," destined to cause a stylistic revolution within poetry written in the Western world. Odd though they seemed at the time, Whitman's poems answered Wordsworth's definition of poetry as "the spontaneous overflow of powerful feelings, recollected in tranquillity."

Studies of creative people often reveal that the spark which initiates a new work or invention or discovery comes suddenly, without conscious attention or forced searching, when the mind is totally relaxed, as in sleep or reverie, or is preoccupied elsewhere. The creative urge forms a design in the medium in which the creator is already accustomed to work—whether words, shapes, colors, musical notes, numbers, ideas, arrangements of materials and mechanisms. For a time the new creation is allowed to take shape and expand naturally on its own. Later the intellect takes over to examine critically, elaborate, discard, and work over the crude early products of inspiration.

Whitman, of course, was already attuned to language as his best means of communication. For years he had written hundreds of thousands of words for publication—enough to qualify him as a facile and practiced professional writer, if not a particularly gifted one. Writing was his customary trade; he was used to framing his feelings and thoughts in words, creating a new and different reality beyond his senses. But now new kinds of words and visions demanded release from within:

> Speech is the twin of my vision, it is unequal to measure itself,
> It provokes me forever, it says sarcastically,
> *Walt you contain enough, why don't you let it out then?*

Many writers have said that they literally "hear" words and rhythms of a new composition which an inner voice recites or dictates to them. Their writing processes commence by setting down what their minds experience in a receptive reverie—either during these auditory hallucinations or afterwards. A number of Whitman's poems obviously were initiated by promptings from his unconscious mind—on his own evidence:

> I lie abstracted and hear beautiful tales of things and the reasons of
> things,
> They are so beautiful I nudge myself to listen.

> I cannot say to any person what I hear—I cannot say it to myself—
> it is very wonderful.

And Walt sometimes felt possessed, like a medium, by disembodied spirits whose bidding he did:

> Melange mine own, the unseen and the seen,
> Mysterious ocean where the streams empty,

Prophetic spirit of materials shifting and flickering around me,
Living beings, identities now doubtless near us in the air that we
    know not of,
Contact daily and hourly that will not release me,
These selecting, these in hints demanded of me.

       •   •   •

O such themes!—equalities! O divine average!
Warblings under the sun, usher'd as now, or at noon, or setting,
Strains musical flowing through ages, now reaching hither,
I take to your reckless and composite chords, add to them, and
    cheerfully pass them forward.

In "Song of Myself" and elsewhere Whitman showed his conviction that he was a chosen instrument by which the democratic
spirit in nature and in mankind expressed itself. This "afflatus" or
breath of divine inspiration sought him out to sing to the whole
world of freedom, equality, and brotherhood:

Through me the afflatus surging and surging, through me the cur-
    rent and index.

I speak the pass-word primeval, I give the sign of democracy,
By God! I will accept nothing which all cannot have their counter-
    part of on the same terms.

Through me many long dumb voices,
Voices of the interminable generations of prisoners and slaves,
Voices of the diseas'd and despairing and of thieves and dwarfs,

       •   •   •

And of the rights of them the others are down upon,
Of the deform'd, trivial, flat, foolish, despised . . .

During the gestation period of *Leaves of Grass*, Whitman's
poetic "daemon" or muse surfaced, to grant him the sounds and
visions which he presented in a new type of poetry—which Walt
would often call "singing."

Most readers of *Leaves of Grass* readily perceive Whitman's
"mystical" side. There is abundant evidence that Walt Whitman
had some of the notable credentials of the mystic. He apparently

experienced sensations which were supernormal or abnormal; he also had thoughts which set him apart from others who lived totally involved and satisfied with the objective or "real" world. He frequently felt the awe and wonder of being alive within a cosmos vast, intricate, harmonious, and beautiful—created and regulated by some great power of whom he and everything else were parts. Happiness over the existence of a morning-glory at his window might reach sheer ecstasy: it too contained a part of divinity and was a message from or manifestation of the all-pervasive life-force or spirit, which he often gave names other than God (such as "the great Camerado") because his own definition hardly fitted the God belonging to most people of his century.

Sometimes this mysterious and benevolent presence in the universe paid the poet intimate and sensuous visits, as revealed in "Song of Myself":

> I am satisfied—I see, dance, laugh, sing;
> As the hugging and loving bed-fellow sleeps at my side through
>   the night, and withdraws at the peep of the day
>   with stealthy tread,
> Leaving me baskets cover'd with white towels swelling the house
>   with their plenty . . .

In the first version, God was this "bed-fellow"; Whitman afterwards made him anonymous. The visitor, by leaving manna, took care of Walt's earthly needs—and seemingly intended to provide such sustenance so long as Walt kept his eyes focused upon the "road" of the spirit, disdaining materialism and greed:

> Shall I . . . scream at my eyes,
> That they turn from gazing after and down the road,
> And forthwith cipher and show me to a cent,
> Exactly the value of one and exactly the value of two, and which is
>   ahead?

Unlike many people who undergo mystical or deeply religious experiences, Whitman proved remarkably able to describe what he had seen and felt, heard and thought, at such times:

There is that in me—I do not know what it is—but I know it is in
me.

Wrench'd and sweaty—calm and cool then my body becomes,
I sleep—I sleep long.

I do not know it—it is without name—it is a word unsaid,
It is not in any dictionary, utterance, symbol.

Something it swings on more than the earth I swing on,
To it the creation is the friend whose embracing awakes me.

Perhaps I might tell more. Outlines! I plead for my brothers and
sisters.

Do you see O my brothers and sisters?
It is not chaos or death—it is form, union, plan—it is eternal life—
it is Happiness.

From its inception to the final edition thirty-seven years later,
Leaves of Grass would be Whitman's proffered "outline" or guide
to his fellow men of his own mystical participation in a meaning-
ful life and his confidence in its perpetuation.

A Canadian psychiatrist interested in psychic phenomena became
a close friend of Whitman in his later years. Dr. Richard Maurice
Bucke said that the poet undeniably possessed what he called "cosmic consciousness," which he defined as an awareness of "the life and
order of the universe." In such a person an "intellectual enlightenment" placed him on a new level of existence, as if a member of
a new species. He would feel "moral exaltation, an indescribable
feeling of elevation, elation, and joyousness, and a quickening of
the moral sense." He also would achieve "a sense of immortality,
a consciousness of eternal life."

Bucke maintained that sometime in the summer of 1853 or
1854 Walt had his first intense "revelation," which caused him to
write most of the poems in the first edition of *Leaves of Grass*
with an obsessive urgency. It is doubtful, however, that a single
dramatic episode initially exposing this "cosmic consciousness"
propelled Whitman into a brief, zealously creative period.

The genesis time of *Leaves of Grass* was long—actually, Walt's
whole lifetime up to its appearance—but in the five or six years
preceding its publication, he was obviously getting ready for some

vast private project. During a lengthy assimilation process he made elaborate researches as preparations; in his private notebooks he experimented with expressing all sorts of feelings and ideas. This writing loosened him, shaking him nearly free of literary conventions; his wide-ranging reading emboldened him to see himself as a special agent for mankind, and also gave him the details to fill in his designs. The poet grew better able to "turn on" whatever lay within him, and then describe it to his satisfaction. The actual period of composition for much of the poetry in the first *Leaves of Grass* may have been comparatively short. However, Walt's notebooks reveal that a number of passages were sketched out in prose or poetic form some while before, and he later "stitched" them together, especially in "Song of Myself."

The loose structure of this early *Leaves of Grass* presented a kaleidoscopic or fluid aspect; the plan permitted Whitman to shuttle back and forth between the external and the internal, the past and the present, the real and the ideal, the actual and the dreamed—to move freely through time and space, investigating the finite and beholding the infinite. "Song of Myself" and "The Sleepers" sometimes seem like surrealistic works of art or "happenings," achieved when Whitman deliberately expanded his consciousness. Some of the most beautiful and fascinating, yet mysterious, passages in his poetry appear to have originated from an almost trancelike state of mind and body.

Whitman's feeling of spiritual ecstasy, involving a harmonious and actually physical contact with some ineffable presence, apparently could be triggered by particular sensations or sensory experiences. Ever since a young child, Walt had known a joyous rapport with nature; in the city he had continuously identified with other people by momentarily submerging himself in their lives and activities. Later on, other experiences too drew Walt away from his single-unit self and a commonplace reality—to unlock, as Emerson had suggested, his "human doors," allowing the "ethereal tides to roll and circulate through him."

Music—in particular the Italian opera so popular in New York in the 1850s—provided one sure means by which Whitman's mind

Walter Whitman and Louisa Van Velsor Whitman: the poet's parents

Walt Whitman's birthplace home in Huntington, Long Island: drawing by Joseph Pennell

Walter Whitman, Jr., as a young New York editor in the early 1840s

Walt Whitman as "The Carpenter": etching by Samuel Hollyer, used as frontispiece in the first edition of *Leaves of Grass* (1855)
New York Public Library

Opposite: A rare page from the manuscript of the first edition of *Leaves of Grass* (Section 14)
The Library of Congress

The wild gander leads his flock through the cool night,
Ya-honk! he says, and sounds it down to me like
        an invitation; ~~it is meaningless~~ closer
The pert suppose it ~~is meaningless~~, but I listen better,
I find ~~it has~~ its place and sign up there toward
    phosphoresed the November sky.—
The ~~clawed cat of the forest~~ moose of the north, the cat on the housesill, the chicken
    ~~the deer~~, the prairie-dog,
The litter of the grunting sow as they tug at her teats,
The brood of the turkey-hen, and she with her
    half-spread wings,
I see in them and myself the same old law.

The press of my foot to the earth springs a hundred
    affections,
They scorn the best I can do to relate them.—

I am enamored of growing outdoors,
~~Of men that live among~~ Of men that live among cattle or taste of the
~~Of the builders of ships—~~ ocean or soil, ~~of axes and malls,~~ — of the
    well drivers of horses
I can eat and sleep with them week in and week out.

    nearest and   and most and easiest
What is commonest and cheapest is Me,
Me going in for my chances,.... spending
~~Spending~~ for vast returns,
Adorning myself to bestow myself on the first
    that will take me,
Not asking the sky to come down to ~~earn~~ my
    good will,
Scattering it freely forever.—

The pure contralto sings in the organ-loft,
The carpenter dresses his plank,.... the tongue of his fore-plane
    whistles its wild ascending lisp,
The married and unmarried children ride home to their
    Thanksgiving dinner,
The pilot seizes the king-pin,.... he heaves down with a strong arp,

Opposite: A page from Walt Whitman's "Blue Book": the poet's copy of the third edition of *Leaves of Grass* in which he made alterations for a new edition
New York Public Library

The "Christ Picture" of Walt Whitman: photograph by Gabriel Harrison, about 1854

Walt Whitman as "The Laborer," probably taken in the late 1850s

As I ebb'd with the ebb of ~~the~~ ocean.

As I walked where the
sea-ripples wash you
Paumanok

Leaves of Grass.

As I ebbed with an ebb
of the ocean of life

1.

1. ELEMENTAL drifts!
O I wish I could impress others as you and the waves
have just been impressing me.

2. As I ebbed with an ebb of the ocean of life,
As I wended the shores I know,
As I walked where the sea-ripples wash you, Pau-
manok,
Where they rustle up, hoarse and sibilant,
Where the fierce old mother endlessly cries for her
castaways,
I musing, late in the autumn day, gazing off south-
ward,
Alone, held by the eternal self of me that threatens
to get the better of me, and stifle me,
Was seized by the spirit that trails in the lines
underfoot,
In the rim, the sediment, that stands for all the water
and all the land of the globe.

(195)

Walt Whitman during the Civil War: photograph by Mathew Brady
U.S. Signal Corps photo; The National Archives

Opposite: "Fall in for Soup": Edwin Forbes' drawing of mess call in a Union Army camp near Falmouth, Virginia, depicting Walt Whitman as the third man in line
The Library of Congress

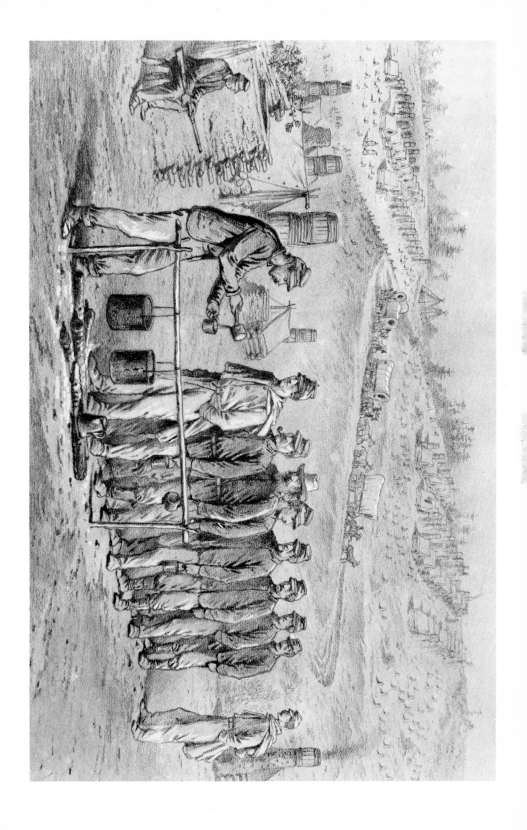

Anne Gilchrist—"My noblest woman-friend"

Walt Whitman in 1872: photograph by Frank Pearsall

Washington City, U.S.
November 3, 1871.

Dear friend,

I have been waiting quite a long while for time & the right mood to answer your letter in a spirit as serious as its own, & in the same unmitigated trust & affection. But more daily work than ever has fallen upon me to do the current season, & though I am well & contented, my best moods seem to shun me. I wished to give to it a day, a sort of Sabbath or holy day apart to itself, under serene & propitious influences—

Walt Whitman's first letter to Anne Gilchrist

confident that I could then write you a letter which would do you good, & me too. But I must at least show, without further delay, that I am not insensible to your love. I too send you my love. And do you feel no disappointment because I now write but briefly. My book is my best letter, my response, my truest explanation of all. In it I have put my body & spirit. You understand this better & fuller & clearer than any one else.

And I too fully & clearly understand the loving & womanly letter it has evoked. Enough that there surely exists between us so beautiful & delicate a relation, accepted by both of us with joy.

Walt Whitman

Whitman in the late 1860s or early 1870s
The Library of Congress

"Walt Whitman, Inciting the Bird of Freedom to Soar": caricature by Max Beerbohm, from *The Poet's Corner* (1904)

Walt Whitman

The "Butterfly Portrait" of Whitman: used in the eighth or "birthday" edition of
Leaves of Grass (1889)   *The Library of Congress*

Drawing of the poet's own
home at 328 Mickle Street,
Camden, New Jersey
Walt Whitman House

Photo-portrait of Walt Whitman
in his mid-sixties

Painting of Walt Whitman, by John W. Alexander (1886)

The Library of Congress

Two views of Walt Whitman's bedroom-sitting room in his Camden home
Walt Whitman House

was released from the bonds of earth to go soaring. "My younger life was so saturated with the emotions, raptures, up-lifts, of such musical experiences that it would be surprising indeed if all my future work had not been colored by them," he later acknowledged. "But for the opera I could never have written *Leaves of Grass.*"

Some music seemed to gather up and transport his very soul into acute bodily sensations:

> The orchestra whirls me wider than Uranus flies,
> It wrenches such ardors from me I did not know I possess'd them,
> It sails me, I dab with bare feet, they are lick'd by the indolent
>   waves,
> I am cut by bitter and angry hail, I lose my breath,
> Steep'd amid honey'd morphine, my windpipe throttled in fakes of
>   death,
> At length let up again to feel the puzzle of puzzles,
> And that we call Being.

Walt was a devotee of music, not a scholar. And when he heard the incomparable singing of tenor Alessandro Bettini or soprano Marietta Alboni, he found his ignorance of Italian actually advantageous. "Ah, welcome that I know not the mere language of the earthly words, in which the melody is embodied, as all words are mean before the language of true music," he rhapsodized. With his own poetry too Whitman would say that the precise meaning of the words was not as important or vital as the emotional "drift" of them and the melody created by their sounds and placements, repetitions, and variations. As with some music, Whitman's best poetic passages often seem almost like incantations.

In "Proud Music of the Storm," a long poem written in mid-career, Whitman explained his own hypersensitivity to sound by recalling some of the sensuously aural memories of his childhood surroundings:

> Ah from a little child,
> Thou knowest soul how to me all sounds became music,
> My mother's voice in lullaby or hymn,

·   ·   ·

> The rain, the growing corn, the breeze among the long-leav'd corn,
> The measur'd sea-surf beating on the sand,
> The twittering bird, the hawk's sharp scream,
> The wild-fowl's notes at night as flying low migrating north or
>   south,
> The psalm in the country church or mid the clustering trees, the
>   open air camp-meeting,
> The fiddler in the tavern, the glee, the long-strung sailor-song,
> The lowing cattle, bleating sheep, the crowing cock at dawn.

Sometimes in *Leaves of Grass,* Whitman would pause and concentrate entirely upon auditory sensations. His ability to organize sound elements, akin to musical composition, provided the loose rhythms and flowing "notes" of his poetic style. It was hardly surprising that as a creator Whitman would classify himself among composers, musicians, and singers—all of whom specialized in sound.

> Composers! mighty maestros!
> And you, sweet singers of old lands, soprani, tenori, bassi!
> To you a new bard caroling in the West,
> Obeisant sends his love.

Whitman's acute sensitivity to sound was only one part of his highly tuned equipment for sensory receptions. His poetry gives ample evidence that his senses of sight, touch, smell, and taste were supernormal too. (It is also arguable that he possessed the much-debated "sixth sense.")

Walt's brain was well stocked with visual materials, as he would tell in "My Picture-Gallery," a poem drafted early but published late in his life.

> In a little house keep I pictures suspended, it is not a fix'd house,
> It is round, it is only a few inches from one side to the other;
> Yet behold, it has room for all the shows of the world, all memories!

Sight details impart a vivid immediacy to many passages in Whitman's poems:

The big doors of the country barn stand open and ready,
The dried grass of the harvest-time loads the slow-drawn wagon,
The clear light plays on the brown gray and green intertinged,
The armfuls are pack'd to the sagging mow.

And Walt confessed a sense of touch so keen that it could be painful:

Mine is no callous shell,
I have instant conductors all over me whether I pass or stop,
They seize every object and lead it harmlessly through me.

I merely stir, press, feel with my fingers, and am happy,
To touch my person to some one else's is about as much as I can
stand.

Blending all senses at once, Whitman effectively told of a sensuous union of body and world:

My respiration and inspiration, the beating of my heart, the passing
of blood and air through my lungs,
The sniff of green leaves and dry leaves, and of the shore and dark-
color'd sea-rocks, and of hay in the barn,
The sound of the belch'd words of my voice loos'd to the eddies of
the wind,
A few light kisses, a few embraces, a reaching around of arms,
A play of shine and shade on the trees as the supple boughs wag,
The delight alone or in the rush of the streets, or along the fields
and hill-sides,
The feeling of health, the full-noon trill, the song of me rising from
bed and meeting the sun.

Although music may have provided Walt with his first "wings" for making the poetic flights in which he soared above lands and peoples, gathering up details for his "catalogues," he often associated these imaginary aerial journeys with the real flights of birds. At times he can be found assuming the guise of birds:

O lands! all so dear to me . . . I putting at random in these songs,
become a part of that, whatever it is,

> Southward there, I screaming, with wings slow flapping, with the
> myriads of gulls wintering along the coasts of
> Florida,
>
> .   .   .
>
> Northward, on the sands, on some shallow bay of Paumanok I with
> parties of snowy herons wading in the wet to
> seek worms and aquatic plants . . .

The bird's freedom to come and go—to observe, absorb, and
then depart—suited Whitman's purpose as a poet perfectly. And
so did its ability to sing. The bird—nature's prime soarer and
singer—became Whitman's favorite symbol for the poet, who
"sang" using human words and "flew" only in his desires and
dreams. Significantly, in two Whitman masterpieces—"Out of the
Cradle Endlessly Rocking" and "When Lilacs Last in the Dooryard Bloom'd"—a bird takes a major role as the poet's spiritual
catalyst and alter ego.

Whitman often referred to himself and other poets as "singers."
They had seemingly been appointed to sing for mankind, just as
birds appeared to voice nature. Sometimes Whitman made the
parallel quite obvious, at the same time displaying some of his
intentions as a poet:

> As I have walk'd in Alabama my morning walk,
> I have seen where the she-bird the mocking-bird sat on her nest in
> the briers hatching her brood.
>
> I have seen the he-bird also,
> I have paus'd to hear him near at hand inflating his throat and joy-
> fully singing.
>
> And while I paus'd it came to me that what he really sang for was
> not there only,
> Nor for his mate nor himself only, nor all sent back by the echoes,
> But subtle, clandestine, away beyond,
> A charge transmitted and gift occult for those being born.
>
> Democracy! near at hand to you a throat is now inflating itself and
> joyfully singing.
>
> Ma femme! for the brood beyond us and of us,
> For those who belong here and those to come,

I exultant to be ready for them will now shake out carols stronger
and haughtier than have ever yet been heard
upon earth.

A bird's flight somewhat resembled a ship upon the water as it
was lifted by wave swells or rocked by tides or moved along by
wind-filled sails or propellers. A ship, too, could "float" in a
smooth, dreamlike manner—or be buffeted about by storms—on a
journey bound for new adventures. Through no mere coincidence
Whitman again and again chose a ship to convey his thoughts,
climbing aboard imagined vessels—most notably, in "Crossing
Brooklyn Ferry" and, much later, "Passage to India." (And he
sometimes referred to *Leaves of Grass* itself as a boat.)

When gazing up at the night sky, the poet-astronaut could take
space flights:

Speeding through space, speeding through heaven and the stars,
Speeding amid the seven satellites and the broad ring, and the
diameter of eighty thousand miles,
Speeding with tail'd meteors, throwing fire-balls like the rest,
.   .   .
I fly those flights of a fluid and swallowing soul,
My course runs below the soundings of plummets.

During such "trips," Whitman's imagination was freed to wander and leap and plunge and fly, in an ecstatic levitation, gathering up bits of wisdom from cosmic journeys.

Space and Time! now I see it is true, what I guess'd at,
What I guess'd when I loaf'd on the grass,
What I guessed while I lay alone in my bed,
And again as I walk'd the beach under the paling stars of the
morning.

My ties and ballasts leave me, my elbows rest in sea-gaps,
I skirt sierras, my palms cover continents,
I am afoot with my vision.

Sleep and dreaming also relaxed the hold of the conscious mind,
to release the unconscious. Dreams supplied sensations and experi-

ences which normal consciousness would discourage, forbid, or repress. In a dream unrelated memory materials became joined, making new patterns. And a dreamer could project himself at random into other bodies, other lives—as Whitman did in his early poem "The Sleepers."

> I go from bedside to bedside, I sleep close with the other sleepers each in turn,
> I dream in my dream all the dreams of the other dreamers,
> And I become the other dreamers.
>
> •   •   •
>
> I am the actor, the actress, the voter, the politician,
> The emigrant and the exile, the criminal that stood in the box,
> He who has been famous and he who shall be famous after to-day,
> The stammerer, the well-formed person, the wasted or feeble person.
> I am she who adorn'd herself and folded her hair expectantly,
> My truant lover has come, and it is dark.

Wandering all night in his vision, the poet visited people one by one, assuming their identities the better to know them. Whatever their virtues and faults, sleep miraculously refreshed them all, making them fully equal in the natural democracy of somnolence:

> I swear they are averaged now—one is no better than the other,
> The night and sleep have liken'd them and restored them.

In sleep, all humanity was united in a bond of loving brotherhood:

> The sleepers are very beautiful as they lie unclothed,
> They flow hand in hand over the whole earth from east to west as they lie unclothed,
> The Asiatic and African are hand in hand, the European and American are hand in hand,
> Learn'd and unlearn'd are hand in hand, and male and female are hand in hand,
>
> •   •   •
>
> The scholar kisses the teacher and the teacher kisses the scholar, the wrong is made right,

The call of the slave is one with the master's call, and the master
    salutes the slave,
The felon steps forth from the prison, the insane becomes sane,
    the suffering of sick persons is reliev'd,

        •   •   •

They pass the invigoration of the night and the chemistry of the
    night, and awake.

During sleep, youth was recaptured and bodily and spiritual
perfection was realized, if only for a brief night. A satisfying deep
sleep resembled the dark, quiet time spent by the fetus in the
mother's womb before emerging into the day-lit world. So one
should welcome night and sleep; each led to daybreak and a refreshed body and revitalized soul.

Why should I be afraid to trust myself to you?
I am not afraid, I have been well brought forward by you,
I love the rich running day, but I do not desert her in whom I lay
    so long,
I know not how I came of you and I know not where I go with
    you, but I know I came well and shall go well.

This nighttime sleep that Whitman praised also bore a striking
similarity to his developing conception of death.

From boyhood on, the seashore and ocean had always appealed
to Walt, and the ocean often would provide a stage or backdrop
for some crucial dramatic event or philosophical realization revealed in his poems. Throughout *Leaves of Grass* marine imagery
recurs, and this was no accident. "Even as a boy," Walt reminisced
in his later years, "I had the fancy, the wish, to write a piece,
perhaps a poem, about the seashore—that suggesting, dividing
line, contact, junction, the solid marrying the liquid . . . blending
the real and ideal, and each made portion of the other."

Leaves of Grass does indeed combine the realities of Whitman's
world with the ideals which he forever cherished; the two are
often inseparable in his poems. "I remember well," he went on,
"I felt that I must one day write a book expressing this liquid,

mystic theme." Afterwards, he realized that "instead of any special lyrical or epical or literary attempt the seashore should be an invisible *influence,* a pervading gauge and tally for me, in my composition." He made this intention explicit in "In Cabin'd Ships at Sea," a poem written in mid-career which he included among the poems in the introductory section of his book.

> *We feel the long pulsation, ebb and flow of endless motion,*
> *The tones of unseen mystery, the vague and vast suggestions of the*
> > *briny world, the liquid-flowing syllables,*
> *The perfume, the faint creaking of the cordage, the melancholy*
> > *rhythm,*
> *The boundless vista and the horizon far and dim are all here,*
> *And this is ocean's poem.*

The very structure of Whitman's book and of individual poems was fluid, shifting, and all-inclusive like the ocean. The cadence of his "free verse" lines can be compared to the irregular beat of the surf upon the shore, sometimes falling gently and caressingly, at other times striking forcefully or fiercely, or coming in hesitantly and dolefully, or joyously and triumphantly—each rhythm suiting the poet's mood and purpose at the time.

Sometimes Whitman portrayed the ocean as the universe in miniature: a perilous, even cruel place for anyone who challenged it—such as the "beautiful gigantic swimmer" in "The Sleepers":

> What are you doing you ruffianly red-trickled waves?
> Will you kill the courageous giant? will you kill him in the prime
> > of his middle age?

More often, the sea was the powerful, profoundly mysterious "savage old mother" of "Out of the Cradle Endlessly Rocking" and "As I Ebb'd with the Ocean of Life." Yet now and then, like a beautiful siren, it summoned the poet to a lover's embrace. Whitman then found it a superb mate, for it mirrored his own vast ambitions and variable soul.

> You sea! I resign myself to you also—I guess what you mean,
> I behold from the beach your crooked inviting fingers,

I believe you refuse to go back without feeling of me,
We must have a turn together, I undress, hurry me out of sight of
    the land,
Cushion me soft, rock me in billowy drowse,
Dash me with amorous wet, I can repay you.

Here, as elsewhere, Whitman used richly sensual imagery in a mystical passage evoking nature. Many of Whitman's early poems —portions of "Song of Myself" most notably—reveal the poet's highly sensuous feelings about scenery, people, animals, activities, even his own body (which he occasionally described in a curiously explicit autoerotic way). In his poetic ecstasies Whitman could express longings—and provide their fulfillments too.

I am he that walks with the tender and growing night,
I call to the earth and sea half-held by the night.

Press close bare-bosom'd night—press close magnetic nourishing
    night!
Night of south winds—night of the large few stars!
Still nodding night—mad naked summer night.

Smile O voluptuous cool-breath'd earth!
Earth of the slumbering and liquid trees!
Earth of departed sunset—earth of the mountains misty-topt!
Earth of the vitreous pour of the full moon just tinged with blue!
Earth of shine and dark mottling the tide of the river!
Earth of the limpid gray of clouds brighter and clearer for my sake!
Far-swooping elbow'd earth—rich apple-blossom'd earth!
Smile, for your lover comes.

Prodigal, you have given me love—therefore I to you give love!
O unspeakable passionate love.

Ecstatic or mystical states of mind, long sought by peoples the whole world over, have been achieved by external means: alcohol, drugs, rhythmic sounds, scents, visual displays, dancing, and orgiastic meetings. Trances and "divine" hallucinations also occur during sensory deprivations, as in fasting, isolation, meditation, chastity—or from a methodical punishment of the body. In the raptures of both religious mystics and participants in ecstatic rites, expressions of universal spiritual love frequently contain sexual imagery. Whitman's sensual poems and passages, for which he would be vilified, were actually mystical in feeling or religious in intention, not pornographic. In his quest for poetic materials and in his own desire to merge with the cosmos, Whitman at times apparently underwent an "auto-intoxication" or self-hypnosis. Needing no intoxicants or drugs to attain a "higher" or enhanced and altered state of consciousness or awareness, his mind provided shifting patterns of richly sensuous or dramatically ideational experiences in a psychic phenomenon which today is commonly labeled "psychedelic."

Some drug-takers have reported "trips" in which they can vaguely "recall" previous existences in lower life-forms. In a remarkable passage which preceded the publication of Darwin's *Origin of Species* by several years, Whitman wrote of his own long and slow development: the evolution of the poet as representative man. Taking place over countless eons beginning with the gestation of the earth itself, Whitman's "ontogeny"—his own physical and spiritual conception and growth—recapitulated "philogeny," or the entire evolutionary history of the species *homo sapiens.*

My feet strike an apex of the apices of the stairs,
On every step bunches of ages, and larger bunches between the
    steps,
All below duly travel'd, and still I mount and mount.

Rise after rise bow the phantoms behind me,
Afar down I see the huge first Nothing, I know I was even there,
I waited unseen and always, and slept through the lethargic mist,
And took my time, and took no hurt from the fetid carbon.

Long was I hugg'd close—long and long.

Immense have been the preparations for me,
Faithful and friendly the arms that have help'd me.

Cycles ferried my cradle, rowing and rowing like cheerful boat-
    men,

For room to me stars kept aside in their own rings,
They sent influences to look after what was to hold me.

Before I was born out of my mother generations guided me,
My embryo has never been torpid, nothing could overlay it.

For it the nebula cohered to an orb,
The long slow strata piled to rest it on,
Vast vegetables gave it sustenance,
Monstrous sauroids transported it in their mouths and deposited it
    with care.

All forces have been steadily employ'd to complete and delight me,
Now on this spot I stand with my robust soul.

During the writing of the first edition of *Leaves of Grass,*
Whitman was responding to a creative impulse strong in special
individuals throughout the history of civilization. Philosophers
and psychologists continuously try to define and explore it, yet
its essence may always remain mysterious, ever defying or escap-
ing analysis. In his essay "Psychology and Literature," Carl
Gustav Jung offered some intriguing explanations for the emergence of great poets in particular times and places. He would
almost seem to be using Walt Whitman as an example, though
he was not.

Jung defined art as "a kind of innate drive that seizes a human
being and makes him its instrument." "The artist is not a person
endowed with a free will who seeks his own ends," he said, "but
one who allows art to realize its purposes through him. As a
human being he may have moods and a will and personal aims,
but as an artist he is 'man' in a higher sense—he is 'collective
man'—one who carries and shapes the unconscious, psychic life
of mankind. To perform this difficult office it is sometimes necessary for him to sacrifice happiness and everything that makes
life worth living for the ordinary human being."

Now, with a "robust soul" that would sing out for all men,
Walt Whitman had arrived in mid-nineteenth-century America,
fully aware of filling a national need and of pursuing a high and

possibly dangerous destiny. Flushed with a mystic's good feeling about his place in the cosmos and prepared to serve with utmost fidelity both his muse and mankind, he was often going to look and sound like a prophet.

*I too am not a bit tamed . . . . I too am
untranslatable,
I sound my barbaric yawp over the roofs of
the world.*

VI

I SOUND MY BARBARIC YAWP

(1855)

In early July of 1855 a new volume of poetry was offered for sale at two dollars. *Leaves of Grass,* in an edition of about a thousand copies, had been printed at the author's expense and under his close supervision. Many of the pages had even been set in type by the poet himself at the Brooklyn printshop of his friends, the Rome brothers. After all, he was an experienced compositor; and who but Walt Whitman would have known how to deal with the peculiarities of this poetic style? Long lines stretched out the entire width of some pages; strung one after another, without a pause that a period would provide, they sometimes piled up so that it took several pages just to finish a single sentence. Strings of dots, looking like ellipses, often took the place of commas and dashes in providing pauses and in separating phrases.

There were twelve different poems in all; six of them bore only the title of the book itself, and the other six were merely separated by space and decorations, having no titles to introduce them. In their later appearances each would have its own special title, but those would be changed again—finally to be called "Song of Myself," "A Song for Occupations," "To Think of Time," "The Sleepers," "I Sing the Body Electric," "Faces," "Song of the Answerer" (strophe 1), "Europe," "A Boston Ballad," "There Was a Child

Went Forth," "Who Learns My Lesson Complete?" and "Great Are the Myths" (the latter to be dropped from the last editions of *Leaves of Grass*).

If this was poetry, it was certainly strange poetry: the likes of it had never been seen before. The author, attempting to place copies for sale in New York bookstores, found that only two were willing to accept them. One of them was Fowler & Wells, a publishing firm and bookstore connected with Fowlers' Phrenological Cabinet, who agreed—possibly to affirm Fowler's earlier estimate of Whitman's natural gifts as a poet—not only to keep the book in stock, but also to serve as its distributor and advertiser. They had a branch store in Boston. The other booksellers were deterred by the odd appearance of the contents. Furthermore, if they actually tried to read the book, they were baffled by the absence of conventional verse, by its curious phraseology, convoluted syntax, and abstruse meanings—and scandalized by crude language and apparent blasphemies. *Leaves of Grass* was simply not a volume they could put on display and offer for sale, especially where ladies were customers.

The outside of *Leaves of Grass* looked conventional enough—thin (ninety-five pages) and quarto-sized (about 9 by 12 inches). The green cloth binding was decorated with entwining leaves, buds, and flowers; the title itself, stamped in gold leaf, sprouted leaves and roots. This florid design typified the books of the time. Nowhere on the cover, however, did the author's name appear. Nor was it to be found on the title page, which faced the frontispiece—a portrait-engraving of a short-bearded man in his thirties, obviously the author himself. He was dressed in a carpenter's outfit, his shirt open at the neck and his wide felt hat tilted at an insouciant angle. Standing with one hand on a hip, the other in a pocket, he seemed a "rough" and nonchalant workman fully at ease with himself and his prospective readers, the possessor of certain secrets he might possibly reveal—exactly the impression he wished to convey.

This hour I tell things in confidence,
I might not tell everybody but I will tell you.

In order to discover the poet's name, one had to look on the reverse side of the title page, where it said that *Leaves of Grass* had been copyrighted by "Walter Whitman." Only in one other place was that name to be seen, presented then in a less formal way by using his nickname—right in the midst of the initial piece: a long, exuberantly discursive section of the book known now as "Song of Myself."

> Walt Whitman, an American, one of the roughs, a kosmos,
> Disorderly fleshy and sensual . . . eating drinking and breeding,
> No sentimentalist . . . no stander above men and women or apart
> from them . . . no more modest than immodest.
>
> Unscrew the locks from the doors!
> Unscrew the doors themselves from their jambs!

Snoopy, boorish, and strange this new poet seemed. And he also had the arrogance to call himself a "kosmos," as though he were a universe all to himself. Apparently he intended to insinuate himself into everybody's lives:

> Undrape . . . you are not guilty to me, nor stale nor discarded,
> I see through the broadcloth and gingham whether or no,
> And am around, tenacious, acquisitive, tireless . . . and can never
> be shaken away.

His intentions sometimes seemed obscene effronteries:

> On women fit for conception I start bigger and nimbler babes,
> This day I am jetting the stuff of far more arrogant republics.

At the same time, he tried to make accomplices out of his readers by claiming that what he was saying was not really so strange or remarkable:

> These are the thoughts of all men in all ages and lands, they are
> not original with me,
> If they are not yours as much as mine they are nothing or next to
> nothing,
>
> •   •   •

This is the grass that grows wherever the land is and the water is,
This is the common air that bathes the globe.

Even his swollen pride appeared to be dilated for others' benefit:

I know perfectly well my own egotism,
And know my omnivorous words, and cannot say any less,
And would fetch you whoever you are flush with myself.

This Walt Whitman felt that he partook of divinity—yet on such vulgar, absurd, and profane terms!

Divine am I inside and out, and I make holy whatever I touch or
    am touched from;
The scent of these arm-pits is aroma finer than prayer,
This head is more than churches or bibles or creeds.

If I worship any particular thing it shall be the spread of my
    body . . .

And then he commenced to list many of his body's anatomical features.
He announced his authoritative concern for both flesh and spirit:

I am the poet of the body,
And I am the poet of the soul.

The pleasures of heaven are with me, and the pains of hell are
    with me,
The first I graft and increase upon myself . . . the latter I translate
    into a new tongue.

He fancied himself the possessor of a magical gift for affecting miracle-cures involving mortal sickness of body or mind:

To any one dying . . . thither I speed and twist the knob of the
    door,
Turn the bed-clothes toward the foot of the bed,
Let the physician and the priest go home.

I seize the descending man . . . I raise him with resistless will.

O despairer, here is my neck,
By God! you shall not go down! Hang your whole weight upon me.

Yet he himself sounded as though he needed a doctor's help, since he often talked like a candidate for an insane asylum:

I find I incorporate gneiss and coal and long-threaded moss and
fruits and grains and esculent roots,
And am stucco'd with quadrupeds and birds all over,
And have distanced what is behind me for good reasons,
And call any thing close again when I desire it.

And was this boastful, rude, peculiar, near-anonymous man the same Walter Whitman who had been a schoolteacher; who had briefly served as editor of the New York *Aurora;* who had written the sentimental, moralizing stories published in the *Democratic Review;* who had composed poems with standard rhyme and meter in the same spirit as his stories; who had produced a preachy "hack" novel about the evils of intemperance; and who had expounded on a variety of subjects for the edification of readers of the Brooklyn *Eagle?*

If style marked the man, this surely was a different fellow entirely. Walter Whitman would hardly have offered such strange and shocking combinations of words, such weird notions, such frequent outrages to human sensibilities. The only readily discernible similarity between this wild-talking, ill-mannered "poet" and the staid writer of old might be a fraternal tendency to lecture, point, admonish, emote, exclaim—all to enjoin and encourage readers to change and improve their lives. Yet surely this *Leaves of Grass* was a barbarian way to approach the moral instruction of a civilized people!

But even Walt Whitman now and then seemed aware of his long-windedness and primitive language:

The spotted hawk swoops by and accuses me . . . he complains of
my gab and my loitering.

I too am not a bit tamed . . . I too am untranslatable,
I sound my barbaric yawp over the roofs of the world.

"Barbaric yawp," then, was Whitman's own phrase for his "poetry"; it was suitable and would stick. But was anybody ever going to try and understand him? Especially since he delighted in making himself difficult and mysterious:

I depart as air . . . I shake my white locks at the runaway sun,
I effuse my flesh in eddies and drift it in lacy jags.

I bequeath myself to the dirt to grow from the grass I love,
If you want me again look for me under your bootsoles.

You will hardly know who I am or what I mean,
But I shall be good health to you nevertheless,
And filter and fibre your blood.

Failing to fetch me at first keep encouraged,
Missing me one place search another,
I stop some where waiting for you.

Thus did a new poet and self-styled prophet of the nineteenth century, a native and resident of the United States of America, announce himself to the world. To explain himself more fully—and therefore appearing even more verbose and inflated than his poetry portrayed him—Walt Whitman had written a lengthy and meandering Preface to his book. Full of ejaculatory utterances, which were set in double columns in hard-to-read small type, it went on and on for a dozen pages.

Anybody who ever undertakes to study Walt Whitman and his poetry uses the famous Preface to the first (1855) edition of *Leaves of Grass* as a basic text. It tells much about Whitman's intentions in writing his early poems, lists his requirements for the "true poet of American democracy," and implies that Whitman was determined to become this idealized modern poet-prophet. Having established his own identity as a poet with a special style and an amplified perspective or vista, Walt was to depart little from the "program" he presented in his Preface for the great new bard.

Whitman's prose in the Preface stylistically conformed with the poems that followed it. His long, complex sentences were strung with words in series, phrases, dependent clauses, and appositions—all tenuously held together by dashes and ellipses. Sometimes, as though in breathless haste, punctuating commas were omitted. The language itself was rhythmic and full of imagery; in the following year Whitman used portions of it almost unchanged—except for dividing passages into poetic lines—when he recast the Preface into new poems.

Whitman saw America's genius best not in its intellectuals but in the common people themselves. The way they walked, talked, looked, dressed, and made friends; their liking for freedom; their anger at injustice and their sensitivity to slights; their respect for citizens of other states; their natural frankness, honesty, curiosity, sympathy, and good temperament; above all, their self-esteem, "the air they have of a person who never knew how it felt to stand in the presence of superiors"—all these, to Whitman, were "unrhymed poetry" which awaited "the gigantic and generous treatment worthy of it" by the poet or bard who was truly "commensurate with a people."

Of this ideal poet Whitman said, "His spirit responds to his country's spirit . . . he incarnates its geography and natural life." The poet would span east and west, stretch from north to south, absorbing and reflecting everything within his nation's boundaries: "To him enter the essences of the real things and past and present events—of the enormous diversity of temperature and agriculture and mines—the tribes of red aborigines—the weatherbeaten vessels entering new ports or making landings on rocky coasts—the first settlements north or south—the rapid stature and muscle—the haughty defiance of '76, and the war and peace and formation of the constitution . . . the union always surrounded by blatherers and always calm and impregnable. . . ."

When this new bard, whom all awaited, composed the "great psalm of the republic," it would have a theme with "vista." A sample of such a continent-containing chant Walt Whitman had written in the long poem which became "Song of Myself." Section 15 presents his earliest full "catalogue" of American life, which

named almost a hundred different activities going on simulta-
neously all over the country, indoors and out:

> The pure contralto sings in the organloft,
> The carpenter dresses his plank . . . the tongue of his foreplane
> > whistles its wild ascending lisp,
> The married and unmarried children ride home to their thanks-
> > giving dinner,
> The pilot seizes the king-pin, he heaves down with a strong arm,
> The mate stands braced in the whaleboat, lance and harpoon are
> > ready,
> The duck-shooter walks by silent and cautious stretches,
> The deacons are ordained with crossed hands at the altar,
> The spinning-girl retreats and advances to the hum of the big
> > wheel,
> The farmer stops by the bars of a Sunday and looks at the oats and
> > rye . . .

In Whitman's catalogue, each person was democratically ac-
corded a place and attention equal to that of the others—each
contributing his part to the absorptive poet as he weaves "the song
of myself."

With inspirational help from Emerson's essays and other sources,
Whitman had put together his portrait of the great modern poet
or bard for America—who might also be variously called a seer,
prophet, answerer, singer, medium, divine literatus, and kosmos.
In the best Greek tradition this poet would tell of his nation's
past, present, and future heroes to all who would gather and listen.
This new Homer, however, would not use as subjects the "feudal"
favorites: kings and queens and well-born nobility whose triumphs
and fates were controlled by the whims of gods and goddesses of
outgrown religions. Instead, he would take as heroic material the
common American men and women, finding an uncommon splendor in their everyday work and attitudes, in their fervent devotion
to their country and to the "grand old cause" of liberty. He was
determined to celebrate, in his own unique way, the "roughs and

beards and space and ruggedness and nonchalance that the soul loves."

In one of Whitman's early notebooks he referred to the project which occupied him as "the New Bible." Undeniably, *Leaves of Grass* was the product of a highly religious mind—if an unconventional and presumptuous one. Whitman was hardly the only person of his time who conceived of a grandiose plan to renovate both individuals and society. Indeed, the nineteenth century in Europe and America abounded in prophets, reformers, visionaries, revolutionists—each with his own special scheme for salvation.

Socialist Karl Marx was one of the century's most original and ultimately influential thinkers. As prophet of radical economic reform, he maintained that personality and society could be altered when the masses revolted against their traditional exploiters—hereditary rulers and bourgeois capitalists—and created a regime in which all men were equal in economic opportunity, social status, and political freedom.

Whitman resembled Marx in his espousal of the common workingman and in his desire to overthrow the idols and thrones of the past which had kept the "lower" classes in thralldom. He delivered his own "manifesto" to the world in the Preface to the first edition of *Leaves of Grass*. But in it he proposed spiritual or religious changes, not economic or political ones; he was already satisfied with democracy's (and perhaps capitalism's) potential. He believed that in order to perfect the social order, man must find a new way of regarding himself as an individual and as a member of a group. To work properly, democracy required a new type of citizen.

During the genesis period of *Leaves of Grass*, Whitman had diligently studied the literature and belief-systems of both primitive and modern world religions. He had gained an understanding of and respect for mankind's religious impulses and needs. A passage in "Song of Myself" attests to his desire to incorporate within himself the whole history of religion:

> I do not despise you priests;
> My faith is the greatest of faiths and the least of faiths,

Enclosing all worship ancient and modern, and all between ancient
and modern,
Believing I shall come again upon the earth after five thousand
years,
Waiting responses from oracles . . . honoring the gods . . . saluting
the sun . . .

A few years later, in "Starting from Paumanok," Whitman would
explicitly state his religious intentions:

I too, following many and follow'd by many, inaugurate a religion,
I descend into the arena,
(It may be I am destin'd to utter the loudest cries there, the win-
ner's pealing shouts,
Who knows? they may rise from me yet, and soar above every
thing.)

Why did Whitman propose himself as the prophet of a new religion? Because he was convinced that his country's future success
depended upon generating and spreading a devotional spirit appropriate for the times among Americans:

I say that the real and permanent grandeur of these States must be
their religion,
Otherwise there is no real and permanent grandeur;
(No character nor life worthy the name without religion,
Nor land nor man or woman without religion.)

In his Preface, Walt Whitman boldly predicted that "there will
soon be no more priests," since the work of the traditional religions
was finished. "A superior breed shall take their place," he said,
"the gangs of kosmos and prophets en masse. . . ." (A *kosmos* in
the Whitman vocabulary was a wise, divinely inspired human
being whose words and actions served as examples and inspira-
tions to his fellow men. The name came from the Greek word
for order and harmony, which was then applied to the universe
itself.)

In his poetry Walt praised the heroic dead; he also empathized with the downtrodden, the despised, and the defective. In imaginary journeys he often assumed the "bodies" and experiences of others, taking onto himself their physical or psychic wounds and equalizing them all by relieving them of sins, pains, or burdens. After such a sequence in "Song of Myself," the poet suddenly realized that he was actually doing what Jesus had done; he then made explicit his identification—indeed, his oneness—with Christ.

> That I could forget the mockers and insults!
> That I could forget the trickling tears and the blows of the bludgeons and hammers!
> That I could look with a separate look on my own crucifixion and bloody crowning!
>
> I remember now,
> I resume the overstaid fraction,
> The grave of rock multiplies what has been confided to it, or to any graves,
> Corpses rise, gashes heal, fastenings roll from me.
>
> I troop forth replenish'd with supreme power, one of an average unending procession,
>
>   •   •   •
>
> Our swift ordinances on their way over the whole earth,
> The blossoms we wear in our hats the growth of thousands of years.

Whitman believed that the spirits of saviors and martyrs embodying the divinity within mankind were perpetually resurrected. Their efforts would be renewed and expanded through all those who, singly or in "gangs," strove, suffered, and even died to establish the "great idea" of "the progress and freedom of the race." Walt clearly found his own special calling in leading people toward the real salvation on earth: the perfect democracy.

Whitman, then, was not just a mystic absorbed in his own solitary visions; wishing to demonstrate them to others, he thereby became a prophet. He later pointed out that people mistakenly narrowed the meaning of the word "prophecy" to mere prediction. "That is not the main sense of the Hebrew word translated 'prophet,'" he said; "it means one whose mind bubbles and pours forth like a fountain from inner divine spontaneities revealing God. . . . The great matter is to reveal and outpour the God-like suggestions pressing for birth in the soul." A good portion of Whitman's poetry would illustrate this Biblical bubbling and flow. He also uttered many cryptic aphorisms which might have come from the mouth of a Delphic oracle; he himself sometimes appeared uncertain as to where they came from or what they meant.

In his Preface, Whitman tried to define what would make the great new poet different from the conventional ones. Writing, he admitted, was not such an uncommon ability. "But to speak in literature with the perfect rectitude and insouciance of animals and the unimpeachableness of the sentiment of trees in the woods and grass by the roadside is the flawless triumph of art," he said. "If you have looked on him who has achieved it you have looked on one of the masters of the artists of all nations and times." Style did not distinguish the great poet so much as his being "the channel of thoughts and things without increase or diminution." He would be "the free channel of himself." And in his offerings in the early *Leaves of Grass* Whitman had done his best to display his qualifications for this role of master-poet.

The Biblical prophets had brought the populace codes of laws. Whitman likewise came with his tablet of commandments. "This is what you shall do," he told readers of his Preface. "Love the earth and sun and the animals, despise riches, give alms to everyone that asks, stand up for the stupid and crazy, devote your income and labor to others, hate tyrants, argue not concerning God, have patience and indulgence toward the people, take off your hat to nothing known or unknown or to any man or number of men, go freely with powerful uneducated persons and with the young and with the mothers of families, read these leaves in the open air every season of every year of your life, re-examine all you have been told at school or church or in any book, dismiss whatever insults your own soul, and your very flesh shall be a great poem. . . ."

Though Whitman spoke as the propagator of a new faith, even a messiah, he echoed the long-established religions because he taught that adherence to a set of moral maxims would guarantee a powerful transformation of both body and soul. Admission into a glorious and immortal afterlife would also be gained.

Walt knew that some individuals had a mysteriously charismatic quality which could affect and alter the people around them. He attributed it to "animal magnetism," a concept popularized by Mesmer which gained favor in the nineteenth century. (Later the phenomenon would be classified as hypnosis.) It was widely believed that particular people possessed or acquired the ability to pass a "magnetic" or "electric" current by body contact, usually the "laying on of hands"; but even the very presence of such a highly charged practitioner could have therapeutic effects on his beholders. Thus Walt would frequently use words like "magnetic" and "electric" when describing the persuasive powers of a great poet, religious and political leaders, or artistic performers— and when depicting sexual attraction or the invisible bonds fraternally linking men in society.

Whitman had found that he exuded a certain "magnetism" himself, and he tried actually to inject it into his poems. He hoped that his readers would feel its peculiar "electric" force emanating from his "leaves" or when in actual bodily contact with his book. And indeed, in the future, many Whitman followers would behave like eager converts.

In his Preface Whitman also maintained that a great poet would prove his worthiness for the role not just in his writing but by embodying within himself, and demonstrating in his own life, all the virtues which he praised. In other words, the poet must "become" his poetry. Again and again, throughout Leaves of Grass, one can see Whitman's attempt to fuse both bodily and spiritually with his poems; and in his own life he tried to fulfill the ideals he had set for America's great new bard.

For prospective poets who might wish to qualify as contenders for the "great poet" position, Whitman had prepared a set of rhetorical questions which, he said, also applied to anyone offering new materials or ideas, laws or entertainments, to the American people—who would be the final judges of their relevance and acceptability. "Is it uniform with my country?" he asked. ". . . Is it something grown fresh out of the fields or drawn from the sea for use to me today here? . . . Does this acknowledge liberty with audible and absolute acknowledgment, and set slavery at naught for life and death? Will it help breed one good shaped and well hung man, and a woman to be his perfect and independent mate? . . . Is it for the nursing of the young of the republic?"

Rare indeed would be the creator of anything capable of filling all the specifications Whitman set. Yet his grand vision was better answered by the first edition of *Leaves of Grass* than by any other piece of American writing hitherto produced—although few would recognize it at the time. Walt Whitman had aimed wide and high and deep—as wide and varied as his growing nation, as high as its great ideals, and as deep as the human soul.

If what Whitman offered to the American public ever really took hold, he predicted the demise of imitative, secondhand verses composed by the American poets who subscribed to foreign standards. Walt recognized that the American people now needed a broad, free, vigorous style which would reflect themselves and their world—and cheer them on to even better accomplishments. Optimistically, he felt that "the largest and wealthiest and proudest nation" would surely go halfway to meet the spirit of its new poets. And how would a poet know if he had passed the test put forward by the people? "The proof of a poet is that his country absorbs him as affectionately as he has absorbed it," Whitman answered. Looking for signs of such acceptance, Walt would find his wait long and arduous.

A would-be prophet speaks out in his most effective way, whether by vocalism from pulpit or public platform or by printed word. Sometimes, too, his voice shouts out from the confines of a mental asylum—for an undeniable relationship exists between the lofty plans and gorgeous visions of the genuine mystic-prophet and the tormented delusions and vehement obsessions of an insane person. Both may "see" things and "hear" voices not perceived by normal people. Since the prophet usually proposes radical alterations in people's ideas and in the very structure of their society, he is often thought to be both dangerous and crazy. Sometimes he is merely ignored or ridiculed; at other times he may fall victim to, and be martyred by, the very people he insists upon leading to salvation.

Both prophetical and deranged minds tend to explain all occurrences in terms of a large system—and here is where a significant difference usually lies. The prophet's universe is beautiful, orderly, and good; within it he is an humble spokesman for a divine, creative force; all its creatures are equals and brothers. The psychopath, on the other hand, lives in the very center of chaos; an ugly, turbulent, malevolent universe seems to direct a destructive force against him. The prophet loves, and the madman hates; the prophet trusts, and the madman fears—both with a passionate intensity and conviction. The world in which each dwells is to him as true and as real—and as readily documented—as the worlds beheld and experienced by normal minds.

The issue of mental peculiarity or derangement has a definite bearing on Whitman's life and poetry. His intense and vastly ambitious plans as a poet show that he was not a normal or "average" person (whatever he claimed to the contrary in his poems); too, many portions of *Leaves of Grass* describe odd or "abnormal" states of mind. A strain of mental instability obviously ran through the Whitman family. Walt's father was unusually moody, and probably on some issues opinionated to the point of fanaticism. Even as a child, Walt's older brother Jesse was difficult; he later became unpredictable, unemployable, and violent—to finish his life in a mental asylum. Both Andrew and Hannah proved to be emotionally unbalanced, and the youngest boy, Eddie, was temperamental and mentally retarded. On the other hand, George and Mary led stable and conventional lives, while Jeff at least made an effort to do so.

It is possible that Walt Whitman experienced life in a "supernormal" or hypersensitive way because of a congenital abnormality or predisposition of his nervous system. Certainly he was neurotic (and what great artist is not?): of that *Leaves of Grass* gives sufficient proof. A neurosis is generally considered a disability or defect; yet its possessor may accomplish wonders by channeling his physical and mental energies in some endeavor wherein

he can capably function. In Walt's case a combination of beneficent factors—a pleasant and stimulating early environment, good
health, cheerful disposition, sturdy intelligence, a loving mother,
a father drawn to ideas and ideals, and a set of fortuitous circumstances which led him toward his ultimate vocation—helped to
make a poet rather than a merely maladjusted and thwarted
human being, with no way of organizing his thoughts and emotions, and continually beset by fears and unacceptable or irrecon-
cilable urges. Creating poetry may have been virtually a life-or-
death matter with Walt. When he addressed the bird in "When
Lilacs Last in the Dooryard Bloom'd," he was really describing
himself:

> ... (for well dear brother I know,
> If thou wast not granted to sing thou would'st surely die.)

Whatever grandiose hopes Walt harbored for himself as poet
and seer, within his own home he was a prophet without honor.
His sober, hard-working brother George resented Walt's absten-
tion from ordinary, lucrative toil. Of what use was he? He got up
late in the morning, sauntered around the neighborhood, and then
came home to sit upstairs in his room for hours, scribbling away
at his "pomes"—if one could call them that.

When Walt brought home the first copy of his *Leaves of Grass*,
just off the press, to show his family, nobody was much impressed.
His mother seemed pleased with her son's new accomplishment,
but she could not comprehend his strange verse. George didn't
even try to read the book; after glancing at it, he cast it aside. At
least when Walt had worked on newspapers he had talked and
written sense—and had done something in which his family could
take real pride.

And what about Walter Whitman's reaction to the book? Did
he realize that these poems of Walt's were his own spiritual grandchildren?

> ... I with my leaves and songs, trustful, admirant,
> As a father to his father going takes his children along with him.

Walt's offerings could hardly interest Walter Whitman as he lay on his deathbed, unconscious and paralyzed. For some while he had been seriously ill. Several years earlier, Walt had taken him on a tour of the old familiar Long Island places which his father wished to see for the last time. Perhaps the nostalgic journey drew closer together the father and son who often were strangers to each other; at any rate, the trip refreshed Walt's own memory of his childhood's people and places—which would so vividly enter into the composition of *Leaves of Grass*.

As Walt printed his poems, his father was dying. Walt must have taken his turn ministering to his father in his sickbed. But if he did possess any of the healing power he claimed as the poet-prophet in "Song of Myself," it proved ineffectual. Just a week after the publication of Walt's book, Walter Whitman died. In "To Think of Time" Walt had already anticipated the death scene:

> The dull nights go over and the dull days also,
> The soreness of lying so much in bed goes over,
> The physician after long putting off gives the silent and terrible
>   look for an answer,
> The children come hurried and weeping, and the brothers and
>   sisters are sent for,
> Medicines stand unused on the shelf, (the camphor-smell has long
>   pervaded the rooms,)
> The faithful hand of the living does not desert the hand of the
>   dying . . .

The poet had long been pondering what life and death meant. Now, with his father's earthly life ended, some of his own words must have come back to him:

> To think of all these wonders of city and country, and others taking
>   interest in them, and we taking no interest in
>   them.
> To think how eager we are in building our houses,
> To think others shall be just as eager, and we quite indifferent.

During his lifetime, Walter Whitman built many houses, including the one in which his son Walt had been born. Few buildings of his own or another's making had ever served him long during his life's peregrinations; none of them would last forever. And now, after sixty-six years, he was finished with house-building and home-inhabiting. But Walt was not. He was determined to build a longer-lasting, more intricate and imposing structure than any carpenter could construct. Whitman would add new "leaves" to the first twelve poems in *Leaves of Grass* until they numbered almost four hundred.

Walt usually thought of his poems as natural, spontaneous growths—like grass, or leaves on trees. Yet sometimes he referred to them in architectural terms, especially when considering their place in his nation's destiny, as in "By Blue Ontario's Shore":

> O America because you build for mankind I build for you,
> O well-beloved stone-cutters, I lead them who plan with decision and science,
> Lead the present with friendly hand toward the future.

Leaves of Grass—ultimately massive in bulk, deliberate in design, ambitious in its creator's intent—might be viewed as Whitman's own personal pyramid-building. Its real purpose perhaps was to baffle death by assuring his immortality. Like the Egyptians whom he admired, Whitman had a decided death-fixation. Block by block, poem by poem, Walt would painstakingly and ceaselessly toil to build his own monument: a record of both his life and his times, which he hoped would last as long as the Pharaohs' great tombs. Frequently he shifted the blocks' positions and removed ones that seemed unstable or unsuitable; here he smoothed rough edges, and there he applied fresh cement—all in a perpetual post-publication meddling which has no parallel in literary history, and is comparable to the dabbling habits of a painter who is never quite through with a studio masterpiece that expresses the essence of his life.

Although Whitman is generally known as the "Poet of Democracy," so much of his poetic attention was devoted to speculations about death—the great leveler, the ultimate democracy—that he might just as fittingly be called the "Poet of Death." His three un-

deniable master-poems—"Out of the Crade Endlessly Rocking,"
"Crossing Brooklyn Ferry," and "When Lilacs Last in the Dooryard Bloom'd"—all have death as a central theme. Many of his
best and most moving shorter poems concern death, and considerations of mortality recur throughout "Song of Myself"—usually
regarded as Whitman's most unique and intriguing poem.

Conventional religions had not given Whitman satisfactory explanations regarding death, so he constructed his own. In "To
Think of Time" he studied the soul's particular and enduring
identity, in which its physical manifestation, the body, played an
important part.

> The earth is not an echo, man and his life and all the things of his
> life are well-consider'd.
>
> You are not thrown to the winds, you gather certainly and safely
> around yourself,
> Yourself, yourself! yourself, for ever and ever!
>
> It is not to diffuse you that you were born of your mother and
> father, it is to identify you,
> It is not that you should be undecided, but that you should be
> decided,
> Something long preparing and formless is arrived and form'd in
> you,
> You are henceforth secure, whatever comes or goes.

Whitman believed in the soul's continued existence after the
body's death: its earthly corporeal life had shaped it for the future.

> ... I have dream'd that the purpose and essence of the known life,
> the transient,
> Is to form and decide identity for the unknown life, the permanent.

He confessed his innate fear of death; but he managed to overcome it.

> If all came but to ashes of dung,
> If maggots and rats ended us, then Alarum! for we are betrayed,
> Then indeed suspicion of death.

> Do you suspect death? if I were to suspect death I should die now,
> Do you think I could walk pleasantly and well-suited toward an-
> nihilation?
>
> Pleasantly and well-suited I walk,
> Whither I walk I cannot define, but I know it is good,
> The whole universe indicates that it is good . . .

As extra insurance, perhaps, so that no portion of one's self would ever be lost, Whitman also discovered a "chemical immortality" of the body. After death the body dissolved and its atoms combined anew to form other living beings, whether plants or animals or people. Whitman's favorite symbol for the endurance of matter through transmutation was the grass: given prime importance, of course, in his book's title, but also appearing often within his poems. (Walt made an intentional *double-entendre* in his use of the word "leaves" in his volume's title, meaning not only the vital part of a plant but also a page in a book—a good reason why he did not call his volume "Blades of Grass.")

Whitman's invocation of his soul—his muse—when commencing "Song of Myself" came while the poet observed a spear of grass. Later on, a child asked the poet a key question, which enabled him to launch his considerations of the possible "meanings" of grass.

> A child said *What is the grass?* fetching it to me with full hands,
> How could I answer the child? I do not know what it is any more
> than he.
>
> I guess it must be the flag of my disposition, out of hopeful green
> stuff woven.
>
> Or I guess it is the handkerchief of the Lord,
> A scented gift and remembrancer designedly dropt,
> Bearing the owner's name someway in the corners, that we may see
> and remark, and say *Whose?*
>
> Or I guess the grass is itself a child, the produced babe of the
> vegetation.
>
> Or I guess it is a uniform hieroglyphic,
> And it means, Sprouting alike in broad zones and narrow zones,
> Growing among black folks as among white . . .

Then, borrowing an image straight from Homer, Whitman introduced the death theme:

> And now it seems to me the beautiful uncut hair of graves.

> Tenderly will I use you curling grass,
> It may be you transpire from the breasts of young men,
> It may be that if I had known them I would have loved them,
> It may be you are from old people, or from offspring taken soon
>   out of their mothers' laps,
> And here you are the mothers' laps.

What had become of all those who died? The poet tried to "translate" the "hints" about them:

> They are alive and well somewhere,
> The smallest sprout shows there is really no death,
> And if ever there was it led forward life, and does not wait at the
>   end to arrest it,
> And ceas'd the moment life appear'd.

> All goes onward and outward, nothing collapses,
> And to die is different from what any one supposed, and luckier.

The grass, then, meant for Whitman the "resurrection of the body" within nature, a universal phenomenon which coincided with the soul's immortality. The soul, likewise, could never be destroyed; it too established an identity elsewhere, in another form, always to seek increasing perfection. In a philosophy of mortality which resembled and perhaps was partly derived from Oriental religious teachings, Walt saw death as a phase of eternal life. Death rested and refreshed the soul before its entrance into a different kind of existence.

> As to you Life I reckon you are the leavings of many deaths,
> (No doubt I have died myself ten thousand times before.)

> I hear you whispering there O stars of heaven,
> O suns—O grass of graves—O perpetual transfers and promotions,
> If you do not say any thing how can I say any thing?

These things decided, Whitman might have let them be. But again and again, with a near-obsessive attention that constantly needed reassurance, Walt continued to write poems about death, immortality, and incarnation.

Thus, in July of 1855 Walt Whitman watched the birth of his book along with the death of his father. His high hopes for the newborn child of his genius probably distracted him from fully participating in domestic sorrow. Here came new life: and would the world welcome it?

The first review of Walt's book appeared in the July 23 edition of the New York *Tribune*. Charles A. Dana, who probably knew Whitman personally at the time, praised the "odd genius" who had written *Leaves of Grass*. "No impartial reader," he said, "can fail to be impressed with the vigor and quaint beauty of isolated portions." But he noted that the language was "too frequently reckless and indecent, though this appears to arise from a naïve unconsciousness rather than from an impure mind."

The review made a fair send-off for the unknown poet who had published the book at his own expense. The other reviews which would follow it later—and there weren't many—would be mostly severe and censorious. Because Walt Whitman virtually claimed to be the great poet whom America wanted and needed, his ingenuous arrogance naturally put critics on the offensive; they overreacted to his brash egotism, among other things.

Several days after the *Tribune* review, Walt received a letter from Ralph Waldo Emerson, who had just read the copy of *Leaves of Grass* sent to him by Fowler & Wells. A good part of the Preface struck home with Emerson; he had been saying many of these things for a long time, but in hardly so brazen and oracular a voice. Emerson recognized, however, that Whitman had ably illustrated his points by writing poems which were remarkable indeed for their vigor, honesty, and sometimes sheer beauty. He had never read anything quite like them.

A responsive and wholly generous man, Emerson wrote at once to Whitman. His letter constitutes the most famous tribute that an unknown writer ever received from a renowned man of letters.

It demonstrates not only Emerson's kindliness, but even more, the acuity of his literary insight.

"Dear Sir," wrote Emerson, "I am not blind to the worth of the wonderful gift of *Leaves of Grass*. I find it the most extraordinary piece of wit and wisdom that America has yet contributed. I am very happy in reading it, as great power makes us happy. It meets the demand I am always making. . . . I give you joy of your free and brave thought. I have great joy in it. I find incomparable things said incomparably well, as they must be. I find the courage of treatment which so delights us, and which large perception only can inspire. I greet you at the beginning of a great career, which yet must have had a long foreground somewhere, for such a start."

Moreover, Emerson declared a wish to "see my benefactor" by visiting New York and paying his respects in person. At that time Whitman and Emerson had no friends in common, which makes Emerson's enthusiasm all the more startling and genuine. The Sage of Concord had detected, beneath Walt's pose of primitivism, the years of preparation behind *Leaves of Grass*. He was aware that Whitman was no workaday carpenter suddenly beset by an odd compulsion to compose poems. The philosopher who treasured the wonders of the human mind responded to the boastfully prophetic, all-encompassing poet who sang so much of the impulses and pleasures of the human body, for he knew—as Whitman knew—that the body nourished the soul.

Naturally Walt was overjoyed to receive such a letter from a man whose opinion he valued above all others. Throughout the summer of 1855 he carried Emerson's letter in his pocket, sustaining some of his initial self-confidence and sense of purpose while his book went ignored by reviewers and buyers.

It had simply never occurred to Emerson, however, that his personal letter to Walt of congratulatory greeting might be used as an open endorsement of both *Leaves of Grass* and its author's talents. (Today, in our promotion-conscious society, such an unsolicited vote of confidence would be written in a far more cautious manner—if at all.) Whitman served as his own publicist as well as publisher. He showed Emerson's epistolary praises to Charles Dana, who then published the letter in an October issue of the *Tribune*. Seemingly ignorant of elementary courtesy in such matters, Walt had not written to obtain Emerson's permission to quote him. And to compound the offense, he inserted copies of the printed letter in copies of his book which he now sent out to other worthies in the literary world.

Emerson's many friends and acquaintances were horrified. Not only did they object to Whitman's public display of a private letter, but most of them were quite unable and unwilling to share Emerson's high opinion of this new poet. John Greenleaf Whittier, it is said, threw his copy of *Leaves of Grass* into a blazing hearthfire; doubtless other complimentary copies met a similar fate. James Russell Lowell, Oliver Wendell Holmes, and Henry Wadsworth Longfellow—major and well-respected poets—were baffled by Emerson's praises, finding nothing good at all about Walt Whitman's poems.

But Whitman's publicity stunt at least stirred up interest—in the autumn of 1855 *Leaves of Grass* began to receive a few reviews, though in them Walt could hardly find the sort of recognition he hoped for. The critic in the *Criterion* confessed that he would have ignored the book but for Emerson's recommendation, and then noted that "an unconsidered letter of introduction has often-times procured the admittance of a scurvy fellow into good society." He gave his own opinion of the volume: "It is impossible to imagine how any man's fancy could have conceived such a mass of stupid filth, unless he were possessed of the soul of a sentimental donkey that had died of disappointed love." A *Putnam's Magazine* reviewer summed up *Leaves of Grass* as "a mixture of Yankee transcendentalism and New York rowdyism"; there was some truth in that.

Emerson himself made few remarks to his friends about Whitman's discourtesy, but he did comment mildly that had he known to what use his letter would be put, he certainly would have enlarged the "*but.*" He continued to like *Leaves of Grass* and recommended it to his visitors, to neighbors like Thoreau and Bronson Alcott, and to his Cambridge and Boston friends. He even sent a copy to Thomas Carlyle in England—along with a cautionary note.

Emerson also asked a friend to visit Whitman while in New

York. Moncure Conway learned that Walt lived in Brooklyn, some distance from the ferry depot. But impressed first by Emerson's enthusiasm and then by his own reading of the book, he made a determined effort to meet the poet. Whitman was not at home when Conway came to call; he could be found at his printers' office, said Mrs. Whitman. And so indeed he was there—dressed in an open-necked striped shirt, revising proof on some new poems —"a man you would not have marked in a thousand." (Would Walt have been pleased or dismayed to know of Conway's confirmation of his "common-man" appearance?)

"His beard and hair are greyer than is usual with a man of thirty-six," Conway reported to Emerson by mail. "His face and eye are interesting, and his head rather narrow behind the eyes; but a thick brow looks as if it might have absorbed much." When Conway told Walt of having recently spent an agreeable evening with Emerson, Walt eagerly asked to know everything possible about Emerson personally and about his opinion of his *Leaves*.

Whitman went cheerfully off to Manhattan with his new acquaintance, who observed Walt's free and easy manner with everybody he saw on street or ferryboat. Although Conway felt that Whitman was "playing Providence a little with the baser sort," he couldn't help but like him. He judged Whitman "clearly his Book"—the very impression Walt had wished to achieve in real life.

Hoping to stimulate interest in his book and to increase its feeble sales, Walt wrote several reviews himself which were published anonymously in publications friendly to him. They show what Whitman wanted people to think of him and his poems. "An American bard at last!" is the way he greeted himself in the *United States Review* (formerly the *Democratic Review* which had published his early stories). The style of Whitman's poems, he continued, was "simply their own style, new-born and red. Nature may have given the hint to the author . . . but there exists no book or fragment of a book which can have given the hint to them." (Walt, of course, was not quite telling the truth—and he knew it.)

An article entitled "Walt Whitman, A Brooklyn Boy" appearing in the Brooklyn *Daily Times* sounded as if the poet himself had composed it—as indeed he had. The poems were the attempt of a "live, naieve, masculine, tenderly affectionate, rowdyish, contemplative, sensual, moral, susceptible and imperious person, to cast into literature not only his own grit and arrogance, but his own flesh and form, undraped, regardless of foreign models, regardless of modesty or law, and ignorant or silently scornful, as at first appears, of all except his own presence and experience, and all outside the fiercely loved land of his birth, and the birth of his parents and their parents for several generations before him." The author-reviewer accurately judged that the poems would appear "devilish" to some readers and "divine" to others.

But if Walt Whitman had really expected the nation to take good notice of him and his *Leaves of Grass,* he was doomed to deep disappointment. Emerson's quick and full recognition of his genius had been a fluke—even, perhaps, a miracle as far as Walt's future was concerned. It is quite possible that without Emerson's gratuitous letter to strengthen his resolve as a fledgling poet, Whitman might have abandoned his new career and discontinued his self-subsidized publications. Then that first editon of the ultimately voluminous *Leaves of Grass* could well have lain in oblivion, eventually to be buried by time because its author, having found no appreciative readers, felt too discouraged to continue his writing and his self-promotion.

What really had convinced Emerson of Whitman's merits as a poet? Walt's various ideas—philosophical, religious, cultural, political—were mostly familiar to him; but the style that enclosed them was not. Like a trail-blazer, Whitman had made a radical departure from the well-traveled road and struck off on his own, launching his lusty songs ahead and behind in a virtuoso's display of human vocalism.

Whitman's style had certain antecedents and possible influences. But whatever it might have owed to the forceful, irregular rhythms and prophetic visions and primal images of the Bible's King James version, to the sacred yet sensual books of the Orient, to Carlyle's odd and spellbinding prose, to Emerson's effulgent suggestions, to the inspired idealism of George Sand, even to the lovingly detailed descriptions of people and things and places in Charles Dickens' novels—Whitman's style was distinctly his own in its fusion of words and ideas and strong emotions.

Whitman took the whole tradition of Anglo-American poetry and set it on a shelf; it was not for him. He had many "Ms. doings and undoings," as he put it—confessing later to the great trouble he had in leaving out the stock "poetical" touches, but finally succeeding. He was after properties more fundamental to the poet than the fashions of past centuries could provide. He would rather appear elemental than civilized. But an artisan, not an untutored primitive, wrote the poems, taking the original products of inspiration and working to refine them—adding, removing, altering again and again, the better to achieve the effects he wanted from his words.

During the preparatory period of the first *Leaves of Grass*, Walt had undertaken a study of linguistics, among his many projects. In his Preface he declared himself glad to be writing in the English language. "It is brawny enough and limber and full enough to suit the grand American expression," he said. He did not forget that it belonged to a tough race which was "never without the idea of political liberty." English pleased him because it was the "powerful language of resistance."

Furthermore, English had attracted and absorbed "the terms of daintier and gayer and subtler and more elegant tongues." This polyglot aspect admirably filled Whitman's ecumenical purpose. America was a "nation of nations" that would lead the whole world toward democracy, so it was only right that other peoples' tongues should be given partial expression in *Leaves of Grass*.

French had contributed many words to the English vocabulary, and Whitman extended the French invasion further. Apparently he felt that certain French words were more effective than their English counterparts because they had a more symbolic content—or a more exotic appearance. He scattered French words throughout his poems, some of them loaded with specific key meanings in the Whitmanian philosophy, others merely idle and distracting: femme, eleve, en-masse, melange, arriere, chansonnier, delicatesse, allons, habitue, feuille, eclat. To a lesser degree he used words of other languages—Latin, Greek, Spanish, German, Italian (the latter notably appearing in connection with music)—along with a few Sanskrit or Hindu terms like avataras and maya.

As if this foreign borrowing were not enough, Whitman also coined his own words and phrases for his own special purposes. Sometimes they had the look of foreign derivation: camerado, lumine, eclaircise, habitans, I exposé. Or they were variations on English words: literats, promulge, harbinge. Often the words seemed awkward, like compassionaters and dispensatress; occasionally they were apt—like Presidentiad, to describe the four-year presidential term of office.

Then to compound such vocabulary innovations, Whitman gave odd spellings: Kanada for Canada, kosmos for cosmos; or he substituted his favored "original" or Indian names for well-known places: Paumanok for Long Island, Mannahatta for Manhattan or New York. At other times he deliberately Americanized foreign place names. In another language peculiarity which may baffle the beginning reader, he would eventually assign numerals instead of names to the months and the days of the week (April became "Fourth month," and Sunday was "First day")—translating all previous references in his earlier poems into this melodious and quaint Quaker form. Another later alteration was his contraction or ellision of the "-ed" in many verbs, past participles, and participial adjectives into "-'d," which gives Whitman's poetry one of its most characteristic (if old-fashioned) features. (Thus, "covered" became "cover'd," "filled" became "fill'd," and so on.)

English-language purists were alarmed by Whitman's obvious delight in American slang words. To them poetry should always present a refined vocabulary; but of course that hardly suited Whitman's intentions. In the essay "Slang in America," written late in his life, Whitman declared slang to be "the lawless germinal element, below all words and sentences, and behind all poetry"— something that naturally earned his high approval. Likening language to "some vast living body," he claimed that slang not only fed it first but also originated fancy, imagination, and humor. By using slang freely, Whitman hoped to keep his idiom informal, relaxed, closer to the common people. And who else would have addressed himself so casually to the globe?

> Earth! you seem to look for something at my hands,
> Say, old top-knot, what do you want?

Whitman's sheer love for words themselves is quite apparent, and some of his special ability as a poet came from his pleasure in experimenting with them. His lexicon was rich and varied, and a vocabulary count puts Whitman far beyond the wordage range of most poets and quite close to the master word-user, Shakespeare. And although Whitman has been criticized for a boring verbosity, especially in his "catalogues," his lengthy surveys of people and places, activities and products, present vital summaries of nineteenth-century United States; as such they well serve social historians.

Whitman utilized a number of special words related to human work, to religion, history and geography, and to science. His virtuosity with technical terms attests to his "omnivorous" interest in many areas; but it also reflects the oft-observed tendency of the ambitious, largely self-educated man to win attention and admiration by his ready acquaintance with abstruse or archaic words or with professional jargon. When these words are used too often, or are not used properly and effectively, the result can be pretentious, even ludicrous—and sometimes this happened with Whitman's poetry.

Sloughing off whatever parts of poetic tradition he did not want, Whitman nevertheless retained some basic and useful forms. Poets can be expected to employ imagery; Whitman gave metaphors and similes powerful and unexpected new uses, often composing whole poems around them. Onomatopoeia came easily and naturally to him; he used or made words which duplicated or approximated the sounds he wished to convey: blab, sluff, clinking, cluck, swash, hiss, wheeze. And he relished assonance and alliteration, the standard techniques of repeating similar vowel and consonant sounds.

To what extent the poet himself consciously exercised his craftmanship is an ever-debatable issue. But critical studies of his numerous alterations through the years in words and lines often show that Whitman knew exactly what he was doing as an artist— far more than either he admitted or his era's critics recognized.

Many people enjoy Whitman's poetry because of its free-flowing aspect, its freedom from the strictures of rhyme and meter; yet it is actually held together by certain techniques, some of them wholly devised by Whitman. Most of Whitman's individual lines do not conform to a regular accenting rhythm or metrical scheme, and their syllable counts are quite variable. But they often contain definite internal beats; they can echo and vary the rhythm of preceding lines and shape a measure for succeeding lines. Accidentally drop a syllable here, a word there—and the small omission may be disturbing to one's sense of proper sound sequence. The beginning and ending words of his lines frequently receive a strong stress. Lines are grouped together in pithily short or enormously lengthy stanzas, or paragraphs. The long poems are usually subdivided into numbered sections; many of these are really poems unto themselves while contributing to the total message or effect.

Whitman's poetic technique sometimes bears a family resemblance to music, especially to the modern and improvisational. Certain poems—most notably, "Out of the Cradle Endlessly Rocking," "Song of the Redwood-Tree," and "When Lilacs Last in the Dooryard Bloom'd"—are presented in paragraphs which may alternate "talking" with "singing," much as the recitative and aria passages in opera. Whitman's stanzaic rhythm patterns pertain to the subject matter or mood within the poem or poetic passage. The first lines of "Song of the Broad-Axe" duplicate the regular pounding of a hatchet or sledge hammer; "Pioneers! O Pioneers!" sets a swift, one-two trochaic marching pace; the italicized bird song in "Out of the Cradle Endlessly Rocking" approximates warbling. (Not surprisingly, a number of composers have set Whitman poems to music.)

Even the notorious "catalogues" use distinctive structural devices to bind their materials together. In a format usually called "parallelism," Whitman could spin out a single sentence for a hundred and more lines, linking them together with verbs or participles all relating to the subject given in the initial lines (or sometimes at the close) who may be the spectator-participant "I," operating in the present tense and giving an immediacy to all that his panoramic vision encounters. The first words of lines repeat and then vary parts of speech (prepositions, articles, conjunctions, adverbs, nouns). Lines themselves may be broken internally into two or three parts, and are separated by ellipses, dashes, commas, or semicolons—providing pauses and occasional surprises.

When Whitman faltered or failed in poems or in passages of poems—and his great ambitions and many experiments inevitably led him into pitfalls and pratfalls—it was frequently because he allowed words to remain abstract symbols of his ideas rather than flesh-and-blood endowments of his known sensory world. Generalized conceptions like democracy, liberty, and union too often turned out to be catchall terms; Whitman trusted that by simply reciting them they would automatically convey his messages and elicit the desired response from readers. Contemporary readers may feel ill at ease, amused, or simply bored with Whitman's effulgent abstractions—usually capitalized—especially those pertaining to a national idealism now faded and worn by a new century's complexities and often-disillusioning experiences. These reactions can be aggravated by the poet's habit of relying upon ejaculatory "O's" and exclamation marks to give dramatic emphasis.

For a poet, compression of statement is an important gift. With all his listings and discourses, his ramblings and raconteuring, Whitman often proved remarkably able to create instantaneously sharp images in a few compact words or phrases. Briefly and unerringly he could reproduce the ache of loneliness, the sheer joy of being alive and well, the ordeal of a wounded man, the torment of self-doubting, the love of humankind, the splendor of a bird's flight or song, the sexual urge, the profound beauty of the night sky, the hatred of tyranny or special privilege, or the strange ecstasy of a visionary "trip." These separate, distinct, yet universal sensations are probably what give Whitman his greatest perennial appeal to young readers; usually in *Leaves of Grass* too they can find revelatory confirmation of their own generation's preoccupying interests and feelings—whatever they might be. Walt Whitman so often "tells it like it is."

Take my leaves America, take them South
and take them North,
Make welcome for them everywhere, for they
are your own offspring . . .

VII

TAKE MY LEAVES AMERICA

(1856-1860)

After publishing *Leaves of Grass,* Walt Whitman returned to journalism. Between the fall of 1855 and the spring of 1856 he wrote a group of informative articles, largely about New York, for *Life Illustrated,* a magazine published by Fowler & Wells. He needed the money he earned: only a few dozen copies of his book of poems had been sold.

During the summer of 1856 Whitman watched while three political parties competed in the presidential election. James Buchanan represented the Democrats, and ex-President Millard Fillmore was the standard-bearer for the Native American (or "Know-Nothing") Party. The new Republican Party, a combination of Free-Soilers and liberal-minded Whigs, chose as their candidate the soldier-explorer John C. Frémont, a hero of national proportions and son-in-law of the abolitionary Senator Thomas Hart Benton.

As his own message to the nation of voters in an election year, Whitman prepared a pamphlet called "The Eighteenth Presidency!" (The title referred to the upcoming eighteenth "Presidentiad," or four-year term of office.) The booklet relayed "The Voice of Walt Whitman to Each Young Man in the Nation, North, South, East and West." Emotional in tone and discursive in treatment—as all Whitman's prose was apt to be—it introduced in a simplified way the principles of an operative democratic government and also demonstrated how and why the Founding Fathers' original ideals had miscarried through the years. Whitman obviously held a low opinion of the current practitioners of government, and as he inveighed against them, he sounded like the youthful editor of the *Aurora* a decade and a half ago.

Walt had his primer on American democracy set in type. Hoping that newspaper editors and "rich persons" would want to circulate it throughout the country to edify working-class men and influence their votes, Whitman sent his "Voice" to various places —but found no takers. His voting instructions, for one thing, were far too nebulous to please the Republicans, whom Whitman was supporting as if by default. He roundly condemned the other two candidates, but failed to endorse Frémont outright. Instead, he asked him to shape up and become the "Redeemer President" whom the nation desperately needed. Whitman's pamphlet was retired to the growing mass of notes and manuscripts to be unearthed and published after his death.

Probably the most fascinating item in "The Eighteenth Presidency!" was Walt's description of the man whom he would consider the ideal candidate. He would have to wait four years; then his dream came astonishingly close to fulfillment. "I would be much pleased," he wrote, "to see some heroic, shrewd, fully-informed, healthy-bodied, middle-aged, beard-faced American blacksmith or boatman come down from the West across the Alleghenies, and walk into the Presidency, dressed in a clean suit of working attire, and with the tan all over his face, breast, and arms; I would certainly vote for that sort of man, possessing the due requirements, before any other candidate."

Although Buchanan and the Democrats won, the Republicans had made a strong enough showing in the 1856 election to assure their continued existence.

All the while, Whitman was busily preparing a new or second edition of *Leaves of Grass*. Still in the flood tide of creativity,

Walt had composed twenty new poems. A few were taken almost bodily from sections of his long Preface; Walt must have decided that his manifesto would be easier read and absorbed when rendered into poetry. He had also made some alterations in his earlier poems. His poems now bore distinct titles, most of them long and awkward—like the original title for "Song for Occupations": "Poem of the Daily Work of the Workmen and Workwomen of These States." The poem to become known as "Song of Myself" was called "A Poem of Walt Whitman, an American." (Eventually, many of Whitman's titles simply came from his poems' first lines.)

Some of Whitman's best-known poems appeared in this new edition, which was published in September of 1856—once more printed at the author's expense and under his surveillance, and distributed by Fowler & Wells. The new *Leaves of Grass* looked quite different. It was a thicker volume but had smaller overall dimensions, so that many more of Whitman's long lines now had to spill over onto indented lines below. The green cover was again adorned with gaudy decorations, now with an extra attraction in gold stamping: "I Greet You at the Beginning of A Great Career— R. W. Emerson."

Emerson had never protested directly to Whitman about the various uses of his letter for publicity purposes, but only grumbled a bit to his friends. He had met Walt in New York before this new edition's appearance, having the first of a number of tête-à-tête dinners which took place whenever Emerson came to town. In addition to employing Emerson's name and remark so boldly upon the book's cover, Walt inserted the whole text of his letter in an appendix called "Correspondence," along with some reviews of the first edition plus a lengthy reply to the man whom he addressed as "Master."

In this long delayed, and now published, response to Emerson Whitman pompously told of other work he had set out to do—"to meet people and the States face to face." (He probably intended to give lectures or recitations around the country, as Emerson did.) "But the work of my life is making poems," Walt acknowledged. Certainly he had an inflated expectation of his own eventual popularity: "A few years, and the average annual call for my Poems is ten or twenty thousand copies—more, quite likely." (It would take far longer than that for *Leaves of Grass* to be studied in courses on American Literature, making possible the large sales he forecast.)

Much of the Preface's material reappeared in the long poem now entitled "By Blue Ontario's Shore," but then called "Poem of Many in One." (It had a dual meaning, referring to the states within the Union—*E Pluribus Unum*—and also to the poet's incorporating within himself the American people and their lands.) A strident pronouncement-poem, it would be often added to in future years as Whitman's visions of himself and his nation shifted.

Again Whitman asked for "bards to corroborate" the democratic nation. He amplified his conviction that the great poet would be the country's real leader because he could sense whatever was lacking and then supply it in his own person and in his poetry. Walt also expanded his list of questions and requirements for poet-candidates, and like an exacting schoolmaster he ticked them off:

> Are you he who would assume a place to teach or be a poet here in the States?
> The place is august, the terms obdurate.
>
> Who would assume to teach here may well prepare himself body and mind,
> He may well survey, ponder, arm, fortify, harden, make lithe himself,
> He shall surely be question'd beforehand by me with many and stern questions.
>
> Who are you indeed who would talk or sing to America?
> Have you studied out the land, its idioms and men?
> Have you learn'd the physiology, phrenology, politics, geography, pride, freedom, friendship of the land? its substratums and objects?

Whitman, of course, judged himself satisfactorily equipped to answer "yes" to his many interrogations.

His conception of democracy never forgot the "great Idea" of creating and sustaining "perfect and free individuals." Behind all that was large and complex, whether nature or nation, there was always the individual person—the all-important single human being to whom Whitman addressed his *Leaves of Grass:*

> I swear I begin to see the meaning of these things,
> It is not the earth, it is not America who is so great,
> It is I who am great or to be great, it is You up there, or any one,
> It is to walk through civilization, governments, theories,
> Through poems, pageants, shows, to form individuals.

The poems in the first edition of Whitman's book had been mainly concerned with presenting the personality of the poet in various moods and guises as he took his prideful stance as a representative American—a new folk hero. The second edition further explored how a great new bard might benefit nationalism, democracy, religion, the future generations, and the self-esteem of the individual citizen.

In "To You, Whoever You Are," Whitman expressed his intense interest in the promise and sanctity of each person, considering it his special duty to awaken each slumbering individual from delusions, self-deprecation, and despair.

> Whoever you are, now I place my hand upon you, that you be my
>   poem,
> I whisper with my lips close to your ear,
> I have loved many women and men, but I love none better than
>   you,
>
>   •   •   •
>
> I only am he who places over you no master, owner, better, God,
>   beyond what waits intrinsically in yourself.

Whitman thus portrayed himself as a sort of psychotherapist who listened, watched, understood, accepted; through his encouraging association he would lead his reader-"patient" into a new feeling about his own identity and a better rapport with the world. How could he have such an effect upon others? In

"Assurances" he gave an answer: because he himself was utterly composed, self-possessed, sure of his own place in the cosmos:

> I need no assurances, I am a man who is pre-occupied of his own
> soul;
>
> •   •   •
>
> I do not doubt I am limitless, and that the universes are limitless,
> in vain I try to think how limitless . . .

Then in "Excelsior" Whitman displayed his determination to be first in everything—the very embodiment of the new American breed's competitive bravado. He would go farthest, be the most just, generous, cautious, benevolent, and passionate—the happiest, boldest, and proudest. And he thought the "amplest thoughts" because he wished with "devouring ecstasy" to enlarge himself to contain everything, so he could compose "joyous hymns for the whole earth."

The whole earth was truly in his thoughts when he wrote "Salut au Monde," "To a Foil'd European Revolutionaire," and "Song of the Broad-Axe." In these poems the poet reached out through space and time—geographically and historically—to embrace and hopefully to affect the residents not only of his nation but of the entire world.

Friends and disciples the poet would need, and in "Song of the Open Road"—one of his most popular poems, always admired by the youthful and by active idealists—Walt asked for boon companions to join him in his unfettered march of the spirit:

> Allons! the road is before us!
> It is safe—I have tried it—my own feet have tried it well—be not
> detain'd!
> Let the paper remain on the desk unwritten, and the book on the
> shelf unopen'd!
> Let the tools remain in the workshop! let the money remain un-
> earned!
> Let the school stand! mind not the cry of the teacher!
> Let the preacher preach in his pulpit! let the lawyer plead in the
> court, and the judge expound the law.

Camerado, I give you my hand!
I give you my love more precious than money,
I give you myself before preaching or law;
Will you give me yourself? will you come travel with me?
Shall we stick by each other as long as we live?

In "A Song of the Rolling Earth" Whitman expressed his belief that real language existed in nature, in people and things, not in the arbitrary human words which were mere symbols:

Were you thinking that those were the words, those upright lines?
those curves, angles, dots?
No, those are not the words, the substantial words are in the
ground and sea,
They are in the air, they are in you.

Walt's lifelong preoccupation with death found an eloquent outlet in "This Compost," which transmuted the poet's momentary morbid fixation on decayed corpses into an exalted vision of the chemical immortality made possible by the earth's antiseptic magic:

Behold this compost! behold it well!
Perhaps every mite has once form'd part of a sick person—yet be-
hold!
The grass of spring covers the prairies,
The bean bursts noiselessly through the mould in the garden,
The delicate spear of the onion pierces upward,
The apple-buds cluster together on the apple-branches,
The resurrection of the wheat appears with pale visage out of its
graves . . .

The second edition of *Leaves of Grass* also advanced the "mysti-cal" side of Whitman in such poems as "On the Beach at Night Alone" and "Crossing Brooklyn Ferry"—first called "Clef Poem" and "Sun-Down Poem." In the first poem the poet briefly ex-pressed, as he watched "the bright stars shining," the kosmos-spirit, the consciousness of universal harmony and purpose for which the heavens supplied a key:

A vast similitude interlocks all,
All spheres, grown, ungrown, small, large, suns, moons, planets,
All distances of place however wide,
All distances of time, all inanimate forms,
All souls, all living bodies though they be ever so different, or in
    different worlds . . .

No poem in the new edition of *Leaves of Grass* would compare in sheer immortal artistry with "Crossing Brooklyn Ferry," Whitman's beautifully rendered consideration of his own resurrection through others' lives. Crossing from shore to shore on the ferry at dusk and flood tide, taking in the myriad details of external reality—river and city, birds, boats, and fellow travelers—Whitman realized that what he saw and felt would be experienced anew by those who rode long after him. Nowhere does the poet's longing to insinuate himself into the future and into other people's lives attain a more powerful and uncanny communion, so that a reader responsive to the poem's mood may feel indeed that the poet stands actually at his side:

It avails not, time nor place—distance avails not,
I am with you, you men and women of a generation, or ever so
    many generations hence,
Just as you feel when you look on the river and sky, so I felt,
Just as any of you is one of a living crowd, I was one of a crowd,
Just as you are refresh'd by the gladness of the river and the bright
    flow, I was refresh'd . . .

And so, exultingly, Whitman would praise the externals which gave shape to the internal or spiritual presence—and whose continued existence guaranteed his own perpetuation:

Fly on, sea-birds! fly sideways, or wheel in large circles high in the
    air;
Receive the summer sky, you water, and faithfully hold it till all
    downcast eyes have time to take it from you!
•   •   •
Appearances, now or henceforth, indicate what you are,
You necessary film, continue to envelop the soul,

About my body for me, and your body for you, be hung our
divinest aromas,
Thrive, cities—bring your freight, bring your shows, ample and
sufficient rivers,
Keep your places, objects than which none else is more lasting.

•　　•　　•

You furnish your parts toward eternity,
Great or small, you furnish your parts toward the soul.

Walt Whitman gave copies of the new edition of *Leaves of
Grass* to two visitors who were Emerson's friends: Bronson Alcott
and Henry David Thoreau. When Alcott first met Whitman, he
confided his impression to his journal. "A nondescript, he is not so
easily described, nor seen to be described," he wrote. "Broad-
shouldered, rough-fleshed, Bacchus-browed, bearded like a satyr,
and rank, he wears his man-Bloomer in defiance of everybody,
having these as everything else after his own fashion, and for
example to all men hereafter. Red flannel undershirt, open-
breasted, exposing his brawny neck; striped calico jacket over
this, the collar Byroneal, with coarse cloth overalls buttoned to it;
cowhide boots; a heavy round-about, with huge outside pockets
and buttons to match; and a slouched hat, for house and street
alike. Eyes gray, unimaginative, cautious yet sagacious; his voice
deep, sharp, tender sometimes and almost melting. When talking
will recline upon the couch at length, pillowing his head upon his
bended arm, and informing you naïvely how lazy he is, and
slow. . . . In fine, an egotist, incapable of omitting, or suffering
any one long to omit, noting Walt Whitman in discourse."

Thoreau, who usually preferred the company of nature to that
of most people, especially in crowds, found his host fascinating.
"He is apparently the greatest democrat the world has seen,"
Thoreau wrote to a friend in a half-ironic, half-admiring vein.
"Kings and aristocracy go by the board at once, as they have long
deserved to. . . . He is essentially a gentleman. I am still somewhat in a quandary about him,—feel that he is essentially strange
to me, at any rate; but I am surprised by the sight of him."

Thoreau told Whitman that aspects of his philosophy were

"wonderfully like the Orientals," but Walt did not admit that the similarities were probably deliberate. For whatever reasons, Walt felt that Thoreau "misapprehended" him and said so. Meanwhile, he noted Thoreau's own brand of individualism, sometimes morbid, sometimes quite undemocratic; but still he found him pleasantly plain and unpretentious. On several occasions in the future Thoreau would return to visit Walt. They intrigued yet baffled each other, and never became good friends.

Walt, then, would never really know how much his poetry had excited the shy, undemonstrative hermit of Walden Pond. Reading the new *Leaves of Grass*, Thoreau was especially impressed with "Song of Myself" and "Crossing Brooklyn Ferry." He wrote at length to a friend about the effect of Whitman's book upon him. "It has done me more good than any reading for a long time," he said. He criticized certain sensual poems, commenting, "He does not celebrate love at all. It is as if the beasts spoke." But he declared that Whitman "has spoken more truth than any American or modern that I know. I have found his poem exhilarating encouraging. . . . On the whole it sounds to me very brave & American after whatever deductions. I do not believe that all the sermons so called that have been preached in this land put together are equal to it for preaching— We ought to rejoice greatly in him. He occasionally suggests something a little more than human. . . . Though rude & sometimes ineffectual, it is a great primitive poem,—an alarum or trumpet-note ringing through the American camp. . . . Since I have seen him, I find that I am not disturbed by any brag or egoism in his book. He may turn out the least of a braggart of all, having a better right to be confident. He is a great fellow."

Walt Whitman also would have liked to learn that in Springfield, Illinois, the man soon to become his "Redeemer President" was reading *Leaves of Grass*. One day Abraham Lincoln had noticed a copy of the book lying on a table in his law office; glancing at it, he became interested. Later he took it home to read more—much to the horror of his "womenfolk," who tried to "purify" the book by burning it. Thereafter the book stayed safely at the office, and often Lincoln picked it up to read at random, sometimes reciting poems aloud to anyone willing to listen.

Whitman would never know of Lincoln's liking for his book. Apart from the bare information of Lincoln's interest—recorded much later by a lawyer who as a young student had worked in the office—there is no direct evidence of any influence *Leaves of Grass* may have exercised upon Lincoln by increasing his self-confidence, reinforcing his opinions, or propelling him into higher political ambitions for his nation's sake. The book may well have contributed some beneficial spark to the future president's spirit: through the years its therapeutic effects upon other readers have often been proclaimed. The Whitman-Lincoln association, always tenuous—for they were never officially to meet—has occasionally been examined by Whitman devotees and scholars. There were many similarities in their political and philosophical thinking. Whitman's eventual apotheosis of President Lincoln was inevitable and fitting.

In the winter of 1856-1857 Walt would surely have benefited from hearing that his poems had stimulated and pleased some readers. He felt discouraged and at loose ends. Despite the merit of the new poems, the second edition of *Leaves of Grass* had scarcely caused a ripple in the literary stream. Fowler & Wells abandoned plans to advertise it, and their standoffish attitude wounded Whitman to the point of rupture. He no longer wrote articles for *Life Illustrated,* which at least had brought him some income. Having to pay his share of family expenses, and probably owing on the publication costs of the book's new edition, Walt borrowed money from supposed friends—a debt that would involve him in unpleasant litigation in the following year.

Now as Walt looked back over his thirty-seven years, he recognized his failure in everything he had really set out to do. He had been dismissed from so many jobs; and far worse, his ambitious and personal creative effort, *Leaves of Grass,* was an apparent disaster both critically and financially. Now, for all the self-vaunting in his poems, he seemed unable to take positive action in any direction. He was a teacher without classroom or pupils, a journalist denied a press, a preacher sans pulpit, an orator speaking in an empty assembly hall, a politician having no party or position, a lover with no beloved, a bard neglected by listeners, a poet unread, a prophet unheeded.

Those who think of Whitman always as the supreme egotist and optimist have failed to read or remember the pessimistic, self-denigrating, and despairing poems, or portions of poems, which he sometimes wrote. In "Crossing Brooklyn Ferry" he had already revealed this other aspect:

> It is not upon you alone the dark patches fall,
> The dark threw its patches down upon me also,
> The best I had done seem'd to me blank and suspicious,
> My great thoughts as I supposed them, were they not in reality
> meagre?

Walt swung high into space in his "up" or happy periods; his converse "down" moods sank him very low. Then he would plunge helplessly into emotional sloughs or severe depressions for days or weeks at a time, whether because of unsolvable inner conflicts or upsetting external events.

The election of James Buchanan, who favored compromise with the South, certainly did not improve Whitman's gloom. Everywhere he looked, Whitman found issues that divided the American people: slavery versus free soil, wealth and poverty, industrialization and agriculture, tariffs and free trade, exploiters and laborers, nativists and immigrants, aristocrats and republicans. . . . This was not a time for a weak presidency. Whitman would soon register his opinion of the three four-year presidential periods tenanted by Taylor, Fillmore, Pierce, and Buchanan in a poetic diatribe—"To the States: To Identify the 16th, 17th, or 18th Presidentiad."

> Why reclining, interrogating? why myself and all drowsing?
> Why deepening twilight—scum floating atop of the waters,
> Why are they as bats and night-dogs askant in the capitol?
> What a filthy Presidentiad! (O South, your torrid suns! O North,
> your arctic freezings!)

> Are those really Congressmen? are those the great Judges? is that
> the President?
> Then I will sleep awhile yet, for I see that these States sleep, for
> reasons;
> (With gathering murk, with muttering thunder and lambent shoots
> we all duly awake,
> South, North, East, West, inland and seaboard, we will surely
> awake.)

Walt was watching and waiting for that turbulent time to come.

The spring of 1857 brought an end to Walt's hibernation. He was asked to be the editor of the Brooklyn *Daily Times,* a liberal newspaper which had supported Frémont in the recent election.

Almost a decade had passed since Whitman had occupied the editor's desk at the *Eagle.* Many things had happened to him, the most notable his being occupied by the *Leaves of Grass* "bee"— Walt's own phrase for that compulsively creative period before his book's publication. Yet he now commenced his duties as if he had never left off daily journalism or had just paused for a brief vacation. Walt easily returned to using the editorial "we." The composite "I" of *Leaves of Grass*—that poet who gave opinions, issued proclamations, coaxed and persuaded and criticized—probably did not find the transfer difficult. The many issues traditionally calling for an editor's attention still concerned and interested Whitman, arousing his responses.

As a newspaper editor again, however, Walt approached certain "taboo" areas in the social sphere cautiously, not punching head-on as he did in his poems. He wanted to keep his job for a while, anyway. Brooklyn had become a popular residence for New York businessmen, who agreed with Walt that in Manhattan "there is no medium between a palatial mansion and a dilapidated hovel." Editor Whitman saluted this bourgeois citizenry: "The most valuable class in any community is the middle class, the men of moderate means." Quite probably, too, they bought the most newspapers, so Walt tried not to offend them. Almost silent now was the primitivistic and radical voice which had addressed the "average" man—Whitman's idealized proletarian. (Yet Walt would find few readers for his *Leaves of Grass* among the working class; usually his most ardent followers were artistic or intellectual types of liberal or iconoclastic persuasions.)

So the exuberant and boastful poet who extolled "roughs," rebels, and sensualists had retreated, for a time at least, into the background—although Whitman did not become so conventional that he abandoned his oddly-assembled workman's garb. In a milder, quieter way he still tried to alter narrow and entrenched attitudes. Promoting individualism and self-reliance, he scolded people for being overly concerned about "What'll they think?" "Who cares?" came Walt's reply, "so long as we have the approval of our own reason and conscience. So long as we wrong no one, assail no just ordinance, social or otherwise, but earnestly go our own way, about our own business, and to our own taste, what should we care for folly's derision or fashion's frown?"

Much as Walt liked the American people, he was aware of their faults. He peered around and critically observed the populace. While fond of dispensing advice to others, they were careless of heeding it themselves, resulting in a hypocritical morality which was deplorable. No change for the better, no easy cure, lay in the offing. "No, and there never will be," said Whitman, "until every individual making up the vast fabric of our social system stops short in his wholesale denunciations against his neighbors and looks to himself—his own principles, his own conduct." (In *Leaves of Grass* Whitman had already directed his attentions to the individual in order to change the group—but who had cared?)

By now Walt was thoroughly disgusted with political parties. A loyal party man, he said, was "the slave of as ruthless a despotism as can well be imagined, and the tyranny of which is the more galling and hurtful, because of its being clothed in the guise of freedom." He had long since ceased calling himself a Democrat.

Walt regarded people's inclination toward hero-worship as a "great evil" in a democracy, for it often caused them to choose the wrong leaders. "The mission of the age," he wrote, "is to correct this tendency—to discourage any man or woman from pinning his faith and confidence blindly and unreflectingly to any central authority whatever." (Would his attitude have been less dour if he had been welcomed as a poet-prophet?)

Yet Whitman himself sometimes lionized people whose deeds impressed him, such as Cyrus W. Field, who had conceived of, and would finally successfully lay, the Atlantic Cable—"that electric chain from the New World to the Old." (Whitman would later praise the feat in "Passage to India.") Obviously, Field's doggedness in the face of perpetual setbacks appealed to Walt. "There is something sublime in the spectacle of this man hoping against hope, battling against chance and fate, persevering in the face of heavy odds," he rhapsodized, "proceeding straight to his goal, utterly unmoved either by covert sneers, or chilly neglect, feeling only one thing—that the cable could be laid and must be laid, and *that he was going to do it*." (Walt was probably thinking too about himself and his book of poems.)

Whitman occasionally summarized the American character in a way which might hold true today. "The greatest fault in our mental constitution," he wrote, "is that we are too hasty and excitable. We are logical enough, but are deficient in the patience necessary to reason out an intricate problem to its legitimate conclusion. Hence Congressional orations are declamatory rather than argumentative, voters are often led away by momentary excitement and sudden impulses, instead of basing their political action on long-cherished principles and calm reflection. In our business affairs . . . we attempt to get rich by bold speculation instead of a long course of steady industry; and in our recreations, even, we rush forward with an avidity which often defeats the object of recreation itself."

Still, Walt found many virtues in Americans. In mundane daily life the brotherhood of humanity was looked upon as a phrase signifying little or nothing; but adversities and great calamities, Whitman pointed out, startled people from apathy and selfishness. "They link us together, for a time at least, by the bond of a mutual sentiment," he said; "they teach us that poor frail human nature can deport itself bravely and well under circumstances the most appalling; they prove to us that the days of heroic self-sacrifice are not yet passed; that in these days, stigmatized as matter of fact and materialistic, the spirit still survives, serene, dauntless, undying, only awaiting the hour of development." (In his "Song of Myself" Whitman had already recorded tales of historical instances of this phenomenon. And four years later, when the Civil War erupted, he would bear witness to a revival of this grand and selfless spirit of brotherhood in men drawn together in a desperately fought common cause.)

Editor Whitman desired to improve the relations between the sexes, the basis for the perpetuation of society. His various proposals and open discussions of sexual matters took editorial courage. During the 1840s and 1850s Victorianism was in full bloom in America, transplanted from England and set into ground already well prepared by the strict and disapproving attitudes toward the body held by Puritans and Calvinists. Victorian ideas essentially belonged to the new middle-class urban population brought to the forefront of society by the Industrial Revolution and the rise of democracy. Wanting to look "genteel" and be judged respectable, they followed the latest fashions and enforced rigid rules for good conduct. Morality was largely concerned with supervising sexual behavior. Since ladies' "limbs" were hidden from the view of the possibly prurient, even piano legs wore ruffled pantalettes. The effect of such prudery was often grotesque. What was normal and natural seemed abnormal and wicked—an attitude which created strictures, tensions, and repressions that were hardly healthful either for society at large or for individuals.

Whitman saw that marriage was becoming a dreadful prospect to many young men; would-be suitors noticed not only the rising cost of living, but also the feminine propensity to follow the absurd and expensive dictates of fashion. Only a return to the "primitive simplicity and economy of former generations," Walt proclaimed, would make the married state more attractive to persons of moderate means.

And to make matters worse, so far as Whitman was concerned, women were hardly prepared in mind and body for a marital life. Females should be taught the general principles of medical science, he declared. He reviewed textbooks on physiology written by doctors who asserted that much of the illness in civilized people came from ignorance and prudishness about bodily functions—inexcusable in an age which considered itself enlightened and scientifically oriented.

"Female health in this country is decidedly at a discount," Walt observed. "Wherever we go we see hundreds of spleeny, sickly, feeble girls who can hardly muster courage to perform the ordinary avocations of life. Tell them about early rising, fresh air and healthy exercise, and they heave a lamentable sigh and are ready to faint away." Ladies dressed in outlandish garments which restricted their movements and often harmed their blood circulation. Since a fair skin and a fragile appearance were much admired, middle-class women avoided sunshine and outdoor activities. Too shy to discuss physical problems with doctors, they suffered from unnecessary ignorance and lack of proper treatment. Childbearing was regarded as an ordeal to be undergone; knowing no way of preventing conception, wives often avoided continuous pregnancies by turning into invalids or by resorting to dangerous operations.

Whitman found all this quite terrible for America. In contrast he recalled "our great grandmothers," who were stout, strong, happy, and hearty, and lived to ripe old ages. They got up early, worked like beavers, and never idled away the hours by dancing. "Instead of being frightened at a mouse at their feet, a beetle on their neck, a fly's foot on their arm," Walt said, "in the absence of their fathers and husbands, they would load their guns and shoot bears and catamounts, and keep at bay a party of savages."

These were the kind of women Whitman hoped would soon reappear and prevail in America. He had already saluted them:

> They are not one jot less than I am,
> They are tann'd in the face by shining suns and blowing winds,
> Their flesh has the old divine suppleness and strength,
> They know how to swim, row, ride, wrestle, shoot, run, strike, re-
>   treat, advance, resist, defend themselves,
> They are ultimate in their own right—they are calm, clear, well-
>   possess'd of themselves.

As for the middle-class American dressed in his business suit and living in the city, he too was trapped by Victorian standards. In order to appear thoroughly civilized, he had relinquished or concealed much of his basic masculinity. But Whitman still saw the aggressive, dominating, honest, and physically vigorous male in the men who did hard labor in the cities or who worked on the land or at sea. America's very survival would depend upon them— not upon the debilitated gentry. This was why, as poet, Whitman celebrated the "roughs": builders, farmers, fishermen, hunters, pioneers, miners. For the good of American democracy, Walt Whitman—as both editor and poet—wanted to restore female and male to a healthy-minded acceptance of their admirable, natural roles.

Walt Whitman the poet had already made a bold sex survey. *Leaves of Grass* was, in part, his tract on the subject of love between the sexes—or "amativeness," in the phrenologists' and Walt's vocabularies. Most of the vehement objections to his *Leaves of Grass* had come from the direct affront he gave to Victorian middle-class sensibilities by mentioning and even praising the body's various functions—sex included—and by exposing raw emotions heretofore ignored by most writers. "Song of Myself" alone had provided good evidence that Whitman was determined to speak his mind on the whole subject of sex:

> Through me forbidden voices,
> Voices of sexes and lusts, voices veil'd and I remove the veil,
> Voices indecent by me clarified and transfigur'd.

Walt maintained that women possessed a sensual nature, as did men. In "Faces" he had not hesitated to describe it in action:

> This is a full-grown lily's face,
> She speaks to the limber-hipp'd man near the garden pickets,
> *Come here* she blushingly cries, *Come nigh to me limber-hipp'd man,*
> *Stand at my side till I lean as high as I can upon you,*
> *Fill me with albescent honey, bend down to me,*

> *Rub to me with your chafing beard, rub to my breast and shoulders.*

Such a passage, appearing with others in the first edition of *Leaves of Grass,* was quite enough to arouse Victorian-American culture against the man who could write thus of pure and innocent womankind, removed far indeed from Eve and the Garden of Eden. But Whitman considered sex highly important, since it was the means by which living creatures were reproduced. In an outspokenly daring way he cast off the veils and fig leaves which so long had concealed parts of the human body from view. In a poem called "A Woman Waits for Me," published in the second edition and destined to cause more furor and misunderstanding than most of his other poems put together, Whitman gave his definition of sex—which "contains all, bodies, souls"—and, he said:

> Without shame the man I like knows and avows the deliciousness
> of his sex,
> Without shame the woman I like knows and avows hers.

In nature the sexes coexisted fruitfully and unashamedly; it should be so with mankind too. Often in Whitman's poems the union of man and woman metaphorically returns them to nature:

> We two, how long we were fool'd,
> Now transmuted, we swiftly escape as Nature escapes,
> We are Nature, long have we been absent, but now we return,
> We become plants, trunks, foliage, roots, bark,
> We are bedded in the ground, we are rocks,
> We are oaks, we grow in the openings side by side,
> We browse, we are two among the wild herds spontaneous as any,
> We are two fishes swimming in the sea together . . .

The poet Whitman's numerous references to reproduction and his descriptive passages demonstrating the sexual impulse in man were extremely shocking and repugnant to most readers living at a time when one simply did not mention any of the "lower" functions of the body. Whatever Walt Whitman might claim of himself, "decent" human beings were not animals. The outrage of Whitman's poetry coincided with the terrible offense given to mankind in 1859 by Charles Darwin's *Origin of Species*, with its theories about man's origin in the animal kingdom. It was widely held that such men were dangerous, even diabolical; consequently, they were treated like outcasts from respectable society.

Today, more than a century later, the public attitude toward sex has radically changed—initially, in America, because of Walt Whitman's courageous pioneering. No longer will most readers of Whitman's poetry be utterly horrified by sensuous passages and sex "catalogues," which may seem sedate indeed when compared with erotic scenes depicted in detail in popular novels, stage plays, or motion pictures that leave nothing to one's imagination—as Whitman did do. And however one feels personally about the advisability of allowing unlimited license in the publishing and entertainment media, it must be recognized that the revolution over viewing sex as an essential ingredient in human life, and portraying it both candidly and aesthetically in literature and art, has been won by those who, like Whitman, promoted the doctrine that the human body has nothing at all to be ashamed of or to hide.

As a journalist, Walt Whitman's propagandistic forays into sex and sex problems did not cause the commotion which his poems had already stirred up. His language was cautious, objective, and almost professorial when he discussed such subjects—in great contrast to the highly personal, strongly emotional, and richly sensual tones in his sex poems. One way or another, though, Walt seemed determined to break through the conventional thinking of his era. Since he knew the journalist's potential power in persuading readers to change their views, at the Brooklyn *Daily Times* Walt often used his circumspect editorials to work away at the same problems he had considered in *Leaves of Grass*.

Editor Whitman noted the increase in the ranks of unmarried women and then examined their predicament. They had the same emotional longings and physical needs as anyone; but whereas unwed men could find "safety valves" or outlets in "bodily and mental exertion," these young spinsters felt miserable as they observed happiness all around them. "It is hard to fast when so many are feasting," Walt said sympathetically.

In a memorable parable in "Song of Myself" he had already shown a woman who wanted love but hid her desire from all but her own imaginings—and the inquisitive poet.

> Twenty-eight young men bathe by the shore,
> Twenty-eight young men and all so friendly;
> Twenty-eight years of womanly life and all so lonesome.
>
> She owns the fine house by the rise of the bank,
> She hides handsome and richly drest aft the blinds of the window.
>
> Which of the young men does she like the best?
> Ah the homeliest of them is beautiful to her.
>
> Where are you off to, lady? for I see you,
> You splash in the water there, yet stay stock still in your room.
>
> Dancing and laughing along the beach came the twenty-ninth bather,
> The rest did not see her, but she saw them and loved them. . . .

But some unmarried women—restless, rebellious, desiring to partake of the joys of loving—no longer would be satisfied by such dreaming in seclusion. Editor Whitman understood them and paraphrased their thinking. Far better than the stale air of the guarded castle in fairyland was "one draught of the fresh outer air—one glimpse of real life and nature—one taste of substantial joys and sorrows that shall wake all the pulses of womanhood." They dared to risk all for an experience "brief and dearly bought." Old age and burial, they knew, would come swiftly enough.

This impulse to ignore society's restrictions and achieve ecstatic sexual lawlessness and union Whitman described in several new poems—as in "One Hour to Madness and Joy":

> To be lost if it must be so!
> To feed the remainder of life with one hour of fulness and freedom!
> With one brief hour of madness and joy.

Whitman then was not just marking time while he earned his salary as a newspaper editor. His career as a journalist had served to prepare him for his vocation as a poet who was interested in all the particulars of his nation and its people. When Walt returned to newspaper work after publishing the first two editions of *Leaves of Grass,* he was still sharpening and expanding his vision of the world at large and of himself—all the while taking satisfaction in instructing a whole community of readers who would have utterly rejected some of the equivalent "lessons" in *Leaves of Grass.* Walt Whitman's assertions that man and woman alike had strong sexual needs, and that the gratification or suppression of them was closely connected with the well-being or distresses of both body and mind, would later be explored at far greater lengths and depths by Sigmund Freud.

When it seemed necessary, Whitman became a muckraker; he dared to find fault with anybody or anything held sacred—such as the local churches and churchmen. One target for his suspicion and censure was Henry Ward Beecher, the enormously popular minister of Brooklyn's Plymouth Church. Beecher's favorite topic for his impassioned sermons was Love, and on Sundays he drew thousands of eager listeners from near and far, many coming from Manhattan on special chartered boats. Whitman dubbed the ladies' feverish attachment to the Reverend as "Beecherolatry." Although Beecher was known to admire *Leaves of Grass,* Walt apparently was not flattered to have his poems praised by a man whom he regarded as a charlatan, and whose own private morality seemed spotty.

Whitman's employers began to receive many protests about the editor's attacks upon various ministers for their failings and hypocrisies as well as his exposures of their buildings' dangerous decrepitude. An office argument in the spring of 1859 resulted in Walt Whitman's resignation from his editorial post on the Brooklyn *Daily Times.* He had lasted there about two years—a long tenure for him.

Walt may have welcomed the release from the constant demands of a job which usually required that he limit his expression to topical matters conventionally considered. Ever since the publication of the second *Leaves of Grass* he had been writing new poems to add to a future third edition. Even during his busy life as a newspaper editor, Walt's muse had hung around.

Although Whitman could feel more like a legitimate, practicing poet again, he still had to contribute to the household and obtain his own spending money. His personal needs were few and modest, but he would have to pay the printing costs for a new *Leaves of Grass;* he was not going to let it wither and die. He earned some money now as a copyist and also wrote free-lance articles for newspapers. His notebooks of the period show that he was working up a few lectures, for he seriously thought again of becoming an orator or "wander-teacher."

Sometimes Walt indulged the hope that some "rich giver," recognizing his worth, would endow him and his enterprise:

> What you give me I cheerfully accept,
> A little sustenance, a hut and garden, a little money, as I rendez-
> vous with my poems,
> A traveler's lodging and breakfast as I journey through the States,—
> why should I be ashamed to own such gifts? why
> to advertise for them?
> For I myself am not one who bestows nothing upon man and
> woman,
> For I bestow upon any man or woman the entrance to all the gifts
> of the universe.

Walt found no friendly patrons, but at least he had good company now in the group of writers, artists, editors, and actors who gathered at Pfaff's Restaurant in New York City. A saloon noted for its hearty and inexpensive cuisine, a list of commendable beers and wines, and an informal atmosphere, it was located in the basement of a building on Broadway near Bleecker Street. During pleasant weather Pfaff's also operated a Continental-style open-air café.

During the late 1850s and early 1860s much of Walt's social life centered around Pfaff's. There the unconventional or rebellious "Bohemians"—artistic or intellectual types who chose to live beyond the pale of proper society—congregated in a noisily talkative camaraderie, accepting each other's quirks and behavior. Of course they welcomed Whitman into their midst. If nothing in his large, benign exterior indicated his qualifications as a social insurgent, his notorious book *Leaves of Grass* gave him a ready entree into the underground social hall which Victorian Americans considered a den of iniquity.

Walt was mostly content to sit quietly back and observe, listen to, and absorb what others were doing and saying. Anything extreme in his emotional life came out in his poetry, not in his behavior. He drank lightly, smoked not at all, and seemed sexually abstemious—all of which made him a "saintly" figure indeed, despite the horrid reputation his poems were earning for him. In his private life Whitman virtually reversed the Victorian norm. Under the cloak of utmost respectability many people behaved hypocritically and immorally. When Whitman sometimes wrote as if he himself were guilty of wicked thoughts and deeds, people were shocked; actually, of course, he was drawing out and recording the hidden feelings of both himself and others, as in this passage from "Crossing Brooklyn Ferry":

Nor is it you alone who know what it is to be evil,
I am he who knew what it was to be evil,
I too knitted the old knot of contrariety,
Blabb'd, blush'd, resented, lied, stole, grudg'd,
Had guile, anger, lust, hot wishes I dared not speak,
Was wayward, vain, greedy, shallow, sly, cowardly, malignant,
The wolf, the snake, the hog, not wanting in me,
The cheating look, the frivolous word, the adulterous wish, not
    wanting,
Refusals, hates, postponements, meanness, laziness, none of these
    wanting,
Was one with the rest, the days and haps of the rest . . .

And it particularly infuriated Victorian-American readers when Whitman hinted of detecting, behind their social masks, never-told thoughts or emotions, or concealed shame over weaknesses and deeds done—such as his revelation in "Song of the Open Road":

Out of the dark confinement! out from behind the screen!
It is useless to protest. I know all and expose it.

Behold through you as bad as the rest,
Through the laughter, dancing, dining, supping, of people,
Inside of dresses and ornaments, inside of those wash'd and
    trimm'd faces,
Behold a secret silent loathing and despair.

No husband, no wife, no friend, trusted to hear the confession,
Another self, a duplicate of every one, skulking and hiding it goes,
Formless and wordless through the streets of the cities, polite and
    bland in the parlors,
In the cars of railroads, in steamboats, in the public assembly,
Home to the houses of men and women, at the table, in the bed-
    room, everywhere,
Smartly attired, countenance smiling, form upright, death under
    the breast-bones, hell under the skull-bones,
Under the broadcloth and gloves, under the ribbons and artificial
    flowers,
Keeping faith with the customs, speaking not a syllable of itself,
Speaking of any thing else but never of itself.

Conventional people abhorred this image of themselves in the mirror which Walt Whitman held before them; he was especially forbidden as an author suitable for ladies.

Among the regulars at Pfaff's was Henry Clapp, editor of the new avant-garde literary magazine, *Saturday Press*. Clapp began to praise and promote Whitman in his weekly paper. He also published a new Whitman poem, "A Child's Reminiscence"—to be much altered in the future, and finally to become known as "Out of the Cradle Endlessly Rocking." Clapp's attentions gave Whitman a needed reassurance. The long poem itself, concerned with the poet's boyhood glimpse of his destiny, showed Walt's own renewal of his real career in life.

All the while Walt frequented Pfaff's he continued his associations with the nonintellectual, unpretentious, and often coarse-mannered workingmen. He relished the reports of his friends the ferryboat pilots and deck hands, who told of the curiosity he invariably aroused among their passengers. Was he a retired sea captain, an actor, a smuggler? As ever, too, Walt enjoyed the swift and hectic rides on the city stagecoaches, and one winter he himself drove one of the horse-drawn Broadway omnibuses to support the family of an ailing driver. Whenever a working-class friend was hospitalized—and their hard, open-air jobs brought them frequent ailments and accidents—Walt came visiting. Gradually he built up acquaintanceships with many of the doctors at New York Hospital, who were much impressed with Walt's perfect bedside manner and his uncanny ability to lift the spirits of the sick or soothe the dying. His poem "To One Shortly to Die" was not just vanity or bragging.

> Softly I lay my right hand upon you, you just feel it,
> I do not argue, I bend my head close and half envelop it,
> I sit quietly by, I remain faithful,
> I am more than nurse, more than parent or neighbor . . .

Walt's very presence, at such times, achieved the palliative effect he had desired from his poems.

Walt became a welcome guest at the doctors' own quarters. Often they joined him at Pfaff's during their off-hours—a time schedule different from that of the Bohemians'. Walt concurrently maintained three quite separate groups of friends, none of whom could have easily commingled with the others.

If Walt Whitman gave the appearance of calm, self-contained majesty as he lolled back in his usual chair at Pfaff's, or sat beside a sick man in a hospital bed, or roared some Shakespearean lines to the winds as he traveled atop a Broadway omnibus, some of the poems he was writing revealed otherwise:

> Earth, my likeness,
> Though you look so impassive, ample and spheric there,
> I now suspect that is not all;
> I now suspect there is something fierce in you eligible to burst
> forth . . .

During this period Whitman was passing through a turmoil of emotions which tossed him from ebullience to black despair. Never before had he felt, never again would he know, such extremes of happiness and sorrow. Heretofore Walt had mostly sung of himself as "an average man, above all"—and then amplified his feelings to include American democracy and the past and future of mankind. Even his sensual poems seemed to be symbolic encounters with idealized female partners for procreative purposes. Perhaps he had never experienced an all-absorbing passion for a real person. His need for some personal attachment to satisfy his deeply emotional nature had gone unrequited as he roamed about, conscious of an intense but diffused longing which he only told in the words of his poems:

> I am he that aches with amorous love;
> Does the earth gravitate; does not all matter, aching, attract all
> matter?
> So the body of me to all I meet or know.

The spirit of American democracy residing in his soul Whitman took as his "femme"—his woman or mate. And perhaps he was so busy in his self-chosen mission of making poems "for the States" that he did not fall in love. As America's great lover, however, he had been unnoticed, unappreciated, unrewarded—and sometimes rudely rejected. Moreover, he was upset by the rapid disintegration of the spirit of national unity and purpose. In times of civil stress, conscious of their inability to remedy society's problems, citizens may withdraw into their own private domains—as Walt did now. He began writing highly intimate poems in the traditional area of the lyric poet: romantic love.

> O you whom I often and silently come where you are that I may
> be with you,
> As I walk by your side or sit near, or remain in the same room with
> you,
> Little you know the subtle electric fire that for your sake is playing
> within me.

As though a wish-fulfillment of his former search for fame, Walt pictured what he might feel "when I heard at the close of the day how my name had been receiv'd with plaudits in the capitol." He was not happy with this imaginary belated success, or from carousing, or from any accomplishment. But then—

> . . . when I thought how my dear friend my lover was on his way
>   coming, O then I was happy,
> O then each breath tasted sweeter, and all that day my food
>   nourish'd me more, and the beautiful day pass'd
>   well,
> And the next came with equal joy, and with the next at evening
>   came my friend . . .

In the poem this "dear friend my lover" was another man—so these were strange love-poems indeed that Walt was composing. He wrote what he truly felt at the time and then published it for all the world to see:

> Recorders ages hence,
> Come, I will take you down underneath this impassive exterior,
>   I will tell you what to say of me,
> Publish my name and hang up my picture as that of the tenderest
>   lover,
>   •   •   •
> Who was not proud of his songs, but of the measureless ocean of
>   love within him, and freely pour'd it forth,
>   •   •   •
> Whose happiest days were far away through fields, in woods, on
>   hills, he and another wandering hand in hand,
>   they twain apart from other men . . .

A number of these poems in the "Calamus" group within *Leaves of Grass* suggest that sometime during the late 1850s Walt Whitman felt a powerful affection for another man. Exactly how conscious he was of any abnormality of his feelings, and to what extent he outwardly expressed them, has long been a major preoccupation of many of his critics and biographers—often to the extent that the focus distorts both his life and his work.

Homosexuality was hardly a new form of sexual emotion or behavior; it had been openly practiced, even celebrated, by certain cultures like the Greek and by prominent artists of the past. In revealing his own feelings, Whitman did not seek to introduce—as he might well have done—any justification on the basis of past "precedents." He wrote at first in a private vein of emotions that were both exquisite and tormenting, giving them the name "calamus" for the wild iris which grew in moist, shady, and wooded areas, bearing tall spearlike leaves that sprang up from a root or rhizome below the soil. Taken altogether, the plant made an obvious phallic symbol; its habitat attested to the reclusiveness of the homoerotic impulse in Whitman. Certainly his feelings were ambivalent:

> O slender leaves! O blossoms of my blood! I permit you to tell in
>   your own way of the heart that is under you,
> O I do not know what you mean there underneath yourselves, you
>   are not happiness,
> You are often more bitter than I can bear, you burn and sting me,
> Yet you are beautiful to me you faint-tinged roots . . .

And of the "Calamus" poems Whitman wrote:

> Here the frailest leaves of me and yet my strongest lasting,
> Here I shade and hide my thoughts, I myself do not expose them,
> And yet they expose me more than all my other poems.

For whatever reasons, the intense friendship ultimately disappointed Whitman, and his anguish found an outlet in writing poetry that bears the mark of a confession.

> Sometimes with one I love I fill myself with rage for fear I effuse
>   unreturn'd love,
> But now I think there is no unreturn'd love, the pay is certain one
>   way or another,
> (I loved a certain person ardently and my love was not return'd,
> Yet out of that I have written these songs.)

The "Calamus" songs were only part of the payment. It is possible that Walt's near-unbearable sense of loss was transmuted into the songs of the bereft mockingbird in "Out of the Cradle Endlessly Rocking." And however oddly unconventional the direction of Walt's romantic longings, some of the poems written at that time place him at his tenderest and most joyous, or in his most perplexed and saddest moods—giving him a touchingly human dimension he seldom achieved elsewhere.

If Whitman felt guilt over his homosexual tendencies, he did not try to hide it from his poetry. His frankness is quite ingenuous—as if he himself did not really understand what he was talking about. Perhaps he could openly publish his feelings because he had nothing really of which he should be ashamed. His homosexuality may actually have been only a romantic and erotic impulse combined with a compulsion to inspire and educate others—potential "eleves" or young disciples—through his "magnetism." Whitman was always attracted to what was impossible and unobtainable, and within his moral framework homosexual practices may have been expressly forbidden.

In Whitman's old age an English correspondent with homosexual leanings hinted to Walt that his "Calamus" poems really praised and promoted homoerotic love. Whitman, genuinely horrified that his poems should be thus interpreted, replied that in his young manhood he had lived "jolly bodily," and in a boastful manner he conjured up a half-dozen illegitimate children as if to prove his normal masculinity. However, his only offspring would seem to be his poems: nobody has yet found definite proof of the existence of one child, let alone six. But neither has anyone produced concrete evidence that Whitman was ever a practicing homosexual.

During Walt's own lifetime few people paid attention to the homoerotic peculiarities of his poetry; the passionate, explicitly physical heterosexual passages were shocking enough. Readers usually accepted the "Calamus" poems as Whitman ingenuously intended them: as chants to bind American democracy with a sacred and loving friendship between men, which he and the phrenologists called "adhesiveness."

> Come, I will make the continent indissoluble,
> I will make the most splendid race the sun ever shone upon,
> I will make divine magnetic lands,
>> With the love of comrades,
>> With the life-long love of comrades.

An open, "manly" affection—hugs, rough kisses, and a comradely arm about the shoulder—Whitman often portrayed in his *Leaves*. It would serve Walt's purpose nobly when he recorded the spirit of the Civil War among the soldiers. Yet it is quite apparent that in his vision of fervent male companionship as the best means of furthering democracy, Walt was actually sublimating his own internal conflicts and torments. He found outlets for his troubling "Calamus" feelings within his poetry.

> I will sing the song of companionship,
>
> .   .   .
>
> I will therefore let flame from me the burning fires that were
>> threatening to consume me,
> I will lift what has too long kept down those smouldering fires,
> I will give them complete abandonment,
> I will write the evangel-poem of comrades and of love,
> For who but I should understand love with all its sorrows and joys?
> And who but I should be the poet of comrades?

It is sometimes suggested that, physically and emotionally, Whitman was almost bisexual or androgynous, belonging to an "intermediate" sex composed of both male and female characteristics and often artistically inclined. A number of Whitman's contemporaries noted his maternal or feminine side—not in a critical manner, but matter-of-factly and usually with admiration. Despite his beard and masculine bearing, Walt was rather passive in demeanor; his skin was soft, clear, pink—almost like a baby's. Within his poems, too, Walt occasionally temporarily assumed for himself the female body and psyche—just as he absorbed and duplicated other life-forms.

Walt Whitman sustained many close relationships with women strictly on a filial or fraternal level. He got along very well with those who were warm and friendly but did not attempt to engulf him physically or emotionally—or legally, in marriage. If Walt had deep love affairs with any women, he managed to hide most of the evidence from his friends and from future biographers. Yet he obviously knew much about the female sex, having considerably expanded his experience since his days as the callow schoolmaster of the "Sun-Down Papers." His information did not come wholly from reading textbooks on anatomy and physiology. Probably Walt had short-term liaisons with women who posed no threats to his bachelorhood; some of them possibly were prostitutes he encountered while carousing with his working-class friends. (As both editor and poet, Whitman sympathized with, and defended, these unfortunate "women of the streets," believing that society should be blamed for the existence of their profession. In the forthcoming edition of his *Leaves,* Walt would offer the poem "To a Common Prostitute," which alarmed the moralists who took it quite literally.)

Probably no single person, man or woman, could have ever kept up for long an intimate physical relationship with Walt Whitman. His passionate intensity, seemingly physical, may have been evanescent, of the moment—its real purpose not direct, as in reciprocated affection or sexual satisfaction, but indirect, in the duplication of his feelings in poetry.

Walt may have preferred to be rejected by a "lover" rather than allow anybody ever to get close enough to him to lay claims which he could neither accept nor satisfy. A perceptive person too would soon discover that Walt was not a whole man to be grasped entire but really a collection of roles tenuously held within the framework of a deliberately artificial, contradictory personality. Whitman's hints, riddles, and talk of "indirections" in *Leaves of Grass* were games devised by a coy spirit who asked or dared the reader to draw near, then pushed him away—sometimes gently, with warnings, and sometimes almost superciliously. As both person and poet Walt enjoyed flirtations. He claimed that he "gave" utterly of himself to friends, passing strangers, and readers; yet all the while he was holding back—part of the paradoxical complexity of his nature.

For the sake of his poetry, Whitman seemed to feel that he must remain chaste and uncommitted to any one person. And complain though he might about his loneliness and longings, he needed to live as a celibate—incompleted emotionally, unfulfilled sexually. He probably felt, or knew, that his "muse" required such continence from him so that he could act upon his sworn "oath of procreation" by writing poems which would germinate a new breed of American men and women. Whitman regarded himself as a modern version of Adam—whose descendants would come from the loins of his spirit, not of his body. He couched this generative act in highly erotic terms, as in "A Woman Waits for Me" and "Spontaneous Me." Whitman's suppressed sexuality was frequently revealed in the poetry he wrote. Some poems or passages of poems indicate that he regarded the creative act as a substitute sex-act: the "love spendings" from his "pent-up rivers" would spawn "sons and daughters fit for these States."

Above all, it appears, Walt longed to establish a relationship with each new reader of his *Leaves* that would be intimate and affectionate, even with undertones of sexuality. He attempted to fuse himself with his poetry, to insinuate himself almost corporeally into his poems, thereby achieving an imagined, satisfying bodily contact with an individual reader which would perpetuate him. In the forthcoming edition of his book, in "So Long!," Walt would show this in these famous lines:

> Camerado, this is no book,
> Who touches this touches a man,
> (Is it night? are we here together alone?)
> It is I you hold and who holds you,
> I spring from the pages into your arms—decease calls me forth.

Henry Clapp's editorial encouragement of Walt Whitman in the *Saturday Press*, which treated *Leaves of Grass* as though it were an urgently current literary event rather than a volume of poetry stillborn and moribund four years ago, helped to renew and maintain Walt's ambitions and self-confidence as a poet. He was gathering up poems for a third edition of his book. In "Starting from Paumanok" he indicated, among his various intentions in making the "true poem of riches," the special territory he was now exploring:

> . . . I will show of male and female that either is but the equal of the other,
> And sexual organs and acts! do you concentrate in me, for I am determin'd to tell you with courageous clear voice to prove you illustrious . . .

His group of "Calamus" poems kept expanding, and as companion-pieces and counterbalances to them he devised the "Enfans d'Adam" group (later called "Children of Adam") to celebrate the procreative or amative instinct in mankind. He included in this assemblage a few earlier poems ("I Sing the Body Electric," "Spontaneous Me," and "A Woman Waits for Me"), but also composed a number of new poems describing the physical and spiritual relations between man and woman.

He contrasted the difference to him between the "amative" and the "adhesive" relationships—the one offering the secure ties of earth, the other a roaming camaraderie of kindred souls:

> Fast-anchor'd eternal O love! O woman I love!
> O bride! O wife! more resistless than I can tell, the thought of you!
> Then separate, as disembodied or another born,
> Ethereal, the last athletic reality, my consolation,
> I ascend, I float in the regions of your love O man,
> O sharer of my roving life.

Still, Walt was a poet without publisher or public. In the winter of 1859-1860 he again suffered a deep depression—doubtless brought on by a combination of internal stresses and external events. In "As I Ebb'd with the Ocean of Life" he likened himself and his poems to the debris cast upon Paumanok's shore.

> O baffled, balk'd, bent to the very earth,
> Oppress'd with myself that I have dared to open my mouth,

> Aware now that amid all that blab whose echoes recoil upon me
>> I have not once had the least idea who or what
>> I am,
> But that before all my arrogant poems the real Me stands yet
>> untouch'd, untold, altogether unreach'd,
> I perceive I have not really understood any thing, not a single
>> object, and that no man ever can,
> Nature here in sight of the sea taking advantage of me to dart upon
>> me and sting me,
> Because I have dared to open my mouth to sing at all.

But while Whitman was doubting his poetry, it had gained some new admirers. In February of 1860 Walt received a letter from the new Boston publishing firm of Thayer & Eldridge. "Dear Sir," it said. "We want to be the publishers of Walt. Whitman's Poems—Leaves of Grass. . . . It is a true poem and writ by a *true* man. When a man dares to speak his thought in this day of refinement—so called—it is difficult to find his mates to act amen to it. Now *we* want to be known as the publishers of Walt. Whitman's books, and put our name as such under his, on title pages.—If you will allow it we can and will put your books into good form, and style attractive to the eye; we can and will sell a large number of copies. . . . We are young men. We 'celebrate' ourselves by acts. Try us. You can do us good. We can do you good—pecuniarily. . . . Are you writing other poems? Are you ready for the press? Will you let us read them? Will you write us?"

The effect of this letter upon Walt's lagging spirits was galvanizing. Since the arrival of Emerson's letter almost five years before, he had not received such startlingly good news or compliments. He would now have publishers who did not simply risk the opprobrium, and probable financial loss, involved in issuing and distributing *Leaves of Grass;* they would undertake their function with pride and enthusiasm—and pay him for the privilege. Walt's near-insurmountable problem of financing a new edition of his work had been solved. He hastened to answer the letter, and terms agreeable to both parties were quickly arranged.

Just one month after he received the summons to publish, Walt went up to Boston with 124 new poems for the third edition of

Leaves of Grass, along with alterations for the older poems. Many of the new poems had already been set in type at the Rome brothers' print shop to provide Walt with "working copies." (And since the printer wisely preserved both Walt's handwritten manuscripts and his altered printed copies, scholars can study the sequence and changes in the composition of the third edition's new poems.)

Almost as soon as Walt arrived, Emerson called on him. Whitman had written him about the promising new circumstance, and he probably sent him some of his new poems to read. The gentle intellectual, bothered by Whitman's numerous graphic attentions to sex in the "Enfans d'Adam" group, intended to persuade Walt to drop the entire section from his forthcoming volume. Emerson, like most intellectuals of his time, was adventuresome mentally and spiritually—but not physically. Walt was something else; he had already acknowledged the province of the body:

> Within there runs blood,
> The same old blood! the same red-running blood!
> There swells and jets a heart, there are passions, desires, reachings,
> aspirations,
> (Do you think they are not there because they are not express'd
> in parlors and lecture-rooms?)

Emerson was thoroughly at home at lectures and in parlors; Walt was not and never would be. For several hours, as the two men walked up and down the Boston Common, Emerson gave Whitman advice. He himself was not shocked by the poems, he said, for he knew that Whitman aimed far higher than bald, literal interpretation. But he knew that most other readers would not see through to Whitman's real intentions and meanings; they would be disgusted, horrified, angered—a reaction bound to have a detrimental effect on the success of the new edition. *Leaves of Grass* would prove far more acceptable and popular, Emerson predicted, if Walt excised the passages on male and female love.

Walt found Emerson's arguments logical, cogent, and objective; he knew he could not respond adequately to offset them. But he still felt strongly that the "Enfans d'Adam" poems were a coherent part of the whole design; they could not be removed without damaging his message and castrating the vitality of his book. (As he grew older, again and again Whitman would re-examine these sex poems which had gained him such notoriety. Sometimes he would deliberately attempt to remove them. "But it would not do," he told a friend. "When I tried to take those pieces out of the scheme, the whole scheme came down about my ears.")

In "Starting from Paumanok" Whitman was promising—

I will make the songs of passion to give them their way,
And your songs outlaw'd offenders, for I scan you with kindred
    eyes, and carry you with me the same as any.

So Whitman told Emerson that he would keep his Adamic children. Certainly from a modern point of view he was right; that group of poems, though fewer in number, helped to balance the overpowering "adhesiveness" of the "Calamus" section and to strengthen the "amativeness" factor while putting Walt's own sexuality in a more normal context. (Apparently Emerson discerned little or nothing in the "Calamus" section to offend his or anybody else's sensibilities; today, of course, this group is far more apt to raise readers' eyebrows than the "Children of Adam" poems. Emerson and others of the time sometimes thought or spoke of their close friends in affectionate terms, using "lover" to describe a spiritual and emotional relationship with one's companions and disciples; in the post-Freudian period, however, this word invariably bears sexual connotations.)

Emerson accepted Whitman's firm decision good-naturedly. He had delivered his warning in the most effective way possible. If Walt disagreed, that was surely his right. As the author, he knew best what he wanted; and he was willing to fight for these poems, even if he had to endure public censure. Without further ado, the two men went off to dine amicably together at a nearby restaurant.

Both Henry Thoreau and Bronson Alcott came to Boston from Concord to greet Walt. They and Emerson too wanted to invite him to their homes, but their womenfolk wouldn't think of associating with this scandalous personage—the usual reaction of "respectable" people throughout Walt's lifetime, whether they had ever read any of *Leaves of Grass* or only knew its reputation as an "immoral" book. Emerson proposed taking Whitman to the exclusive and literary Saturday Club, but its other members hurriedly vetoed his plan. (Usually, however, when genteel people actually met Walt, they were charmed by his calm and gentle manner and his obvious moral purity—for all the braggadocio and blatant sexuality in his book. Indeed, his modest behavior and conventional opinions often disappointed the admirers of his poetry. "Walt, you really should read *Leaves of Grass* sometime," one acquaintance suggested.)

New Yorkers were familiar with the sight of Walt Whitman— dressed in a wide- and bent-brimmed hat, workman's clothes and boots—striding along Broadway as though he owned it. Now in Boston he created "an immense sensation"—as he put it in a letter. "Everybody here is so like everybody else—and I am Walt Whitman!—Yankee curiosity and cuteness for once is thoroughly stumped, confounded, petrified, made desperate."

The news of Walt's presence got around to the few who already knew and liked his book. John T. Trowbridge scurried off to introduce himself; he found Whitman at his publishers', correcting proofs. The writer expected Whitman to be "proud, alert, grandiose, defiant of the usages of society," so was taken aback to find him "the quietest of men." He asked Walt how he felt when he reread his early poems. "I am astonished to find myself capable of feeling so much," Walt replied, as if verifying that much of his poetry originated in regions within him about which he knew very little.

As for Whitman's new publishers, they gave him freedom to do whatever he liked with *Leaves of Grass*. It was a gratifying novelty to be treated with respect. Making no suggestions as to the book's contents or arrangement of the poems, Thayer and Eldridge busied themselves in other ways: asking the printer to follow Walt's every request, seeing that the cover and internal designs were rendered to his satisfaction, providing a strong binding and a good paper stock, and advancing a sizable royalty on the anticipated future sales of the volume.

Walt's optimistic mood was reflected in the invitation in "Starting from Paumanok" which he extended to his countrymen:

Take my leaves America, take them South and take them North,
Make welcome for them everywhere, for they are your own off-
spring,
Surround them East and West, for they would surround you . . .

When the third edition of *Leaves of Grass* was published in May of 1860, it got ample coverage—in Clapp's *Saturday Press*, of course, where it was advertised, but also in magazines and newspapers in Eastern, Southern, and Midwestern cities, and even in England. The expected reactions of outrage appeared; in the new *Leaves of Grass* strict moralists naturally found more material than ever to decry. But there were praises too in a dawning recognition of a vibrant and genuine American literary talent. Whitman was now viewed by some critics in the way he wanted: a strong personality, almost a folk hero, who encompassed the whole spiritual, historical, biographical, and geographical landscape of the United States.

Although many readers were still unwilling to read Walt Whitman's poems, he was at least becoming known. Parodies of his style began to be printed in newspapers and magazines. In the Pfaff circle Walt was much admired by the actresses Adah Isaacs Mencken and Ada Claire, who were poetesses too; their published verses now imitated Whitman's.

Clapp had asked a literary-minded lady named Mrs. Juliette Beach to review Whitman's book, doubtless knowing that she liked its first two versions. A review was sent to him from her address; to Clapp's dismay, it was quite condemnatory, but he printed it. "Walt Whitman assumes to regard women only as an instrument for the gratification of his desires, and the propagation of the species," it stated. "His exposition of his thoughts shows conclusively that with him the congress of the sexes is a purely animal affair, and with his ridiculous egotism he vaunts his prowess as a stock-breeder might that of the pick of his herd."

It turned out that Mrs. Beach did not write these words at all; her irate husband had. A letter subsequently published in the *Saturday Press* and signed by "A Woman" was probably Mrs. Beach's own opinion of Whitman's volume: "These bold and truthful pages will inevitably form the standard book of poems in the future of America. . . . It is all good, the sudden transition, the obscure connection, the grand sublimity and boldness, but far better the spirit of the writer, so raised beyond everything else, sometimes even beyond himself, grasping at ideas too great for words. God bless him. I know that through 'Leaves of Grass,' Walt Whitman on earth is immortal as well as beyond it."

If a violent disagreement went on within the Beach household, it is noteworthy that the wife liked and defended Whitman's book whereas it enraged her husband. Often the "weaker" sex— whom men might wish to protect from the sight of Walt's *Leaves* —was not at all offended by Whitman's poems of sexuality. ("It is very curious that the girls have been my sturdiest defenders, upholders," Walt observed late in his life.) Sometimes intelligent, emancipated women readers could better comprehend Whitman's metaphors and symbolism than men, who were apt to take his boasting as direct assaults upon their own masculinity.

On the national scene, the month of May, 1860, was notable not for the publication of a third *Leaves of Grass* but for the youthful Republican Party's convention in Chicago. To the surprise of many Americans who had hardly heard of him, Abraham Lincoln was nominated as a presidential candidate. (Walt Whitman had first noticed him while editor of the Brooklyn *Daily Times*, when the famous Lincoln-Douglas debates took place in Illinois.)

Lincoln had said enough against slavery to make himself wholly disliked by most Southerners. He wanted to have slavery banished entirely from the Western territories; and he also maintained that the Union could not continue to exist half-slave and half-free.

The Democrats had picked Senator Stephen A. Douglas, who took a compromising stand on slavery because he believed it was an archaic institution that would soon disappear. The Northern

Democrats believed that only Douglas's election could save national unity. But the Southern Democrats supported a proslavery candidate, John C. Breckinridge, while the Constitutional Union Party offered John Bell and a conservative, patriotic platform—so that the Democratic votes were split three ways.

In early 1859, Walt Whitman, in one of his last editorials for the Brooklyn *Daily Times,* had predicted that the Democrats in the next year's election would have to choose between "two Ds— Douglas and Defeat." He observed then that, "judging from the present temper of the ultra Southerners, they will accept the latter, hoping thereby to precipitate a disruption of the Union."

Clearly the South was on the road to fulfilling Whitman's prophecy. The deeply concerned Douglas, the gallant "Little Giant," campaigned vigorously in the South, trying to convince its people to accept the election results, whatever they might be. He warned them that the North would never permit the South to secede from the Union.

As for the man from the West, Walt did not immediately recognize Lincoln's resemblance to the "Redeemer President" for whom he had asked four years earlier. But a Republican now, Walt Whitman cast his vote for Abraham Lincoln, though he knew that his election would imperil the nation he loved.

During the period when he composed the new poems for the third edition of *Leaves of Grass,* Walt Whitman had often felt intimations of his own impending mortality, which he expressed in some of the "Songs of Parting": "Song at Sunset," "So Long!," and "As the Time Draws Nigh."

> As the time draws nigh glooming a cloud,
> A dread beyond of I know not what darkens me.
>
> I shall go forth,
> I shall traverse the States awhile, but I cannot tell whither or how
>   long,
> Perhaps soon some day or night while I am singing my voice will
>   suddenly cease.
>
> O book, O chants! must all then amount to but this?

Must we barely arrive at this beginning of us?—and yet it is
        enough, O soul;
O soul, we have positively appear'd—that is enough.

Walt Whitman was not dying: an outmoded way of life in
American democracy was. And during its death throes Whitman
would sing new kinds of songs.

In peace I chanted peace, but now the drum
of war is mine,
War, red war is my song through your streets,
O city!

VIII

NOW THE DRUM OF WAR IS MINE

(1861-1865)

In mid-February of 1861 Walt Whitman went over to New York to watch a public spectacle. To get a commanding view of the whole scene, he perched on the top of an omnibus pulled to the side of Broadway, where some thirty thousand people were gathered to await the arrival of the President-elect. Abraham Lincoln was stopping briefly in Manhattan on his way from Illinois to Washington, D. C. Usually visiting dignitaries were greeted in the city streets with cheers, flag-waving, and parades, but now the massed crowd stood silent and tense, feeling both curious and resentful toward Lincoln.

Lincoln's victory in the past November had caused the nation to split in two; the Southern states were now acting on their long-voiced threat to secede from the Union. People tended to blame Lincoln personally for the formation of the new Confederacy. The whole country, poised on the brink of disaster, wanted to know what the new President was going to do; New Yorkers apparently thought they could find clues just by looking at him.

Some people were still angry that the Republicans had passed over New York's own William Henry Seward to select Lincoln as their candidate. Lincoln was heartily disliked by the many "Copperhead" Democrats who sympathized with the South, and he was already mistrusted by the Radical Republicans, who feared that he would be too moderate on the slavery issue and too conciliatory towards the rebellious states. Altogether, the collective mood of the crowd was hostile. Expecting actual violence, Walt Whitman pictured "many an assassin's knife and pistol lurk'd in hip or breast-pocket there, ready, soon as break and riot came."

A barouche finally arrived and stopped in front of the Astor House. Walt saw Abraham Lincoln get out, afterwards noting "his perfect composure and coolness—the unusual and uncouth height, his dress of complete black, stovepipe hat push'd back on the head, dark-brown complexion, seam'd and wrinkled yet canny-looking face, black, bushy head of hair, disproportionately long neck, and his hands held behind as he stood observing the people."

Lincoln seemed fully aware of the crowd's temper, but he gazed back at them with quiet courage and his own brand of curiosity—and perhaps a hint of the humor that would help to alleviate the darkest times during the coming years. He seemed neither unfriendly nor overfriendly. No shout or sudden movement broke the stillness of the long, awkward encounter. At last Lincoln stretched his arms and legs, turned his back on the assembled spectators, and slowly walked up the stairs to the hotel. His personal peril was over: he had somehow passed a spontaneous, nonverbal public test of his demeanor and will.

The impression which Abraham Lincoln had made upon Whitman—and doubtless upon many others there—was quite favorable. The new President—this gangling, ugly, self-composed man—looked wholly human; no longer was he a name, a cardboard figure, a face on a poster. He was obviously a strong-minded "man of the people"—neither an aristocrat who treated others condescendingly nor a changeable "dough-face" who readily truckled to the whims of populace or party. Lincoln seemed prepared to deal with the great problems of the presidency in his own particular way, without undue haste or delay, but with wisdom and justice and fortitude. Certainly nobody envied Lincoln the difficult tasks ahead of him.

Walt Whitman too was about to undertake a new role. The issues dividing the nation had long been clear to him; he knew which side he would be on when war came. Foretelling a national catastrophe in his poetry and prose, he had urged people to change their ideas—even their way of life. But now it was too late; his words and those of others had gone unheard and unheeded as various factions proceeded stubbornly on their separate courses, bound to collide where and when they intersected.

In "Song of the Banner at Daybreak," a long poem on which he had been working, Whitman gave an urgent vitality to a poet stirred by the sight of a battle pennant and the nation's banner flying above him. He would avoid "book-words" and sing angry new songs out in the open air:

> I'll put the bayonet's flashing point, I'll let bullets and slugs whiz,
> (As one carrying a symbol and menace far into the future,
> Crying with trumpet voice, *Arouse and beware! Beware and arouse!*)
> I'll pour the verse with streams of blood, full of volition, full of joy,
> Then loosen, launch forth, to go and compete,
> With the banner and pennant a-flapping.

A month after Lincoln's inauguration, Whitman was walking down Broadway at midnight. He had just attended the opera and now headed for the Brooklyn ferry and home. Noticing an unusual racket from the newsboys, Walt bought a paper. He took it over to a lighted hotel lobby, where several dozen people were already gathered, and read that the Confederates had just attacked Fort Sumter in Charleston harbor. In shocked silence the men tried to absorb the full implication of the South's assault upon United States property and upon the national flag itself. The War Between the States, the Secession War, or the Civil War— call it what one would; war had come to America.

That night Whitman's ferry ride was not the customary convivial event; he was somber and deep in thought. He had been expecting this war all along, but now he did not feel ready for it.

He wanted to prepare body and soul for the ordeal ahead by dedicating himself as if in some religious rite. In a notebook he wrote: "I have this day, this hour, resolved to inaugurate for myself a pure, perfect, sweet, clean-blooded robust body, by ignoring all drinks but water and pure milk, and all fat meats, late suppers —a great body, a purged, cleansed, spiritualized, invigorated body."

Just what did Walt intend to do with a superb condition of physique and psyche? He was nearly forty-two years old, almost overage to be a fighting soldier. And despite his poetic militancy, he abhorred bloodshed, an attitude acquired in his Quaker-type upbringing, combined with his own innately pacific nature. His brother George, however, who was ten years younger, at once went out to join a volunteer regiment. And Andrew tried to enlist but was rejected because of poor health.

Walt probably felt he would need all his resources just to function as a poet of warlike democracy. Watching all around him the dramatic changes in New Yorkers following the news from Fort Sumter, Walt described them in "First O Songs for a Prelude":

> From the houses then and the workshops, and through all the
> doorways,
> Leapt they tumultuous, and lo! Manhattan arming.
>
> To the drum-taps prompt,
> The young men falling in and arming . . .

With a journalist's eye and a poet's feeling, Whitman recorded the details of the myriad preparations for warfare as mechanics, lawyers, shop clerks, and wagon drivers all dropped their tasks to go off to battle for the Union.

> Squads gather everywhere by common consent and arm,
> The new recruits, even boys, the old men show them how to wear
> their accoutrements, they buckle the straps care-
> fully,
> Outdoors arming, indoors arming, the flash of the musket-barrels,
> The white tents cluster in camps, the arm'd sentries around, the
> sunrise cannon and again at sunset,

> Arm'd regiments arrive every day, pass through the city, and
> embark from the wharves,
>
> •   •   •
>
> The blood of the city up—arm'd! arm'd! the cry everywhere,
> The flags flung out from the steeples of churches and from all the
> public buildings and stores,
> The tearful parting, the mother kisses her son, the son kisses his
> mother . . .

And just as Walt's beloved "Mannahatta" altered with the
coming of the war, so did his role as a poet—in his "City of Ships":

> In peace I chanted peace, but now the drum of war is mine,
> War, red war is my song through your streets, O city!

Whitman would not soon experience a "manly life in the camp,"
but he was already serving his country. In the first year of the war
his new poems bespoke a resurgence of vigor and purposefulness.
Better than any other American poet, he was ready to sing out
the songs for "Eighteen Sixty-one":

> Arm'd year—year of the struggle,
> No dainty rhymes or sentimental love verses for you terrible year,
> Not you as some pale poetling seated at a desk lisping cadenzas
> piano,
> But as a strong man erect, clothed in blue clothes, advancing,
> carrying a rifle on your shoulder,
> With well-gristled body and sunburnt face and hands, with a knife
> in the belt at your side,
> As I heard you shouting loud, your sonorous voice ringing across
> the continent . . .

New Yorkers expected a quick and easy end to the South's
secession attempt. Young soldiers like George Whitman, who had
enlisted for a hundred days, carried stout ropes with which they
naïvely expected to capture Rebels. Their overconfidence was
shattered in July, when the first battle of Bull Run smashed the
Federal forces under General McClellan's command. Yankees,
more humble about their military prowess, faced the probability

of years of war ahead of them. Discouraged people now listened to the Copperheads and agreed that the Southern states should be allowed to depart peaceably from the Union.

Walt Whitman read accounts of that early battle in the New York papers, and later he listened to stories told by soldiers who had taken part in the rout and panicky retreat. In the prose volume *Specimen Days,* which contains much of Whitman's Civil War reporting, he recreated the scene as the exhausted and humiliated Union troops limped back the twenty miles to Washington, D. C., while a drizzling summer rain turned to mud the dust on their bodies and the dirt of the roads.

"Where are the vaunts, and the proud boasts with which you went forth?" asked Whitman. "Where are your banners, and your bands of music, and your ropes to bring back prisoners? Well, there isn't a band playing—and there isn't a flag but clings ashamed and lank to its staff." As the weary men straggled back into the city, a few good souls brewed vats of soup and coffee, sliced chunks of bread, and set tables out on the sidewalks to feed the soldiers.

Meanwhile in the stunned capital angry, fearful, despairing, and disloyal moods ran rampant among the citizens, especially among the bureaucrats. The "secesh generals, with their victorious hordes" would invade at any moment. "The dream of humanity, the vaunted Union we thought so strong, so impregnable—lo! it seems already smash'd like a china plate," wrote Whitman, recapturing that terrible crisis time. "One bitter, bitter hour—perhaps proud America will never again know such an hour. She must pack and fly—no time to spare. Those white palaces—the dome-crown'd capitol there on the hill, so stately over the trees—shall they be left—or destroy'd first?" The overwhelming sentiment just after Bull Run was to have Lincoln abdicate and depart, and then turn the city over to Southern rule.

Yet the Confederate generals neglected to follow up their victory by marching into the disarrayed capital. And President Lincoln, quickly recovered from his shock, began with firm determination to strengthen his own authority and to organize the military forces. "If there were nothing else of Abraham Lincoln for history to stamp him with," said Whitman, "it is enough to send him with his wreath to the memory of all future time, that he endured that hour, that day, bitterer than gall—indeed a crucifixion day—that it did not conquer him—that he unflinchingly stemm'd it, and re-solv'd to lift himself and the Union out of it."

In New York the newspapers told of the President's iron will to hold the Union together and to preserve its capital. With rousing editorials they supported him, helping to turn the North's humiliation over the Bull Run defeat into renewed efforts to fight. Patriotic men like George Whitman, when their period of service had expired, immediately re-enlisted. As for Walt Whitman, Bull Run stirred him to write fervid poems for recruitment:

> Beat! beat! drums—blow! bugles, blow!
> Through the windows—through doors—burst like a ruthless force,
> Into the solemn church, and scatter the congregation,
> Into the school where the scholar is studying;
> Leave not the bridegroom quiet—no happiness must he have now
> with his bride,
> Nor the peaceful farmer any peace, ploughing his field or gathering
> his grain,
> So fierce you whirr and pound you drums—so shrill you bugles
> blow.

After some months of strenuous poem-making, Whitman re-treated into a period of tense watching and hoping. Although the North remained steadfast in its desire to win, it was engaged in a prolonged seesaw struggle with the South in which neither opponent gained major or lasting victories on the various battle fronts. "Quicksand years that whirl me I know not whither—" was how Walt described this time. He could not keep up perpetually a militant spirit and often, as before, sought the restful country-side or the refreshing seascape. Tired of the war's strife and the city's din, he felt like living close to nature forever. In such a mood he composed "Give Me the Splendid Silent Sun":

> Give me odorous at sunrise a garden of beautiful flowers where
> I can walk undisturb'd,

Give me for marriage a sweet-breath'd woman of whom I should
  never tire,
Give me a perfect child, give me away aside from the noise of the
  world a rural domestic life,
Give me to warble spontaneous songs recluse by myself, for my
  own ears only,
Give me solitude, give me Nature, give me again O Nature your
  primal sanities!

But while dreaming of this ideal rusticity, the poet realized
that he still half-belonged to the city and to democracy; so he
dismissed his longing for pure nature and welcomed anew the
busy New York scenes he had loved since a boy, made even more
exciting by the war:

Give me the shores and wharves heavy-fringed with black ships!
O such for me! O an intense life, full of repletion and varied!
The life of the theatre, bar-room, huge hotel, for me!
The saloon of the steamer! the crowded excursion for me! the
  torchlight procession!
The dense brigade bound for the war, with high piled military
  wagons following;
People, endless, streaming, with strong voices, passions, pageants,
Manhattan streets with their powerful throbs, with beating drums
  as now . . .

Walt no longer frequented Pfaff's Restaurant: the toasts and
boasts of the many Copperheads gathering there offended him.
Clapp's circle of Bohemians had broken up, and his *Saturday
Press* was temporarily defunct. But the worst blow of all to Walt
was the bankruptcy of Thayer & Eldridge, shortly after announcing the forthcoming publication of a new book by Whitman.
Once more Walt had no regular publisher for his poems, although
he managed to get some of his war-mood poems published in
newspapers and magazines.

To earn money now, Walt did free-lance journalism: pieces
about the history of Brooklyn and Long Island, descriptions of
city and country, and medical reports on New York Hospital,

where he still was friendly with the doctors. His hospital visits to sick or injured horse-bus drivers had expanded to chatting with wounded soldiers recuperating in New York. He was impressed when the men happily showed him special gifts—both treats and useful items—given to them by a kind lady who visited almost daily.

Doubtless Walt felt guilty that he himself was not a soldier too, despite his vocal patriotism and the "drum-taps" he sounded for others to fight for the Union. But direct participation in warfare—like other firm and physical commitments in life—was not for Walt. His rousing battle cries were symbolic; others would deal with the perils and details of a real response.

At least Walt could vicariously follow George's career as a soldier, who because of his courage had received several field promotions and was now a first lieutenant. So far he had been lucky, having gone unscathed through many skirmishes. In his letters home, George thoughtfully spared his family most of the grim aspects of a soldier's life in camp and battle—though Walt probably would have liked to know of them.

Then just after the disastrous battle of First Fredericksburg in mid-December of 1862, as Walt was looking over the casualty list in the *Herald,* he spotted the name "George W. Whitmore" listed among the wounded of the 51st New York Volunteers—his brother's regiment. Walt instantly decided that it was George's name, misspelled. Yet while frantically searching the other papers' lists, he could not find the name again.

When Walt came home with his gloomy news, the Whitman family went into a turmoil. Everyone wanted to do something right away; even Jeff's young wife Martha ("Matt") offered to go off to nurse poor George. Walt set out for Washington that very afternoon with fifty dollars of the family's money in his pocket. The journey was complicated: ferry to Manhattan, across the city on an omnibus, ferry to New Jersey, the train to Philadelphia, and then transfer to another train. In the rush and confusion a pickpocket managed to snatch Walt's money purse; he arrived penniless in Washington, D. C.

In his anxiety to locate George, Walt had no time to spare for sight-seeing in the national capital, where he had never been before. For two days, tired and famished, Walt walked from hospital to hospital, his discouragement growing, for he could get no information as to George's whereabouts. Fortunately he encountered an acquaintance from Boston—the Abolitionist writer William D. O'Connor, who was employed as a clerk in the Treasury Department. O'Connor gave Walt food and money and suggested that George might still be with his own regiment just across the river from the Fredericksburg battlefield.

Walt left Washington at once for Virginia, to continue his search for his wounded brother, traveling by boat and train for another day and night. Given directions for the 51st New York Volunteers' camp, he trudged down a road that wound past an improvised army hospital. Under a tree were shallow, freshly dug graves—and a great pile of arms and legs. Whitman's first direct encounter with the real horrors of battle shocked him; no longer did the war seem the inspiring and ennobling venture he had celebrated in his poetry.

Walt now pictured George lying in a communal grave—or, at best, one of those wounded men who had given a limb or two to the grisly pile. Faint with dread, he walked on toward the regimental encampment—there, to his vast joy, finding George all in one piece and on active duty, a gash in his cheek from a shell fragment nearly healed. George was surprised but pleased to see Walt. Knowing that his wound was not serious, George had tried to keep his name off the casualty lists, to avoid alarming his family; he did not know that he had not wholly succeeded.

After sending off a reassuring telegram to the family, Walt settled down in camp like a veteran. For several weeks he shared a tent and mess with George and his men, spending Christmas with the Union Army, surrounded by the war's devastation. Walt noticed with brotherly pride how the soldiers liked and respected George. Methodical, considerate, responsible, and brave, George made a prime officer; he was not one of the conceited, weakling "shoulder straps" whom Walt despised, who bossed underlings but then fled combat. Walt was delighted to be on hand when

George was given a captain's commission for his deeds at Fredericksburg.

Still the inveterate journalist, Walt observed everything, asked questions of everyone, and made notes for future usage. "I took the first scrap of paper, the first doorstep, the first desk, and wrote, wrote, wrote," Whitman recalled later. "No prepared picture, no elaborated poem, no after-narrative could be what the thing itself was . . . You want to catch the first spirit, to tally its birth. By writing at the instant, the very heartbeat of life is caught. . . ."

Not wishing to be only a scribbler and chatterbox while so much needed doing, Whitman began to make the rounds of the camp hospitals. His ministrations to omnibus drivers and soldiers in New York had accustomed him to sickness, wounds, and death; but he had never seen them as he did now in the crude field hospitals, most of them tents. Since there were no cots and few mattresses, the wounded men lay on blankets upon the cold ground, lucky if cushioned by pine needles or leaves. "I go around from one case to another," Whitman wrote in a notebook. "I do not see that I do much good to these wounded and dying; but I cannot leave them. Once in a while some youngster holds on to me convulsively, and I do what I can for him; at any rate, stop with him and sit near him for hours, if he wishes it."

Death was a constant occurrence. "As you step out in the morning from your tent to wash your face," Walt said, "you see before you on a stretcher a shapeless, extended object, and over it is thrown a dark gray blanket. It is the corpse of some wounded or sick soldier of the regiment who died in the hospital tent during the night; perhaps there is a row of three or four of these corpses lying covered over. No one makes an ado. There is a detail of men to bury them; all useless ceremony is omitted."

The poet in Walt Whitman gave his own silent and ceremonious salutes to these departed human spirits. He could not help but wonder what kind of man each had been while living.

> A sight in camp in the daybreak gray and dim,
> As from my tent I emerge so early sleepless,

As slow I walk in the cool fresh air the path near by the hospital
    tent,
Three forms I see on stretchers lying, brought out there untended
    lying,
Over each the blanket spread, ample brownish woolen blanket,
Gray and heavy blanket, folding, covering all.

Curious I halt and silent stand,
Then with light fingers I from the face of the nearest the first just
    lift the blanket;
Who are you elderly man so gaunt and grim, with well-gray'd hair,
    and flesh all sunken about the eyes?
Who are you my dear comrade?

Then to the second I step—and who are you my child and darling?
Who are you sweet boy with cheeks yet blooming?

Then to the third—a face nor child nor old, very calm, as of
    beautiful yellow-white ivory;
Young man I think I know you—I think this face is the face of the
    Christ himself,
Dead and divine and brother of all, and here again he lies.

Walt would not have been surprised to encounter among the
Union soldiers the facsimile of Jesus. He admired their courage,
patience, and humor and found them dedicated not only to duty
but to the larger ideals of national unity and democracy. Walt
also saw a loving comradeship among these men who daily faced
death together—something he had long dreamed of but never
really witnessed "en masse" until now. So many of Walt's "Drum-
Taps" war poems would poignantly capture this perfect "adhesiveness."

At December's end Whitman took charge of a trainload of
wounded soldiers being sent to Washington. He did his best to
ease the long, rough trip. After he got all the patients settled in
hospitals, he stopped by William O'Connor's apartment. He had
decided to stay for a while in the city and needed help in finding
a cheap place to live. O'Connor's wife Nelly, meeting Walt for the
first time, liked him immediately. The couple found Walt a room
in their own building, and they invited him to take his breakfasts

and dinners with them. Walt's former publisher, Charles Eldridge, also living in Washington, got a part-time copyist job for him in the Army paymaster's office. Whitman would earn enough money to live simply—with enough free time to visit the disabled men in the army hospitals scattered throughout the city.

When Walt left New York, he expected to return after being assured that George was safe and sound. Now his life had taken a sudden dramatic shift. For several years Whitman was to be a Civil War "wound-dresser," a role he undertook with a sense of both mission and predestiny. It never occurred to him that he had any choice in the matter, he acknowledged later. "It was a religion with me," he told a friend. To him religion was whatever really turned a man on: "something in heaven or earth which he will give up everything else for—something which absorbs him, possesses itself of him, makes him over in its image. . ." Just as the Leaves of Grass "bee" had caused Walt to set aside all other ambitions in the past, he was now seized by a desire to comfort and tend the war's casualties.

Tapping the drum as a call to arms in New York, Whitman had sounded militant and menacing. But now he had seen war for himself: the havoc wrought on Virginia's battlefields and the maimed soldiers. His shrill confidence in a democracy warlike and dazzlingly triumphant was muted; his new poems became personal and tragic in tone.

> Arous'd and angry, I'd thought to beat the alarum, and urge
>   relentless war,
> But soon my fingers fail'd me, my face droop'd and I resign'd
>   myself,
> To sit by the wounded and soothe them, or silently watch the
>   dead.

Walt Whitman portrayed himself now as the "Wound-Dresser," who, after the battles were over, came to tally their terrible costs in human suffering and death. He nursed the wounded, consoled the dying, and listened to tales of bloody skirmishes he had not seen:

Bearing the bandages, water and sponge,
Straight and swift to my wounded I go,
Where they lie on the ground after the battle brought in,
Where their priceless blood reddens the grass the ground,
Or to the rows of the hospital tent, or under the roof'd hospital,
To the long rows of cots up and down each side I return,
To each and all one after another I draw near, not one do I miss,

.   .   .

With hinged knees and steady hand to dress wounds,
I am firm with each, the pangs are sharp yet unavoidable,
One turns to me his appealing eyes—poor boy! I never knew you,
Yet I think I could not refuse this moment to die for you, if that
would save you.

Whitman's poetry could never be accused of offering "dulcet rhymes" or tinkling "piano-tunes." Now he realistically recorded for those of his own generation and for posterity the gruesome details of the stricken humanity awaiting the wound-dresser's tender, loving care:

The crush'd head I dress, (poor crazed hand tear not the bandage
away,)
The neck of the cavalry-man with the bullet through and through
I examine,
Hard the breathing rattles, quite glazed already the eye, yet life
struggles hard,
(Come sweet death! be persuaded O beautiful death!
In mercy come quickly.)

Walt always carried little notebooks made by pinning or sewing together loose sheets of paper. Almost every date had entries, principally notations and reminders about the men seen in the hospitals. Many patients had been wounded in battle, but even more had succumbed to the communicable diseases that afflicted the army camps. A number of these cases Whitman later introduced in his Civil War recollections within *Specimen Days*. "In one bed a young man, Marcus Small, company K, 7th Maine—sick with dysentery and typhoid fever—pretty critical case. . . . I let him talk to me a little, but not much; advise him to keep very quiet—

do most of the talking myself—stay quite a while with him, as he holds on to my hand—talk to him in a cheering, but slow, low and measured manner . . . . Thomas Lindly, 1st Pennsylvania Cavalry, shot very badly through the foot—poor young man he suffers horribly, has to be constantly dosed with morphine, his face ashy and glazed, bright young eyes—I give him a large handsome apple, lay it in sight, tell him to have it roasted in the morning, as he generally feels easier then, and can eat a little breakfast . . . ."

Whitman prepared himself carefully for his daily rounds. "In my visits to the hospitals," he recalled, "I found it was in the simple matter of personal presence, and emanating ordinary cheer and magnetism, that I succeeded and help'd more than by medical nursing, or delicacies, or gifts of money, or anything else. During the war I possess'd the perfection of physical health. My habit, when practicable, was to prepare for starting out on one of those daily or nightly tours of from a couple to four or five hours, by fortifying myself with previous rest, the bath, clean clothes, a good meal, and as cheerful an appearance as possible."

"I believe I weigh about two hundred, and as to my face (so scarlet) and my beard and neck, they are terrible to behold," Walt wrote his mother, describing his effect on others. "I fancy the reason I am able to do some good in the hospitals among the poor languishing and wounded boys is that I am so large and well —indeed like a great wild buffalo, with much hair. Many of the soldiers are from the West and far North, and they take to a man that has not the bleached, shiny, and shaved cut of the cities and the East."

A big and benign Walt Whitman entered the wards like Santa Claus, with graying beard and shaggy mane, a ruddy face, a kindly smile, and a bulging knapsack. He carried an astounding variety of things: a jar of fruit jelly for doling out in spoonfuls to those who craved sweets; an orange to be sliced, then coaxed into the mouth of someone refusing to eat at all; a bottle of fruit syrup to combine with ice water for a refreshing treat for the whole ward; pickles and dried fruit; pouches or plugs of tobacco for smokers and chewers; a ten-cent or fifty-cent bill—a "shin-plaster"—for anybody without funds; a rice pudding specially baked by Nelly O'Connor for a soldier who desired this and nothing more; writing paper, envelopes, stamps; current newspapers and magazines, books, and Bibles on loan; clean clothes for men going home on furlough or for good.

Whitman was never a regular paid nurse. And although he carried a "pass" given to him by the Christian Commission—a civilian group that encouraged hospital visitors and volunteers and collected funds for the needs of the hospitalized soldiers—Walt was really a "free-lancer." He went wherever he was welcomed and made his own schedule, at first financing these altruistic expeditions from his own meager pocketbook. When it soon became apparent that his money would scarcely suffice, he solicited funds from Washington people and from his acquaintances in New York and New England.

Walt would instinctively know or deftly seek out each person's need, and if he could not supply it then and there, he would make a special note to do so unfailingly in a day or two. Yet often the main matter involved no material contribution—instead, a smile of friendly concern, a few gentle words of encouragement, a warm handclasp to one who felt cut off from or abandoned by others. Whitman's love for his fellow men had sometimes been intense enough to disturb his equilibrium; now he had literally thousands of comrades upon whom he could bestow his healing and "magnetic" personality.

"Most of these sick or hurt are evidently young fellows from the country, farmers' sons, and such like," Whitman noted. "Most of them are entirely without friends or acquaintances here—no familiar face, and hardly a word of judicious cheer, through their sometimes long and tedious sickness, or the pangs of aggravated wounds." What they really needed, Walt believed, was a reassuring physical affection, especially since so many of the soldiers were very young, still in their teens and away from home and family for the first time.

During the Civil War, America began to make use of women's capabilities in caring for the sick and the wounded—following Florence Nightingale's example during the Crimean War a decade before. Walt, however, thought that simply having female nurses in the hospitals was not necessarily the best solution. Young ladies, though dedicated to their work, had often been hastily and poorly trained; moreover, their usually diffident attitude toward the body made it hard for them to dress wounds, give sponge baths, and administer bedpans—so their uneasiness was communicated to the patients.

Walt believed that the middle-aged mothers of many children, and Negro "mammies," made the best nurses. They knew from long personal experience how to tend invalids, and nothing about the male form could shock or repel them. Above all, they radiated a strong, beneficent maternal affection—which Walt himself could also readily give:

> The hurt and wounded I pacify with soothing hand,
> I sit by the restless all the dark night, some are so young,
> Some suffer so much, I recall the experience sweet and sad,
> (Many a soldier's loving arms about this neck have cross'd and
>   rested,
> Many a soldier's kiss dwells on these bearded lips.)

Whitman complained that some volunteer nurses and society matrons making dutiful ward visits picked out favorites to dote upon, and thereby neglected patients far more needful of special attention. And he criticized the hospitals for not giving proper attention to maintaining order, cleanliness, antiseptic conditions, and diets appropriate for invalids.

Walt knew that most of the doctors were conscientious and capable; but they were also overworked, rushing from bed to bed, ward to ward, in and out of operating rooms. Few had either the time or the ability to soothe a sick man's spirits or raise his will to live; they dealt with the body's disorders, not with the area of the elusive but all-important human soul. As they discovered Walt's uncanny talent in that terrain, the doctors gave him liberty to come and go as he liked, in difficult cases even inviting his opinions and seriously heeding them.

Armory Square was Walt's favorite hospital, and its head surgeon, Dr. Bliss, later said that from his own knowledge of Whitman's work there and elsewhere, he believed that "no one person who assisted in the hospitals during the War accomplished so much good to the soldiers and for the government as Mr. Whitman." Soldiers who recovered and later returned to civilian life often named their sons "Walt." And grateful veterans afterwards told of an arm or leg spared unnecessary amputation or of a will to live restored through Walt's persuasiveness. That this "angel of mercy" happened to be a poet was quite irrelevant to them.

Besides passing out gifts and helping with medical attentions, Walt would frequently read to a group of patients: dramatic stories, declamatory poetry, or passages from the Bible—but never, so far as he could recall, anything from *Leaves of Grass*. He liked to play the game of Twenty Questions with them. At other times Walt sat at the bedside of a sick and lonely man to talk quietly with him; or he listened attentively while someone told him of his family or of a battle incident. Like President Lincoln, who often visited the hospitals too, Walt did not differentiate between the Yankee and Rebel invalids. To him they were brothers and equals, and the tragic controversy which had divided their nation should not be allowed to invade the hospitals and retard their recovery. Some of Walt's dearest friends among the patients were Confederate soldiers.

If a patient was incapacitated, Walt would write to his family or sweetheart for him. Meanwhile, the poet within imagined what might happen after the soldier's letter arrived home—and depicted such a sequence in "Come Up from the Fields Father." The sister called the father away from his harvest-gathering, and the mother came in from the kitchen:

> Fast as she can she hurries, something ominous, her steps trembling,
> She does not tarry to smooth her hair nor adjust her cap.
>
> Open the envelope quickly,
> O this is not our son's writing, yet his name is sign'd,
> O a strange hand writes for our dear son, O stricken mother's soul!
> All swims before her eyes, flashes with black, she catches the main words only,

Sentences broken, *gunshot wound in the breast, cavalry skirmish,*
taken to hospital,
At present low, but will soon be better.

•   •   •

Alas poor boy, he will never be better, (nor may-be needs to be
        better, that brave and simple soul,)
While they stand at home at the door he is dead already,
The only son is dead.

But the mother needs to be better,
She with thin form presently drest in black,
By day her meals untouch'd, then at night fitfully sleeping, often
        waking,
In the midnight waking, weeping, longing with one deep longing,
O that she might withdraw unnoticed, silent from life escape and
        withdraw,
To follow, to seek, to be with her dear dead son.

Whitman knew that it was the bereft living who suffered now,
not the dead man. So frequently, to supplement the government's
terse communication, Walt wrote his own consolatory letter to
parents or wife, telling of the deceased soldier's last days and
hours and of how easily and painlessly he had died.

Whitman maintained that "so much of a race depends on how
it faces death, and how it stands personal anguish and sickness."
The Civil War amply reassured him about the American breed of
men. Witnessing many soldiers die before his very eyes, and hearing of uncounted other deaths on battlefield or in sickbed, he was
impressed that these men always died courageously and peace-
fully, as though confirming his assertion in "Song of Myself" that
to die was to be luckier than one supposed.

Although Walt's life centered about the army hospitals, he did
not confine himself to them: for his own well-being he could not.
"It is curious," he wrote to his mother, "when I am present at
the most appalling things—deaths, operations, sickening wounds
(perhaps full of maggots)—I do not fail, although my sympathies
are very much excited, but keep singularly cool; but often hours
afterward, perhaps when I am home or out walking alone, I feel

sick and actually tremble when I recall the thing and have it in my mind again before me."

Seeking some brief respite and distraction away from the grim spectacles and from his intense feelings for the hospitalized men, Walt took long walks around Washington, especially at night, often describing in his notebooks what he had seen on these jaunts—some to be preserved later in *Specimen Days*. On a balmy moonlit night in February he visited the President's house, finding "everything so white, so marbly pure and dazzling, yet soft . . . under the lustrous flooding moon, full of reality, full of illusion— the forms of the trees, leafless, silent, in trunk and myriad-angles of branches, under the stars and sky—the White House of the land, and of beauty and night. . . ."

And as though on a pilgrimage, Walt went to see the rebuilt and refurbished Capitol. Although he commended Lincoln's decision to continue the work on it, he found its "incredible gorgeousness" too lush to suit the nation's spirit and particularly inappropriate for these austere and tormented times. "Filled as I am from top to toe of late with scenes and thoughts of the hospitals (America seems to me now—though only in her youth but brought already here—feeble, bandaged, and bloody in hospital)," he wrote, " . . . all the poppy-show goddesses and all the pretty blue and gold in which the interior Capitol is got up seem to me out of place beyond anything I could tell. . . ." Overwhelmed, he made a quick escape from its premises.

In Washington Walt himself lived as he always had—simply and frugally. But now he reduced his possessions and needs to an ab- solute minimum; his room was as bare as a monk's cell. After the O'Connors moved into their own house, Walt took an attic room on Sixth Street, cater-cornered to the mansion owned by the Sec- retary of the Treasury, Salmon P. Chase.

John T. Trowbridge of Boston was writing a biography of Chase and came to Washington as his guest. He heard that Whit- man lived just across the street, so he paid him a call. He was fascinated with the dramatic contrast between two styles of living: "In the fine, large mansion, sumptuously furnished, cared for by sleek and silent colored servants, and thronged by distinguished guests, dwelt the great statesman; in the old tenement opposite, in a bare and desolate back room, up three flights of stairs, quite alone, lived the poet." Walt's garret was furnished only with a cot, a cheap pine table, several rickety chairs, and a small iron stove. Yet Walt cleared the chairs of their piles of papers and invited his visitors "to sit down and stop awhile, with as simple and sweet hospitality as if he had been offering us the luxuries of the great mansion across the square."

When Trowbridge dropped by Whitman's place several days later, he watched the poet prepare his breakfast from a few provisions kept in a wooden crate. Walt brewed tea in a plain tin pan, sliced a loaf of bread with a jackknife and toasted the pieces upon the stove with the aid of a sharp stick. The brown paper bag serving as his plate was burned as soon as the simple meal was over.

Whitman sporadically went office-seeking; he wanted to have a permanent job with the government—such as Eldridge and O'Connor had—in order to pay for more hospital treats and to send money home to his mother. Emerson had given Walt several letters of recommendation to prominent Washington statesmen, and Trowbridge delivered the one to Salmon P. Chase. In it Emerson mentioned that Whitman had written *Leaves of Grass*. Had he never learned of Walt's authorship of that notorious book, Chase doubtless would have offered him a job. As it was, he refused to help—but, to Trowbridge's astonishment, insisted upon keeping the letter as a souvenir of Emerson.

Walt's stay in wartime Washington was instructive, if frequently discouraging. He was giving his all to help those men who dedicated their very lives to preserve the Union. Understandably, he regarded with enormous disgust the arrogant or petty-minded officials in positions of real or fancied importance, which the war had made available to many of them; he also noticed the large number of near-disloyal Copperheads working in governmental jobs. And he watched wily and selfish men rapidly become rich by supplying the government with goods and services it desperately needed for the conduct of the war—people who could hardly be called patriots.

During his first year in the capital, Walt often felt depressed not only from his contacts with some of its citizens and his hospital experiences, but from the discouraging succession of Union defeats. He began to doubt that the North would be able to continue the war, let alone win it. Briefly he recorded his mood for 1863:

Year that trembled and reel'd beneath me!
Your summer wind was warm enough, yet the air I breathed froze me,
A thick gloom fell through the sunshine and darken'd me,
Must I change my triumphant songs? said I to myself,
Must I indeed learn to chant the cold dirges of the baffled?
And sullen hymns of defeat?

But Walt would then reassert his convictions. "The war *must* be carried on," he wrote his mother. "I would willingly go in the ranks myself if I thought it would profit more than as at present, and I don't know sometimes but I shall, as it is." For the time being, however, Walt was more useful in the hospitals.

A terrible blow to Union morale came in May of 1863 with the rout of General Hooker's forces at Chancellorsville. A boastful Hooker, overconfident of smashing Generals Lee and "Stonewall" Jackson, had his own troops surrounded and nearly obliterated by the Confederates in a nighttime battle. Whitman hurried to tend the wounded soldiers as soon as they arrived in the city, and from them and the news reports he pieced together the scene. In *Specimen Days* he provided an "eyewitness" account of Chancellorsville in "those shadowy-tangled, flashing moonbeam'd woods." History would never yield all the details of the fight, he said; but deftly the poet-journalist evoked "the cries, the din, the cracking guns and pistols—the distant cannon—the cheers and calls and threats and awful music of the oaths . . . the devils fully rous'd in human hearts—the strong shout, *Charge, men, charge*—the flash of naked sword, and rolling flame and smoke. . . ."

And, said Whitman, no history or poem or music—"no formal general's report nor book in the library, nor column in the paper"— could ever tell all the individual deeds of heroism. Then he portrayed a composite American hero, the plain Civil War soldier, as he "crawls to some bush clump, or ferny tuft, on receiving his death shot—there sheltering a little while, soaking roots, grass and soil, with red blood . . . perhaps the burial squads, in truce, a week afterwards, search not the secluded spot—and there, at last, the Bravest Soldier crumbles in mother earth, unburied and unknown."

But the poet would immortalize this Unknown Soldier of the Civil War in "Vigil Strange I Kept on the Field One Night," in which he symbolically buried a young "comrade" after keeping an all-night vigil next to him—

> Vigil of silence, love and death, vigil for you my son and my
> soldier,
> As onward silently stars aloft, eastward new ones upward stole,
> Vigil final for you brave boy, (I could not save you, swift was your
> death,
> I faithfully loved you and cared for you living, I think we shall
> surely meet again,) . . .

The grim war at least was confirming Whitman's long-held confidence in the common man, America's product and best representative, whom Walt found in plentiful supply among the ordinary soldiers. It was they who gave new funds of faith and courage to the Union—and to the poet too.

> Long, too long America,
> Traveling roads all even and peaceful you learn'd from joys and
> prosperity only,
> But now, ah now, to learn from crises of anguish, advancing,
> grappling with direst fate and recoiling not,
> And now to conceive and show to the world what your children
> en-masse really are . . .

The Union Army's victory over Lee's forces at Gettysburg in early July of 1863 also helped to dispel Whitman's gloom. No settlement yet seemed near. "But I do not lose the solid feeling, in myself," Walt wrote to his mother, "that the Union triumph is assured, whether it be sooner or whether it be later, or whatever roundabout way we may be led there; and I find I don't change that conviction from any reserves we meet, nor delays, nor blunders."

Whitman had been studying Abraham Lincoln at close range. "I think well of the President," he wrote to a friend a few months after settling in Washington. "He has a face like a Hoosier Michael Angelo, so awful ugly it becomes beautiful, with its strange mouth, its deep cut, criss-cross lines, and its doughnut complexion. —My notion is too, that underneath his outside smutched mannerism . . . Mr. Lincoln keeps a fountain of first-class practical telling wisdom. . . . He has shown, I sometimes think an almost supernatural tact in keeping the ship afloat at all with head steady, not only not going down, and now certain not to, but with proud and resolute spirit, and flag flying in sight of the world, menacing and high as ever. I say never yet captain, never ruler, had such a perplexing dangerous task as his, the past two years. I more and more rely upon his idiomatic western genius, careless of court dress or court decorum." (This early image of Lincoln as the chief officer of the "ship of state" would eventually appear in "O Captain! My Captain!," Whitman's best-known poem.)

During the hot summer of 1863 the Lincolns stayed in a house on the outskirts of town, and Walt watched the President pass by in his barouche almost every morning, on his way to the White House. He especially noticed Lincoln's eyes, "with a deep latent sadness in the expression." It seemed that the President got to know Whitman by sight, for he would smile and nod toward him. "I love the President personally," Whitman declared. Walt thought of Lincoln as the ideal American leader; he gave less attention now to physical perfection, more to an energetic and valiant spirit— with which the President obviously was well endowed.

All through the Civil War Walt Whitman kept on writing, filling his little makeshift notebooks with a thousand observations. He composed poems based on things he saw and felt about the war. And besides the many personal letters written to his mother and to friends giving details of his life and work and the current happenings in the capital, he wrote a number of letters and news dispatches for various New York and Brooklyn papers.

Whitman planned two books. The first would be a compact record of events and his own experiences during 1863, to be entitled *Memoranda of a Year*. Secondly, he was preparing a new collection of poems, a few written before the war's outbreak but most of them concerned with it. The former project, in note form, was never completed because Walt could not find an interested publisher. But *Drum-Taps*, as he called it, expanded as the months went by and he wrote more and more poems to go into it.

The O'Connors and Charles Eldridge remained Whitman's good friends and admirers. During the war Walt also formed his close association with John Burroughs, a young naturalist and writer from the Hudson Valley. A few years before, John had been powerfully affected when reading *Leaves of Grass*. Hearing that Whitman now lived in Washington, he abandoned a schoolteaching job and went to the capital, his main ambition being to know the poet personally.

Meeting in the shop of a mutual friend, the young man from the country (he was in his mid-twenties) and the middle-aged man of the city instantly took to each other. "I have been much with Walt," Burroughs wrote soon after to a friend. "I love him very much. The more I see and talk with him, the greater he becomes to me. He is as vast as the earth, and as loving and noble. . . . He walks very leisurely, rather saunters, and looks straight forward, not down at his feet. He does not talk readily, but his conversation is rich and suggestive. . . . Walt has all types of men in him, there is not one left out."

Pleased with this prospering friendship, Burroughs found a clerical job in the Treasury Department, then sent for his wife to join him in Washington. The sensible, oft-severe Ursula came, but did not warm up at once to Walt, as Nelly O'Connor had, doubtless at first resenting or disapproving of her husband's admiration for him. But gradually she began to understand and accept the important influence Walt exercised upon John's life and career—and to notice at the same time how John had possibly become equally beneficial to Walt.

Each man was to have a strong and permanent effect upon the other. Whitman encouraged Burroughs to write, suggested subjects and titles for his essays and books about nature, inspired John's own versifying, and gave good editorial advice. Burroughs in turn proved certainly the most satisfactory, yet independent-minded, Whitmanian disciple. They shared many similar ideas and feelings—especially a kinship with nature. John was a sturdy walker and a keen observer. (Walt would sometimes borrow John's descriptions, especially those relating to birds.) In town and country both he made a boon companion, for he was a stimulating talker and a responsive listener who unleashed Walt's tongue on a variety of subjects. (Although abnormally "adhesive" emotions sometimes beset Whitman, his deep and lasting friendship with Burroughs seemed thoroughly normal.)

In November of 1863 Walt returned to Brooklyn for a sorely needed rest from his hospital work. But peace and quiet were rare within the Whitman household nowadays. Mrs. Whitman, having a sympathetic interest in Walt's "wound-dressing" experiences, listened attentively for hours as he told of so much he had seen and done. The rest of the time she had a multitude of her own woes to disclose to him.

Jeff and his wife "Matt" were inconsiderate and selfish, she complained; although they lived in the family home, they did not contribute their fair share to its support. Furthermore, they gallivanted around town, night and day, leaving their spoiled little girl "Hattie" (named Mannahatta by Jeff to please Walt) in the care of her already harassed grandmother. Mrs. Whitman constantly worried that Jeff would be drafted into the army; despite his shortcomings, she could not spare him, for with both George and Walt away, he was the only real man around. . . . Eddie, crippled and mentally dim, yet very stubborn, had always been a burden to her. Jesse's mind and erratic behavior were going from bad to worse; his violent spells, especially during the night, frightened her terribly. Poor Andrew, living nearby, was near death from some disease of the throat. Meanwhile, his wife got drunk, let their small children fend for themselves out on the streets, and earned bits of money as a prostitute. . . . And to make matters still worse, sister Hannah, who lived in Vermont with her unemployed artist-husband, wrote long whining letters about her sad fate and planned to return home to her family. Hannah's spouse penned his own complaints: Hannah kept a filthy house and would not feed him properly, so he was going to throw her out. (Walt was bound to feel somewhat responsible for the situation, since he had introduced the couple to each other. Yet for all their many grievances through the years, they never separated. Hannah had her peculiarities, but she was the only Whitman who apparently ever really read and liked *Leaves of Grass;* for this alone Walt would have cherished her.)

After a few weeks of this home-visiting, Walt must have returned to Washington with a sense of relief at putting some distance between himself and these domestic troubles.

During the early months of 1864 Whitman made a tour of the camps around Culpeper, Virginia, again experiencing army life in the rough. The Union regiments perpetually moved around, tense from expecting an attack from Lee's forces at any moment.

One night Walt was aroused from sleep by the noise of soldiers returning from some maneuver. "It was a curious sight to see those shadowy columns moving through the night," he recalled. "I stood unobserv'd in the darkness and watch'd them long. The mud was very deep. The men had their usual burdens, overcoats, knapsacks, guns and blankets. Along and along they filed by me, with often a laugh, a song, a cheerful word, but never once a murmur. It may have been odd, but I never before so realized the majesty and reality of the American people *en masse.*"

Walt told his mother that he had no difficulty at all in getting along with the soldiers or teamsters—or anyone else in camp. "I most always find they like to have me very much. . . . No doubt they soon feel that my heart and sympathies are truly with them, and it is both a novelty and pleases them and touches their feelings, and so doubtless does them good—and I am sure it does that to me."

With pleasure the poet observed the army's every preparatory motion. Quickly and deftly he sketched vignettes of the war as he saw it, his words fitting companions to Mathew Brady's photographs and Winslow Homer's watercolors. Here was how Whitman saw "Cavalry Crossing a Ford":

> A line in long array where they wind betwixt green islands,
> They take a serpentine course, their arms flash in the sun—hark to
>   the musical clank,
> Behold the silvery river, in it the splashing horses loitering stop to
>   drink,
> Behold the brown-faced men, each group, each person a picture,
>   the negligent rest on their saddles,
> Some emerge on the opposite bank, others are just entering the
>   ford—while,
> Scarlet and blue and snowy white,
> The guidon flags flutter gayly in the wind.

Walt also looked at the surrounding Virginia countryside, "dilapidated, fenceless, and trodden with war." In a customary journalistic assessment, he praised its "capacity for products, improvements, human life, nourishment and expansion." He admired the scenery, the sunshine, the mountains, the nights. Beholding a delicate new moon, he wished upon it: "Ah, if it might prove an omen and good prophecy for this unhappy State."

But Virginia would see more warfare. In March of 1864 Ulysses S. Grant took over the supreme command of the Union Army, then launched his relentless Wilderness Campaign through Virginia, determined to capture the Confederacy's capital at Richmond.

Now that the Civil War was definitely turning in the Union's favor, Walt Whitman should have felt exhilarated; but he could not. His once-superb health had been overtaxed by the rigorous hospital rounds. Walt suffered from a chronic sore throat, dizziness, and head pains. Some doctors surmised that his blood was poisoned when an open cut in his hand became infected by a soldier's gangrenous wound; others diagnosed a mild case of "hospital" malaria—or said that he had had a sunstroke. In June Walt returned home to Brooklyn to recuperate. The Whitman family's problems were somewhat changed: Andrew had died, and now Walt's mother fretted over his neglected children; Jesse's behavior had become so unpredictable and dangerous that Walt had him committed to an insane asylum.

As Walt's health improved, he began to write a series of newspaper articles about the hospital facilities in New York and Brooklyn. A main activity, however, was attending political rallies—for Walt was in New York during the crucial presidential contest in 1864. He went to see what the Democrats were up to, for he could rarely resist crowds of people, fireworks, flags flying, cannon salutes, and placards. President Lincoln ran on the Republican or Union ticket; he was opposed by General George B. McClellan, the erstwhile commander of the army who had proved so ineffectual that Lincoln had dismissed him. Since McClellan loathed Lincoln and favored making a peace treaty with the South, he was enthusiastically supported by the Copperhead Democrats. The Radical Republicans had shrilly denounced Lincoln for being slow in banishing slavery and too gentle toward the Southern rebels, and they talked of choosing somebody else as their candidate. But now they found McClellan so abominable as a presidential prospect that they joined with the moderate Republicans to assure Lincoln's re-election. Walt Whitman once again cast his vote for Lincoln—this time with absolute trust in his worth.

In early October the Whitmans learned that George had been captured by the Confederates. Walt was greatly worried, for he had talked with many exchanged or escaped prisoners and knew how wretched the Southern prisons were—especially now, when even the Rebel soldiers themselves had skimpy supplies. On the day after Christmas George's trunk arrived home, returned by the army. It took several hours for the Whitmans to summon up enough courage to open it. "There were his uniform coat, pants, sash, &c.," Walt said. "There were many things reminded us of him. Papers, memoranda, books, nick-nacks, a revolver, a small diary, roll of his company, a case of photographs of his comrades (several of them I knew as killed in battle) with other stuff such as a soldier accumulates. Mother looked everything over, laid out the shirts to be washed, the coats and pants to hang up, & all the rest were carefully put back. It made us feel pretty solemn."

Walt read George's diary and was deeply moved. Although it

just recorded facts and happenings, he pronounced it "a perfect poem of the war." Walt's sensible, practical young brother had led a life which seemed truly heroic, "living poetry" in itself.

Hoping to rescue George with words, Walt wrote letters to the newspapers, protesting General Grant's recent order that stopped all exchanges of prisoners. He also contacted influential friends who might be able to obtain special permission from Grant for his brother's return. Just before Walt left for Washington, his family received a letter from George, who was in a prison in Virginia; it had taken several months to get there. Back in the capital, Walt sent George a package of food and clothing. Closer to the war action, he kept up his barrage in his brother's behalf and must have succeeded, for in February George was on his way home, exchanged for a Confederate prisoner.

In early January of 1865 Whitman had returned to Washington in the near-certainty of getting a job, thanks to William O'Connor's persistence. Rested and back in reasonably good health, Whitman passed an examination which made him a clerk in the Department of the Interior. He now enjoyed a good and secure income; his duties were not especially demanding, allowing him time and energy to continue his hospital visits.

Ensconsed in the Indian Bureau, Walt liked to watch the visiting chiefs. Admiring these colorful and noble representatives of the primal American now on the retreat, Whitman felt sad as he thought of their ultimate disappearance—to be told later in the poem "Yonnondio," an Iroquois word meaning "lament for the aborigines."

> Yonnondio—I see far in the west or north, a limitless ravine, with
> plains and mountains dark,
> I see swarms of stalwart chieftains, medicine-men, and warriors,
> As flitting by like clouds of ghosts, they pass and are gone in the
> twilight,
> (Race of the woods, the landscapes free, and the falls!
> No picture, poem, statement, passing them to the future:)
> Yonnondio! Yonnondio!—unlimn'd they disappear . . .

Walt Whitman celebrated the present time and anticipated the future, but he was also attracted to the past. He could therefore feel compassion for the South, whose old pattern of life was doomed to fade away, like that of the American Indians.

In early March of 1865 Walt witnessed Lincoln's second inauguration. The weather on the night before had been stormy, but next day the sun shone brightly down upon the crowds gathered to watch the long and gaudy parade and to see Lincoln take the oath of office again.

Walt thought that Lincoln looked haggard—"demands of life and death, cut deeper than ever upon his dark brown face." But he still glimpsed "all the goodness, tenderness, sadness, and canny shrewdness, underneath the furrows." After the ceremony, the President stepped out on the Capitol's portico, and Walt noticed that a small fleecy white cloud hovered above him like a bird, which he interpreted as a good sign for both Lincoln and the nation.

That evening Whitman went along with the great throng that rushed into the White House to gawk at the furnishings and the famous personalities. "I saw Mr. Lincoln, drest all in black," Whitman recorded, "with white kid gloves and a claw-hammer coat, receiving, as in duty bound, shaking hands, looking very disconsolate, and as if he would give anything to be somewhere else." Walt at least could escape the unruly people who made souvenirs out of wallpaper and curtains and carried off almost every object not bolted down or too heavy to handle.

In quiet solitude, after the noisy excitement of the inaugural festivities, Walt gazed up at the heavens and afterwards described his impressions in a notebook: "The western star, Venus, in the earlier hours of evening, has never been so large, so clear; it seems as if it told something, as if it held rapport indulgent with humanity, with us Americans. . . . The sky, dark blue, the transparent night, the planets, the moderate west wind, the elastic temperature, the miracle of that great star, and the young and swelling moon swimming in the west, suffused the soul. . . ."

Shortly thereafter Whitman obtained a leave of absence from his job. He wanted to visit George, resting at home and eating well after his months of imprisonment. He also wished to oversee the printing in New York of his book of Civil War poems.

Whitman entertained high hopes for *Drum-Taps*. "I feel at last, & for the first time without any demur," he had written to O'Connor, "that I am satisfied with it—content to have it go to the world verbatim and punctuatim. It is in my opinion superior to *Leaves of Grass*—certainly more perfect as a work of art, being adjusted in all its proportions, & its passion having the indispensable merit that though to the ordinary reader let loose with wildest abandon, the true artist can see it is yet under control. But I am perhaps mainly satisfied with *Drum-Taps* because it delivers my ambition of the task that has haunted me, namely, to express in a poem (& in the way I like, which is not at all by directly stating it) the pending action of this *Time & Land we swim in,* with all their large and conflicting fluctuations of despair & hope, the shiftings, masses, & the whirl & deafening din, (yet over all, as by invisible hand, a definite purport & idea)—with the unprecedented anguish of wounded & suffering, the beautiful young men, in wholesale death & agony, everything sometimes as if blood color, & dripping. The book is therefore unprecedently sad, (as these days are, are they not?)—but it also has the blast of the trumpet, & the drum pounds & whirrs in it, & then an undertone of sweetest comradeship & human love, threading its steady thread inside the chaos, & heard at every lull & interstice thereof—truly, also it has clear notes of faith & triumph."

While Walt Whitman was staying in Brooklyn, the Union's victory finally came. On April 3 Grant's army captured Richmond, and when General Robert E. Lee surrendered at Appomattox a week later, the doom of the Southern states' secession attempt was sealed. The Confederate capital, removed to Montgomery, Alabama, capitulated on the twelfth of April. The Civil War, fought for more than four arduous years at the cost of over half a million lives, had ended. The Union would be whole again, and the soldiers, North and South, would return to their homes and families. President Lincoln issued an amnesty which would allow the Southerners to rebuild their ravaged land while adjusting to a way of life without slavery.

Like Lincoln and other moderate men of the North, Walt Whitman viewed the Union's triumph not as an opportunity for vindictive action toward the rebellious states, but as the start of a new friendship possible between two regions so different in character but truly equal—like comrades or brothers. In "Reconciliation," Whitman gave tragic stature to the South's defeat by personifying it in the death of a Confederate soldier:

> For my enemy is dead, a man divine as myself is dead,
> I look where he lies white-faced and still in the coffin—I draw near,
> Bend down and touch lightly with my lips the white face in the coffin.

Shut not your doors to me proud libraries,
For that which was lacking on all your well-
fill'd shelves, yet needed most, I bring,
Forth from the war emerging, a book I have
made . . .

IX

SHUT NOT YOUR DOORS TO ME

(1865-1869)

In mid-April of 1865 there was much for which the Whitman family could be thankful. The Civil War had ended. George was home, alive and well, having survived many battles and then sickness and near-starvation during his Southern imprisonment. In a peaceable capacity Walt too had done his part in the war to save the Union, and his experiences had greatly aged him. His hair and beard were now quite gray; although only forty-five years old, he looked almost like an old man.

Walt Whitman felt vigorous enough, however, to attend busily to the printing of his war poems, *Drum-Taps*. In them he had recorded his many moods and observations during the war, as well as the overall experience of the American people themselves. Whitman had graphically described the horrors of battlefield and hospital, but his poems were equally remarkable for their portrayals of the powerful and sustaining comradeship among the soldiers which the war had engendered. Walt believed that this open "manly affection" made the best basis for reuniting the nation:

Over the carnage rose prophetic a voice,
Be not dishearten'd, affection shall solve the problems of freedom
    yet,
Those who love each other shall become invincible,
They shall yet make Columbia victorious.

       •   •   •

One from Massachusetts shall be a Missourian's comrade,
From Maine and from hot Carolina, and another an Oregonese,
    shall be friends triune,
More precious to each other than all the riches of the earth.

The Civil War had shown to the world the viability of the Republic's ideals and the determination of the vast majority of the people of the North to keep the Union together as originally created by their forefathers. Walt maintained that the events leading up to victory had renewed his faith in the nation's, and democracy's, course. "I feel, more than ever," he said, "how America has been entirely re-stated by them—and they will shape the destinies of the future of the whole of mankind."

It was springtime. The season meant a new beginning, a rebirth of the earth and of all that lived upon it. Past cultures had often celebrated spring as the resurrection of a beloved young god untimely taken away from them, who returned annually to a mournful land that suddenly became joyous as his spirit was revealed in the warmer sunshine, the renewed greenery, and new life.

Good Friday, the funereal day commemorating the crucifixion of Jesus, came on April 14. That evening, President Abraham Lincoln was assassinated. The United States of America now had a martyred spiritual leader of its own.

When they heard the dreadful news the next morning, the Whitmans were stunned. "Mother prepared breakfast—and other meals afterwards—as usual," Walt remembered; "but not a mouthful was eaten all day by either of us. We each drank half a cup of coffee; that was all. Little was said. We got every newspaper morning and evening, and the frequent extras of that period, and pass'd them silently to each other."

If the war had struck down any member of his family, Walt

could not have grieved more than he did now. During his past years in Washington, often studying the President and hearing approving reports of him, Walt had concluded that the safety and perhaps even the perpetuation of the Union depended upon Lincoln's wisdom, forceful will, and compassion. During the war he had proven to be a firm leader, a paternal guiding spirit which the nation sorely needed. In the postwar period his abilities would be equally important: peace was going to be as hard to achieve as victory had been. And now Lincoln was dead.

Walt felt unbearably restless with a soul-deep anguish that now required human companionship and the illusion at least of doing something, rather than sorrowful solitude. "When a great event happens, or the news of some great solemn thing spreads out among the people, it is curious to go forth and wander a while in the public ways," he explained. Late Saturday afternoon he took the ferry to Manhattan. He found the usually bustling Broadway thoroughfare almost deserted. Most of the store windows had been emptied of their goods on display and were draped in black crepe. People gathered together in front of the newspaper offices, seeking consolation in groups and hopeful of hearing of the capture of Lincoln's assassin.

Americans spent Easter Sunday in mourning, not in celebrating the coming of spring and the resurrection of Christ. Ironically, only in the shock of his assassination did the people adequately understand and appreciate Lincoln as their nation's savior. Whitman would regard Lincoln's death as a religious, even Messianic event. "There is a cement to the whole people, subtler, more underlying, than anything in written constitution or courts or armies," he would later say, "—namely, the cement of a death identified thoroughly with that people, at its head and for its sake. Strange (is it not?) that battles, martyrs, agonies, blood, even assassination, should so condense—perhaps only really, lastingly condense— a Nationality."

Whitman cut his vacation short and hurried back to Washington, where on Monday all government offices were closed. Lincoln's body lay in state, for public viewing, first at the White House and then in the Capitol's rotunda, but Walt declined to look upon it. He did watch the great procession passing down Pennsylvania Avenue, part of the most impressive funeral ever conducted in America, preceding the return of Lincoln's remains to Illinois. Lincoln's favorite horse followed the caisson-hearse, his master's empty boots held in the stirrups. About thirty thousand civilians walked in the solemn parade along with thousands of marching soldiers and sailors, who carried reversed arms and furled banners.

Whitman felt that Lincoln's death saddened the soldiers more than anyone else. Their commander-in-chief, he had been confident of their mettle and persisted in seeking a worthy general to lead them from setbacks and stalemates to victory—which Grant had finally done. The soldiers had known and loved Lincoln, supporting his convictions with their lives. And now the President had paid for the Union's salvation with his own life, as if mysteriously fated as a final sacrificial victim. In "Hush'd Be the Camps To-day" Whitman recorded what he knew to be the soldiers' feelings on the day of the capital's memorial parade for Lincoln. And in it he imagined their request of himself:

> . . . Sing poet in our name,
> Sing of the love we bore him—because you, dweller in camps,
>   know it truly.

Already stirring within the poet were songs that told of his own great sorrow over the death of a man who, at a distance, had become a beloved friend and father-figure. The rapport and kinship Walt felt for the slain president lasted for the rest of his life. Lincoln embodied two of Whitman's deepest interests: the national hero and the meaning of death.

Whitman now wanted to speak out not only for himself, but to summarize the American people's grief. In the past he had likened the President to the captain of a ship sailing over turbulent seas toward a distant harbor. He had also compared a single soul's journey through life, or a nation's course through history, with the voyages of ships. The spirit-ship of the United States had been traveling across the perilous ocean of war, where huge waves had dashed against it, sometimes nearly engulfing or capsizing it; and all the while its courageous captain stayed at the helm, determined to bring his ship safely into port. At last the stormy passage was over and the peaceful harbor gained. A large crowd of grateful citizens waited, greeting ship and captain with cheers and bou-quets. But the ship of state came in without its master: the captain was dead.

In his desire to reproduce the nation's mood and possibly to make himself readily understood by everyone, Whitman composed his famous dirge, "O Captain! My Captain!":

O Captain! my captain! our fearful trip is done,
The ship has weather'd every rack, the prize we sought is won,
The port is near, the bells I hear, the people all exulting,
While follow eyes the steady keel, the vessel grim and daring;
But O heart! heart! heart!
O the bleeding drops of red,
Where on the deck my Captain lies,
Fallen cold and dead.

With its near-regular metrical rhythm and conventional stanzas and rhyming, the poem hardly typified Whitman's usual free-verse style, but it succeeded even better than he had hoped. First published in the *Saturday Press*, it soon began to be reprinted in anthologies and has been committed to memory by generations of students. It was the only poem Whitman wrote which became popular during his lifetime—sometimes a matter of annoyance to him, because he was not particularly proud of it. ("I'm almost sorry I ever wrote the poem," he remarked to a friend in his old age.)

During the period following Lincoln's death, Whitman—still a journalist by habit—collected anecdotes about the assassination, either directly from eyewitnesses or gleaned from the newspapers. (Walt would use the material in "The Death of Abraham Lincoln," a written lecture he read aloud many times in his later years.) Whitman also followed the accounts of the train trip taking Lincoln's body on the long ceremonial route toward Springfield and burial, which passed over the same ground that Lincoln had traversed four years before on his way to assuming the presidency. Walt was especially touched to learn of the hundreds of wreaths and flowers which mourners placed on the coffin as the cortege paused in large cities to allow the residents to pay their last respects.

In Brooklyn, when Walt had heard of Lincoln's death, the lilac buds—his childhood's cherished flowers—were just beginning to open. In Washington the flowers were in full bloom, for spring came earlier to the South. With Walt, lilacs made a lasting sensory connection with Lincoln's assassination. "By one of those caprices that enter and give tinge to events without being at all a part of them," he later observed, "I find myself always reminded of the great tragedy of that day by the sight and odor of these blossoms. It never fails."

Whitman now linked the funeral train's journey and the lilacs with two favorite symbols—bird and star—to shape a long poem in which the poet's mood moved from dark despair to an exulting acceptance of death as the final ornament and explanation to life: the traditional elegiac progression. "When Lilacs Last in the Dooryard Bloom'd" is usually considered Whitman's greatest poem. (Since nowhere in it did he mention the name Lincoln or the word President, the subject of the poet's loss might not be readily known to readers wholly unaware of when and why the poem was composed. Within *Leaves of Grass* itself, however, the poem appears in the section "Memories of President Lincoln.")

Whitman had long portrayed himself as a representative American, and now he cast himself in a chief mourner's role; within it he could embody and then assuage the sorrow felt by millions of citizens in the North and South.

Whitman knew that his sadness, his acute sense of loss, would return ever afterwards with springtime and lilacs.

> When lilacs last in the dooryard bloom'd,
> And the great star early droop'd in the western sky in the night,
> I mourn'd, and yet shall mourn with ever-returning spring.
>
> Ever-returning spring, trinity sure to me you bring,
> Lilac blooming perennial and drooping star in the west,
> And thought of him I love.

The cloud and star (actually, the planet Venus) which Whitman had observed during Lincoln's inauguration, earlier interpreted as good omens, now gloomily portended disaster. The star was Lincoln's spirit; and his death was the murky night-cloud that obscured it and took the poet captive.

> O powerful western fallen star!
> O shades of night—O moody, tearful night!
> O great star disappear'd—O the black murk that hides the star!
> O cruel hands that hold me powerless—O helpless soul of me!
> O harsh surrounding cloud that will not free my soul.

The poet figuratively plucked a sacrificial offering from the lilac bush of his childhood—symbolic of purity and the renewing power of springtime:

> In the dooryard fronting an old farm-house near the white-wash'd
>   palings,
> Stands the lilac-bush tall-growing with heart-shaped leaves of rich
>   green,
> With many a pointed blossom rising delicate, with the perfume
>   strong I love,
> With every leaf a miracle—and from this bush in the dooryard,
> With delicate-color'd blossoms and heart-shaped leaves of rich
>   green,
> A sprig with its flower I break.

Meanwhile, hidden in a swamp, a hermit thrush sang to voice all of nature's sorrow—also reflecting the poet's own urge to create a song that would sum up and then release his pent-up grief.

> Solitary the thrush,
> The hermit withdrawn to himself, avoiding the settlements,
> Sings by himself a song.

At the same time a coffin traveled across the land, "over the breast of the spring." The poet pictured the reception it received everywhere, and then gave his own floral tribute:

Coffin that passes through lanes and streets,
Through day and night with the great cloud darkening the land,
With the pomp of the inloop'd flags with the cities draped in black,
With the show of the States themselves as of crape-veil'd women
      standing,
With processions long and winding and the flambeaus of the night,
With the countless torches lit, with the silent sea of faces and the
      unbared heads,
With the waiting depot, the arriving coffin, and the sombre faces,
With dirges through the night, with the thousand voices rising
      strong and solemn,
With all the mournful voices of the dirges pour'd around the coffin,
The dim-lit churches and the shuddering organs—where amid these
      you journey,
With the tolling tolling bells' perpetual clang,
Here, coffin that slowly passes,
I give you my sprig of lilac.

The poet's "bouquet" for the deceased man actually was his
poem or song—and his offering was given not just for one man
but for all mortal men, and even for death itself.

(Nor for you, for one alone,
Blossoms and branches green to coffins all I bring,
For fresh as the morning, thus would I chant a song for you O sane
      and sacred death.

All over bouquets of roses,
O death, I cover you over with roses and early lilies,
But mostly and now the lilac that blooms the first,
Copious I break, I break the sprigs from the bushes,
With loaded arms I come, pouring for you,
For you and the coffins all of you O death.)

The poet now realized what the star in the west had been trying to warn him during the previous month. (Whitman often
connected stars with human events in his own brand of astrology.)

O western orb sailing the heaven,
Now I know what you must have meant as a month since I walk'd,

As I walk'd in silence the transparent shadowy night,
As I saw you had something to tell as you bent to me night after
        night,
As you droop'd from the sky low down as if to my side . . .

The poet then turned from the star to address the thrush, encouraging him to sing on but explaining that he could not yet
come and listen to him, for he was detained by "the lustrous
star," "my departing comrade"—and he still had his own song to
sing, his dirge for the deceased. He asked himself,

O how shall I warble myself for the dead one there I loved?
O how shall I deck my song for the large sweet soul that has gone?

        •   •   •

O what shall I hang on the chamber walls?
And what shall the pictures be that I hang on the walls,
To adorn the burial-house of him I love?

Probably thinking of those scenes painted on the walls of Egyptian Pharaohs' tombs—reminders of nature's bounties and human
activities—the poet proposed typical American vistas for the dead
President:

Pictures of growing spring and farms and homes,
With the Fourth-month eve at sundown, and the gray smoke lucid
        and bright,
With floods of the yellow gold of the gorgeous, indolent, sinking
        sun, burning, expanding the air,
With the fresh sweet herbage under foot, and the pale green leaves
        of the trees prolific,
In the distance the flowing glaze, the breast of the river, with a
        wind-dapple here and there,
With ranging hills on the banks, with many a line against the sky,
        and shadows,
And the city at hand with dwellings so dense, and stacks of
        chimneys,
And all the scenes of life and the workshops, and the workmen
        homeward returning.

Earth and its people had vital, abiding wonders, and while considering them the poet suddenly took a joyful and sensuous tone:

> Lo, the most excellent sun so calm and haughty,
> The violet and purple morn with just-felt breezes,
> The gentle soft-born measureless light,
> The miracle spreading bathing all, the fulfill'd noon,
> The coming eve delicious, the welcome night and the stars,
> Over my cities shining all, enveloping man and land.

The sun and the day had passed through their part of the circle; now night and the stars came. So, too, did a man live and then die, as part of the natural cycle within the universe. With new vigor the poet again called out to the thrush, asking him to continue his warbling:

> Sing on, sing on you gray-brown bird,
> Sing from the swamps, the recesses, pour your chant from the
> bushes,
> Limitless out of the dusk, out of the cedars and pines.
>
> Sing on dearest brother, warble your reedy song,
> Loud human song, with voice of uttermost woe.
>
> O liquid and free and tender!
> O wild and loose to my soul—O wondrous singer!

Finally the poet felt ready to face the dark cloud that had hidden the star and then enveloped the whole land:

> And I knew death, its thought, and the sacred knowledge of death.

The "thought" of death—the realization that all life was mortal—and the "sacred knowledge"—a conviction that death was a necessary part of the cosmic scheme—now became companions to the poet as he walked out in the evening and down to the swamp to listen to the shy bird singing his "carol of death":

Come lovely and soothing death,
Undulate round the world, serenely arriving, arriving,
In the day, in the night, to all, to each,
Sooner or later delicate death.

      •   •   •

Approach strong deliveress,
When it is so, when thou hast taken them I joyously sing the dead,
Lost in the loving floating ocean of thee,
Laved in the flood of thy bliss O death.

The bird sang on melodiously and jubilantly in the night, "tally-ing" the poet's own feelings. Then abruptly his singing aroused shocking visual memories in the poet:

And I saw askant the armies,
I saw as in noiseless dreams hundreds of battle-flags,
Borne through the smoke of the battles and pierc'd with missiles
    I saw them,

      •   •   •

I saw battle-corpses, myriads of them,
And the white skeletons of young men, I saw them,
I saw the debris and debris of all the slain soldiers of the war . . .

But these ghastly images of war's destructiveness vanished when the poet realized that the dead rested now in a peace well-earned, having given their lives to a cause in which they believed; it was their bereft families, the living, who continued to suffer.

The thrush's "powerful psalm" of death had miraculously helped the poet to accept not only Lincoln's death, but all the deaths caused by the Civil War. But the becalmed poet would never forget any of the elements that had contributed to this concilia-tion with mortality:

Yet each to keep and all, retrievements out of the night,
The song, the wondrous chant of the gray-brown bird,
And the tallying chant, the echo arous'd in my soul,
With the lustrous and drooping star with the countenance full of
      woe,
With the holders holding my hand nearing the call of the bird,

> Comrades mine and I in the midst, and their memory ever to keep,
> for the dead I loved so well,
> For the sweetest, wisest soul of all my days and lands—and this for
> his dear sake,
> Lilac and star and bird twined with the chant of my soul,
> There in the fragrant pines and cedars dusk and dim.

Thus Whitman closed his threnody for Lincoln, for the war's slain soldiers and civilians, and for death itself. Just as the body of the President had been taken across his mourning nation to its final resting place, so the poet's soul had passed through a catharsis period of terrible grief to reach at last a new and harmonious acceptance of mortality.

Drum-Taps was published in May of 1865 (too early to include Whitman's Lincoln elegies and the poems about the war's end). The volume contained fifty-three new poems, most of them about the Civil War: but some of them were written before it, and others, like "Pioneers! O Pioneers!", were not directly concerned with war.

After a five-year hiatus in book publication, Walt felt anxious to take up his staked claim as the "Poet of Democracy." Naturally he hoped that *Drum-Taps* would be well received by the critics; even more, he wanted it to become popular among ordinary readers, who would find in it some of their own wartime experiences and feelings. Walt's plea for a fair audience, contained within his new book, had a touching sincerity:

> Shut not your doors to me proud libraries,
> For that which was lacking on all your well-fill'd shelves, yet
> needed most, I bring,
> Forth from the war emerging, a book I have made . . .

Awaiting reactions to *Drum-Taps*, Whitman continued his clerkship in the Department of the Interior, and also recorded the events going on around him in "Washington City." In late May came the Grand Review of the Union Armies. Down the long, broad Pennsylvania Avenue for two days trooped solid ranks of men, twenty and more abreast, stretching out as far as Walt's eyes could see. George Whitman, back with his 51st Regiment now as a major, marched with them.

During the parade Walt saw the new President, Andrew Johnson. "He is very plain & substantial," he wrote his mother afterward; "it seemed wonderful that just that plain middling-sized ordinary man, dressed in black, without the least badge or ornament, should be the master of all these myriads of soldiers, the best that ever trode the earth. . . ." Whitman knew that Johnson had the difficult, if not impossible, task of reconciling the North and South and restoring the devastated, rebellious states to full status within the Union, as Lincoln had intended.

Watching this long procession of victorious soldiers, Whitman sensed the bellicose "Spirit Whose Work Is Done"—the spirit of liberty and democracy—marching among them:

> As your ranks, your immortal ranks, return, return from the battles,
> As the muskets of the young men yet lean over their shoulders,
> As I look on the bayonets bristling over their shoulders,
> As those slanted bayonets, whole forests of them appearing in the
>   distance, approach and pass on, returning home-
>   ward,
> Moving with steady motion, swaying to and fro to the right and
>   left . . .

And the poet asked this "spirit of dreadful hours" to infuse him with its elements before it too departed with the soldiers:

> Touch my mouth ere you depart, press my lips close,
> Leave me your pulses of rage—bequeath them to me—fill me with
>   currents convulsive,
> Let them scorch and blister out of my chants when you are gone,
> Let them identify you to the future in these songs.

Walt Whitman now intended to take on the task of reminding the nation, then and in the coming years, of how and why the Civil War was fought. The soldiers who died would become part of the "leaven'd soil" of America; the others were going back to work, in their cities and on farms and seacoasts. The soldiers' war was over, but Walt's idealistic battles with the hostile forces of oppression, injustice, prejudice, privilege, and disunity would still be waged. He would call out his songs to the fields and hills and rivers, to the rocks and trees and winds of America. Meanwhile, he intended to stay on in Washington. He had his salaried job there, and something in the very atmosphere seemed important to his poetic inspiration.

> The prairie draws me close, as the father to bosom broad the son,
> The Northern ice and rain that began me nourish me to the end,
> But the hot sun of the South is to fully ripen my songs.

Then Walt suffered an unexpected crisis. In mid-May of 1865 the Department of the Interior got a new Secretary. James Harlan, a former Methodist minister and Senator, immediately launched a thorough check on the loyalty and "moral character" of each of his employees. Someone possibly told him of Whitman's authorship of *Leaves of Grass,* or perhaps he discovered it for himself while inspecting Walt's desk one evening. At any rate, he read a copy of the book, containing Walt's handwritten revisions of a number of his poems.

Harlan was shocked. He swiftly sent a notice firing Whitman from his job. Baffled and upset, Walt took the official rejection to William O'Connor. He in turn hurried off to his friend J. H. Ashton, the Assistant Attorney General, who had initially obtained the position for Whitman.

The ever-flammable O'Connor guessed that Walt had been dismissed because of his connection with *Leaves of Grass*—though the letter had not said so. "I fancy that there never was before such an outpouring of impassioned eloquence in the presence of an audience of *one*," Ashton wrote later of the scene enacted in his office. "The wrong committed, as O'Connor said," he went on, "was the ignominious dismissal from the public service of the greatest poet America has produced, an offense against the honor and dignity of American letters, and against humanity itself as consecrated in 'Leaves of Grass.'"

Ashton's own feelings were hardly as vehement, but he did agree that a great harm had been done to Walt. He was annoyed that the United States government, through one of its cabinet members, had dismissed the poet from its employ as an "unworthy person"—although during the war it had welcomed this same man's unselfish services to its hospitalized soldiers.

Ashton went to see Harlan, who told him that not even the President himself could make him reinstate Whitman. Harlan became so adamant on the subject that only after extreme diplomacy did Ashton persuade him not to interfere with Whitman's employment elsewhere in the government. Ashton then arranged to have Walt transferred at once to his own department. "The result of it all," he said later, "was that the Government finally became the friend and protector, instead of the enemy and persecutor, of our poet."

Walt's move turned out to be advantageous. In the Attorney General's office Whitman was always treated with respect; nobody scorned or vilified him because of his poems. Indeed, the officials in the department often utilized Walt's literary talents by asking him to write papers, letters, and speeches for them.

In another pleasant repercussion, Walt received a sympathetic letter from a man named Van Rensellaer. He told of a time when he and a friend in Congress had been talking with Lincoln and Walt came strolling by. When the President wanted to know who he was, Van Rensellaer identified Whitman as the author of *Leaves of Grass*. "Mr. Lincoln didn't say anything," Walt's correspondent recounted, "but took a good long look till you were quite gone by. . . . 'Well,' he says, '*he* looks like a *man*.'" This was said by Lincoln in a special emphatic way which Van Rensellaer could only hint at. In his whole life Whitman surely never received so pleasing a compliment, even if given indirectly.

The story of Whitman's removal from office got into certain newspapers. The Brooklyn *Eagle* naturally seized upon it gleefully: "Our eccentric fellow citizen Walt Whitman has lost his position . . . under the general order discharging immoral persons. . . . Most of our readers probably know Whitman by sight; he used, in his own language to 'celebrate himself' so conspicuously along the streets of Brooklyn." The editorial acknowledged Walt's humane hospital work, but obviously regarded his governmental employment as a reward for services rendered in wartime. He was now provided, it told, with a desk in the Attorney General's office—"where we suppose they are not so particular about morals."

William O'Connor was not going to let the whole insulting episode pass him or Whitman by. Feeling an urge to cudgel Harlan verbally, he wrote the fiercely defensive pamphlet, *The Good Gray Poet*—the title, for better or for worse, to stick with Whitman forevermore. In his diatribe O'Connor effectively disproved the charges of immorality and indecency against both Whitman personally and his poetry. In the process O'Connor made Walt a saintlike character even nobler and more perfect than Whitman had willed himself to be.

At the same time O'Connor used his essay to discuss the issue of censorship of literary material pertaining to sex. Courageously he mocked the extreme prudery of the century, in which Bowdler had purified Shakespeare for Victorian readers by excising supposedly offensive passages. O'Connor asserted that Whitman's occasional eroticisms characterized a universal poetic genius that also appeared in portions of the Bible, Homer's epics, Dante, Shakespeare, and Byron. Such passages demonstrated the richness of the poet's language and the depth of his feelings; they were also essential in conveying his full meaning. Those who misinterpreted or distorted Whitman's erotic poetry were just numbskulls, the impatient O'Connor concluded.

Meanwhile, Whitman was diligently finishing up a group of new poems gathered under the title of *Sequel to Drum-Taps*. Notable among them were his Lincoln elegies. The twenty-four-page printed booklet was put together with as yet unbound sheets of *Drum-Taps* to make a single volume.

Neither *Drum-Taps*, by itself or with its sequel, attracted the critical attention, whether positive or negative, received by the first three editions of *Leaves of Grass*. Nobody seemed very eager to review or buy it. A short flurry of interest was awakened in

Whitman's poetry following the publication of O'Connor's defense, but it rapidly subsided.

When *Drum-Taps* was reviewed at all, it generally evoked the sort of disdainful criticism which had usually greeted *Leaves of Grass*. Such was the critique appearing in the *Nation*, written by the young novelist-to-be Henry James. "To become adopted as a national poet," he wrote, "it is not enough to discard everything in particular and to accept everything in general, to amass crudity upon crudity, to discharge the undigested contents of your blotting-book into the lap of the public. You must respect the public which you address; for it has taste, if you have not." (Later in his career, James was to find, to his great surprise, that much of Whitman's poetry deeply moved him—almost in spite of his aristocratically discriminating taste.)

Which were worse? Denigrating remarks or years of neglect? Used to them both though Whitman was by now, he was hurt by the failure of *Drum-Taps* and its *Sequel* to gain a wide readership. The poor reception also bothered him because he knew that no other writers in the period just after the Civil War had published anything better, in either poetry or prose. Into his war poems Walt had put so much of his real feelings and of his actual experiences in camp among the soldiers or in the hospitals. Perhaps busy people just wanted to forget the war scenes now; nor did they wish to be reminded of Lincoln's death.

But at least in Washington Walt enjoyed a small coterie of friends who buttressed his ego against rebuffs or a disinterested public. Almost every evening he went to the O'Connors' home. Always among the guests were Whitman admirers—his personal friends or people who had asked to meet him. ("We talked of everything that the human mind could conceive," Charles Eldridge recalled later of those years.) They all suspected a conspiracy of silence or condemnation toward Whitman's poetry within the literary establishment, which deliberately cast aspersions upon his morality, misread his poems or quoted lines out of context, and prevented the publication of his poetry in the "respectable" magazines. These "Whitmanites" (someone later gave them the epithet "Whitmaniacs," and indeed there was a rabid element in their loyalty) sustained Walt's self-confidence and kept him good company, but sometimes they went to extremes in their hero-worship. William O'Connor, for example, published a thinly disguised story about Whitman in which he likened his protagonist to Christ.

Walt had a standing invitation for pancake breakfasts on Sundays at the Burroughs' house on Capitol Hill. (The Senate Office Building now occupies the site of the little farm where John raised pigs and chickens, milked his cow, and grew vegetables and fruits.) To Ursula's annoyance, Walt invariably arrived late. But so genial was he when he finally appeared, and so unmindful of the distress he had inadvertently caused, that his tardiness was quickly forgotten—until the following Sunday morning. After a filling meal, John and Walt walked around town, discussing the many topics of keen mutual interest. (Burroughs, who described the hermit thrush to Walt, had certainly been responsible for the poet's choice of that bird as the "death carol" singer in "When Lilacs Last in the Dooryard Bloom'd.")

O'Connor was Whitman's comrade-in-arms: fervid, fierce, stimulating. In a calmer, steadier way John Burroughs proved as good and loyal a friend. O'Connor was especially responsive to the social and political portions of Whitman's poetry, while Burroughs was drawn to its lyrical and philosophical passages, particularly those pertaining to nature. O'Connor and Burroughs probably interpreted Whitman's poetry more skillfully than he himself did or could, and through the years they made gallant efforts to widen his readership by writing sensitive and knowledgeable articles about Whitman and his poems.

John Burroughs too prepared a book about his friend: *Notes on Walt Whitman as Poet and Person.* (Whitman perhaps wrote sizable parts of it; certainly he went over the material carefully to be sure John had said the proper things.) As though watching some specimen of a rare avian species, John observed Walt; very early in their association he had noted details of Whitman's appearance and behavior. "There is something indescribable in his look, in his eye, as in that of the mother of many children," he said. And he tried to put into words the odd or uncanny aspect about Whitman that made him truly different from ordinary people. This something, he decided, was revealed primarily in Walt's gray-blue eyes. Though beautiful and expressive, now and then an expression in them almost frightened John and caused him to draw away. "I cannot explain it—whether it is more, or less, than human," Burroughs wrote. "It is as if the Earth itself looked at me—dumb, yearning, relentless, immodest, unhuman. If the impersonal elements and forces were concentrated in an eye, that would be it. It is not piercing, but absorbing and devouring—the pupil expanded, the lid slightly drooping, and the eye set and fixed."

Deep and firmly rooted though Walt's friendships with O'Connor and Burroughs were, they were basically intellectual. For a different sort of relationship—simple, relaxed, affectionate—Walt relied upon a young horse-car conductor named Peter Doyle. An ex-Confederate soldier, Pete was like the working-class men with whom Whitman had often consorted in New York when shunning salons and literary conversations.

During his hospital visits Whitman had become attached to particular men whose characters appealed to him, and when they returned to their camps or homes he had greatly missed them. Now, as if replacing all the departed soldiers, Walt established a close companionship with Doyle. He helped Pete on the job by taking fares, and in odd hours they sauntered around the capital in easy fellowship, occasionally roistering among Pete's friends. With Pete, Walt did not have to play the Good Gray Poet; he knew that Pete liked him simply for himself, not for any special poetic genius he possessed. Whitman also recognized that Pete did not admire whatever small bits of *Leaves of Grass* he had managed to read. In a letter to Pete he guessed Doyle's opinion of the book: "a great mess of crazy talk and hard words all tangled up, without sense or meaning."

Walt had a gentle, plain-talking, fatherly way with Doyle—quite probably how he would have been with a son of his own. He took interest in all matters large and small in Pete's life, sometimes fussing over him like a brood-hen. When out of town, he wrote letters regularly (to be posthumously published as a book entitled *Calamus*) in which he told jokes, sent money, advised or admonished Pete, talked of bringing him bouquets of wildflowers, and described what he had been seeing and doing. Walt could be pleased that his attachment was reciprocal. (And though there is evidence that Walt's feelings for Pete were occasionally bothered by excessive "adhesiveness," the overt relationship apparently remained normal.)

Most of Walt's intellectual, sophisticated associates in Washington could not comprehend his attachment to Peter Doyle; they had nothing at all in common with Pete except Walt's friendship. The perceptive Burroughs, however, viewed Doyle in a less scornful way. "He was an inarticulate Walt Whitman," he later observed, having noticed a rough similarity in basic character, like that of father and son, between the aging poet and the amiable, unpretentious young horse-car driver.

In August of 1866 Walt took another vacation from his job. He went up to New York to visit his family and to supervise the printing of yet another—the fourth—edition of *Leaves of Grass,* "that unkillable work," as he called it. As usual, it would receive little attention from the critics or the public, but Walt realized that he must keep on publishing his book—or it would perish.

This new version included both *Drum-Taps* and its sequel, but they were added as appendages, not integrated with the rest of the text. However, Walt had inserted various references to the recent war into his revisions of other poems. He continued his practice of altering or eliminating not only passages which seemed inferior, but also some which perhaps had already exposed too much of him, psychologically. In this edition too Whitman, with both new poems and old, concluded many verbs and participles with "-'d"—an orthographic peculiarity now a trademark of his poetry.

Busy though he was with job and friends and poetry, Walt did not neglect the soldiers who still lingered in the Washington hospitals. These men perhaps needed more cheering up than the wartime invalids had, for many of them were considered hopeless cases. Walt visited often and frequently provided special treats, such as the festive Christmas dinner he arranged for a group of them in 1866.

Walt was always solicitous too with his mother. In her old age and increasing frailty, she found more reasons than ever to be worried about, or take offense at, the behavior of her children, their spouses, and her grandchildren. . . . George must be courting a girl, she reported to Walt; he was preoccupied and away from home a lot—and irritable whenever she asked for a little spending money. Yet how gay and generous he had been while a soldier! . . . Jeff and Matt were still spendthrifts and runabouts; they had a place of their own now, but often dumped their two rambunctious little girls upon their grandmother—and much as she loved them, her patience was wearing thin. . . . Feeble-minded Eddie at least could make himself useful doing chores around the house, but Jeff unkindly refused ever to give him a meal at his own home because of Eddie's sloppy table manners. In fact, Jeff wanted to "put him away," as they had done earlier with Jesse. (As for poor Jesse, he would soon die in the mental asylum—and, before his family knew about it, be buried in a pauper's grave. Mrs. Whitman naturally would take his death hard. "Of course Walt if he has done ever so wrong he was my first born," she wrote her second and oldest-surviving son.) . . . Hannah and her husband kept up their epistolary barrage from Vermont; but though perpetually complaining, neither budged from their married martyrdom. . . . Only Walt and Mary, who was busy and happy with her family in Greenport, Long Island, caused their mother no distress. Patiently, Walt wrote back sympathetic letters, offering whatever advice and encouragement he could without arousing further animosity within the family. He also regularly sent money home to help his mother pay her expenses. In spite of his absorption in poem-making, Walt was not wholly impractical and irresponsible.

When Whitman received a job promotion with a raise in salary, he left his unheated garret and moved into a small but comfortable attic room in a boardinghouse. He really spent little time there, however. During leisure hours, if he was not at the O'Connors' or the Burroughs' or visiting other friends or strolling around town

with Pete, Walt was reading or writing or revising poems (an endless process with him) in his office at the Treasury Building, where
the Attorney General's department was located. Walt had access
to the building, always warm in winter, at all hours. He could
order whatever books he wanted from its library, then read them
in comfort by the light of a newfangled gas tube called an "astral
lamp."

Happy with his immediate surroundings, Whitman was not so
satisfied with the conditions in Washington, D. C., itself, where
the notorious Reconstruction Era had commenced. Lincoln had
wanted the postwar period to be a time for cooperative reassess-
ment of human values and readjustment in economic interests of
the two diverse and divided sections of the nation. It would
necessarily involve restraint of emotions on both sides—as Lincoln
had described it in his second Inaugural Address, "with malice
toward none; with charity for all." But Lincoln's death had made
a calm and sensible approach to reuniting the nation virtually
impossible. The North did not feel conciliatory; the South's pride
had been severely wounded, its livelihood nearly wrecked.

Although few Radical Republicans had truly mourned Lincoln,
they now used his assassination to satisfy the Northern demand
for vengeance over the war's cost in lives and dollars and the
reckless killing of the Union's leader. The Radicals at first welcomed Andrew Johnson as a "pushover" President, but when he
tried to implement Lincoln's moderate plan for renewing relations
between the states, he encountered angry opposition from Congress. The new President, with none of Lincoln's wily diplomacy
or self-control, took his stand bluntly and stubbornly. The heavily
Republican Congress opposed most of his programs and began to
do whatever it wanted, enacting severe measures against the
Southern states. They divided the South into five provinces ruled
over by military governors as if conquered countries, removed
voting rights from many white citizens while granting suffrage
to all male ex-slaves (without yet allowing Negroes in the North to
vote), and imposed an onerous taxation which discouraged the
rebuilding of cities, farmlands, industries, and railroads. Northern
"carpetbagger" politicians and business speculators—many of

whom had already profited from the war—invaded the South with schemes of quickly seizing political power through manipulations of Negro votes and of amassing fortunes by investing in crucial industries and land.

Secretary of War Edwin M. Stanton, who supervised the military "occupation" of the South, especially incurred the President's dislike. In 1868, when Johnson tried to oust Stanton from his cabinet, most Congressmen and Senators were furious; they decided they had had enough of Johnson. In the impeachment trial the President was spared expulsion by a single vote.

Throughout President Johnson's ordeal in office Whitman sympathized with him. Walt realized that he was trying to make a just peace and to heal the nation's wounds—and that probably no single human being, even Lincoln himself, could have managed Reconstruction without angering and alienating many Americans.

The new magazine *Galaxy* printed a few poems by Walt Whitman. Its editors then asked the poet to write several articles that would effectively answer some serious charges against American democracy recently made by Thomas Carlyle. In "Shooting Niagara: And After?" the Scottish philosopher had dourly predicted that democracy would destroy civilization. Whitman, as democracy's staunch advocate, naturally accepted the assignment.

As Walt began systematically to scrutinize American society, what he mainly observed seemed neither praiseworthy nor promising. He may have been disgruntled in part because the American people had neglected to recognize him as a bona fide prophet; but history largely confirms his opinions of the post-Civil War period. If anybody harbors the misconception that Whitman had only praises for his nation's political and economic systems and took a roseate view of its future, he should read *Democratic Vistas*, the title for Whitman's three magazine articles combined into one essay and published in book form in 1871. His most important prose work, the long piece makes many a forceful point, and is surprisingly relevant to democracy and culture in the United States of the present day.

Whitman's first two articles, "Democracy" and "Personalism," were printed in *Galaxy* in late 1867 and early 1868. A third, "Literature," was eventually declined, probably because of subscribers' protests over Whitman's previous commentaries on the state of the nation. A few readers, however, had been most interested in what Whitman had to say. Bronson Alcott wrote an approving letter to Walt. He also recorded his enthusiasm in his journal: "Read 'Personalism' again after day's work. Verily, great grand doctrine, and great grand Walt, grown since I saw him in his Brooklyn garret in 185- . . . . Another American besides Thoreau and Emerson." (Alcott was to incorporate Walt's concept of "Personalism" into his own philosophy.)

Most of Whitman's poems about democracy, real or ideal, had rung with a positive, optimistic tone. Now his prose treatments of the same subject—allowing him a wider range to ramble, rant, digress, expand—were markedly, even savagely critical. Yet Whitman also made numerous proposals—most of them visionary rather than practicable—to offset conditions which he regarded as deplorable or dangerous.

The somber essay showed a dramatic mood change from the hopeful, oft-ecstatic attitude of the poet-prophet who, some fifteen years before, had written the Preface to the 1855 edition of *Leaves of Grass*. Nevertheless, Whitman reaffirmed in it his basic principles; he amply avowed his faith in the democratic spirit and process and his confidence in the average man, product of American democracy and type-progenitor of its future citizenry. But more than ever before, Whitman realized that democracy must be constantly re-examined and worked at; and unless it was—and by the right people—it might soon go disastrously astray. (Aspects of his new forebodings now crept into his new poems and altered versions of old poems, such as "By Blue Ontario's Shore.")

Walt had good reason to feel disillusioned, for he was witnessing the start of the most corrupt epoch in American history. He had believed that the Civil War was fought for a great cause: the preservation of the youthful Union with its democratic principles, along with granting freedom and equality and dignity to all men. The soldiers themselves, whether of North or South, had reinforced his belief in the essential goodness, even greatness, of Americans—a "grand, common stock."

Whitman was horrified to discover that the war to some Americans merely meant furthering purely selfish, materialistic motives. In the war's aftermath came the "Gilded Age" in which many people tended to forget all humane ideals and thought only of their own advancements, profits, and pleasures. As a government employee, Whitman learned much from what he saw for himself and from what he heard from his associates. Avarice, cynicism, hypocrisy, and self-indulgence had seized the nation. Looking upon these corruptions with an irate and melancholy eye, Walt penned in his *Democratic Vistas* a furious indictment of the times. "Society, in these States, is cankered, crude, superstitious and rotten," he intoned. "I say we had best look our times and land searchingly in the face, like a physician diagnosing some deep disease. Never was there, perhaps, more hollowness at heart than at present, and here in the United States. Genuine belief seems to have left us." This disorder, he found, had infected all classes of Americans. (It would soon reach its fever peak during the two administrations of Ulysses S. Grant.)

Hushed now was the jingoistic tone of the young journalist Walter Whitman, Jr. Whitman now feared that New World democracy, despite its obvious materialistic progress and its granting new political and economic opportunities to the ordinary man, could prove "the most tremendous failure of time" when it came to producing a "great moral and religious civilization"—the only justification, to him, of a great material one. And like a social pathologist Walt turned his "moral microscope" upon Americans, sketching various signs of degeneracy which had accompanied the decline and fall of past cultures. "Confess that everywhere, in shop, street, church, theatre, barroom, official chair, are pervading flippancy and vulgarity, low cunning, infidelity," he said, "—everywhere the youth puny, impudent, foppish, prematurely ripe—everywhere an abnormal libidinousness, unhealthy forms, male, female, painted, padded, dyed, chignoned, muddy complexions, bad blood, the capacity for motherhood decreasing or deceased, shallow notions of beauty, with a range of manners, or rather lack of manners . . . probably the meanest to be seen in the world."

Many Americans could now read and write; and Walt described with a journalist's relish the new printing presses for mass publications. But of what good were these improvements and inventions? He complained that most writers simply aimed "to amuse, to titillate, to pass away time, to circulate the news, and rumors of news, to rhyme, and read rhyme." He still found the "main things" woefully lacking in his country's literature, which ideally should permeate "the whole mass of American mentality, taste, belief, breathing into it a new breath of life, giving it decision, affecting politics far more than the popular superficial suffrage . . . radiating, begetting appropriate teachers, schools, manners." Such writings could establish "a religious and moral character beneath the political and productive and intellectual bases of the States." He pointed to the great classics of the past to demonstrate his thesis.

Not surprisingly, Whitman believed that the best way of renewing the moral conscience of Americans, and of re-establishing a necessary faith in democracy, would come from "a cluster of mighty poets, artists, teachers, fit for us, national expressers, comprehending and infusing for the men and women of the States, what is universal, native, common to all, inland and seaboard, northern and southern." But most writers of the age, he saw, were inadequate to this all-important task—partly because they disdained to write for and about the common people, whom these "literats" judged "ungrammatical, untidy, and their sins gaunt and ill bred." Naturally, their books tended to make "mostly critical and querulous men," rather than citizens with a sympathetic concern for others.

Whitman did not deny that the average man had his imperfections. He had studied "the specimens and vast collections of the ignorant, the credulous, the unfit and uncouth, the incapable, and the very low and poor." Nevertheless, his overall impression was positive. "When I mix with these interminable swarms of alert, turbulent, good-natured, independent citizens, mechanics, clerks, young persons—at the idea of this mass of men, so fresh and free, so loving and so proud, a singular awe falls upon me." And he felt sorry indeed that so few fellow writers had bothered to absorb and praise this democratic spirit.

Walt also knew that anyone who thought himself superior to the common people would find it hard to believe that a nation's politics could ever be improved by "absorbing such morbid collections and qualities therein." He recognized that there would always be "numbers of solid and reflective citizens" who would never get over their distrust of democracy. He himself readily admitted "the appalling dangers of universal suffrage in the United States." But he was confident that democracy—like nature's soil, with its "cosmical, antiseptic power"—would gradually work all sorts of people, as a fertile compost, into its ground; they could contribute their own special nutriments to the ensemble, making democracy all the richer and stronger.

Whitman warned that the greatest danger to any nation was "having certain portions of the people set off from the rest by a line drawn—they are not privileged as others, but degraded, humiliated, made of no account." And he knew that democracy "looks with suspicious, ill-satisfied eye upon the very poor, the ignorant, and on those out of business. She asks for men and women with occupations, well-off, owners of houses and acres, and with cash in the bank. . . ." Proposing "a more universal ownership of property, general homesteads, general comfort—a vast, intertwining reticulation of wealth," he regarded the practical, energetic, and materialistic character of Americans fundamental in preparing the results he demanded.

Social reformers, even revolutionists, Walt welcomed to "counterbalance the inertness and fossilism making so large a part of human institutions. The latter will always take care of themselves—the danger being that they rapidly tend to ossify us." Though radicals might be overzealous or fanatical and make "inconsiderate appeals," their free activity was as fundamental to democracy "as circulation to air." Whitman found a function for such agitation. "A nation like ours, in a sort of geological formation state, trying continually new experiments . . . is not served by the best men only, but sometimes more by those that provoke it—by the combats they arouse. Thus national rage, fury, discussion, etc., better than content. Thus, also, the warning signals, invaluable for after times." Declaring that he knew of nothing grander than "a well-contested American national election," Walt encouraged young men to engage in politics: "Always inform yourself; always do the best you can; always vote." But he also advised them to steer clear of political parties.

Despite certain reservations about democracy in America, Whitman maintained that the "democratic formula is the only safe and preservative one for coming times." He called democracy "a training school for first-class men" as well as "the best training for immortal souls." In a democracy, "man, properly trained in sanest, highest freedom, may and must become a law, and series of laws, unto himself, surrounding and providing for, not only his own personal control, but all his relations to other individuals, and to the State." Other times had had their own theories and conditions; but for today, for the modern world, democracy was the only plan worth establishing—with the hope that it would become self-perpetuating, like nature's laws. Christ had made all men equal in the "moral-spiritual" sphere; democracy now was putting them all on the same broad platform in social, economic, and political terms—each with a right to be free, prideful, comfortable, and happy.

Since a good citizen was a distinct person as well as part of the mass of men, the design of democracy must include and support equally the individual's own development and his participation in society. Everyone should have both a personal identity and a group function. "Our task is to reconcile them," said Whitman. One always had to struggle against a conformity to group demands or expectations: "To prune, gather, trim, conform, and ever cram and stuff, and be genteel and proper, is the pressure of our days."

Whitman called his own type of individualism "Personalism." It was basically a religious conception, because Walt asked each person to identify and privately cultivate his soul, to counterbalance the leveling tendencies in a democratic society. "Only in the perfect uncontamination and solitariness of individuality may the spirituality of religion positively come forth at all," Whitman said. "Only here, and on such terms, the meditation, the devout ecstasy, the soaring flight. . . . Alone, and silent thought and awe, and aspiration—and then the interior consciousness, like a hitherto unseen inscription, in magic ink, beams out its wondrous lines to the sense." In Whitman's own soul this Personalism expressed a particular aim: "To take expression, to incarnate, to endow a literature with grand and archetypal models—to fill with pride and love the utmost capacity, and to achieve spiritual meanings, and suggest the future."

At the same time, Whitman also encouraged the new nineteenth-century spirit of scientific inquiry. "Side by side with the unflagging stimulation of the elements of religion and conscience," he asserted, "must henceforth move with equal sway science, absolute reason, and the general proportionate development of the whole man. These scientific facts, deductions, are divine too—precious counted parts of moral civilization, and, with physical health, indispensable to it, to prevent fanaticism."

With science's help, Whitman proposed, people should also start to beget superior offspring. "Parentage must consider itself in advance," he said, anticipating eugenics. And, like a health cultist, he described the attributes of his model American: "A clear-blooded, strong-fibered physique is indispensable; the questions of food, drink, air, exercise, assimilation, digestion, can never be intermitted. Out of these we descry a well-begotten selfhood . . . of the bodily figure, the movements easy, the complexion showing the best blood, somewhat flushed, breast expanded, an erect attitude, a voice whose sound outvies music, eyes of calm and steady gaze, yet capable also of flashing—and a general presence that holds its own in the company of the highest." This "native personality"—Whitman's idealized self, obviously—would be truly equipped to carry forward "the banner of the divine pride of man in himself."

Nor did Walt neglect women in his recommendations for an improved citizenry. After all, their role was "to endow the birthstock of a New World." He wanted democracy to construct its own type of women, "extricated from this daze, this fossil and unhealthy air which hangs about the word *lady*." They should be raised "to become the robust equals, workers, and, it may be, even practical and political deciders with the men." Women were superior in their "divine maternity." But to achieve equality with men in other matters, Walt required that they "give up toys and fictions, and launch forth, as men do, amid real, independent, stormy life." Here he supported in principle the feminist movement in mid-nineteenth century America which advocated women's rights to vote, own property, receive higher educations, and occupy professional positions.

Above all else in *Democratic Vistas*, Walt offered his vision of democracy as an ideal still to be realized. "Far, far, indeed, stretch, in distance, our Vistas! How much is still to be disentangled, freed! How long it takes to make this American world see that it is, in itself, the final authority and reliance." He knew now that he would never see the ultimate triumph of democracy: "Not for us the joy of entering at last the conquered city—not ours the chance ever to see with our own eyes the peerless power and splendid *éclat* of the democratic principle, arrived at meridian, filling the world with effulgence and majesty." But he found consolation that he had been among those who had known "the prophetic vision, the joy of being tossed in the brave turmoil of these times—the promulgation and the path, obedient, lowly reverent to the voice, the gesture of the god, or holy ghost, which others see not, hear not—with the proud consciousness that amid whatever clouds, seductions, or heart-wearying postponements, we have never deserted, never despaired, never abandoned the faith."

Walt Whitman saw himself now as a pathfinder to democracy for the future generations—and described his role in "Thou Mother with Thy Equal Brood":

> The paths to the house I seek to make,
> But leave to those to come the house itself.

If in America Walt Whitman was generally ignored or scorned, in Europe in the late 1860s he began to be widely accepted as the best spokesman for American democracy.

Walt Whitman's poetry was first "discovered" abroad by the

English. Copies of the first edition of *Leaves of Grass* had been introduced into England in 1856. Auctioned off by a literary peddler, one of these books came into the hands of the poet and critic William Michael Rossetti. (Rossetti had helped to found the avant-garde Pre-Raphaelite Brotherhood of English writers and painters whose rallying motto was "art for art's sake." Their odd dress, attitudes, and behavior—just as with Pfaff's Bohemian circle in the United States—aroused both alarm and derision among the prim and practical Victorian society around them, against which they were obviously reacting.) Rossetti became fascinated with Whitman's poetry. He passed the copy of *Leaves of Grass* around to his friends, but few of them cared for it. Rossetti, off to other enthusiasms, put it aside.

Ten years later, Rossetti's interest in Whitman was rekindled when he read William O'Connor's *The Good Gray Poet* and also met Moncure Conway, the friend of Emerson who had visited Walt right after the publication of the first *Leaves of Grass*. (Conway reported on that early encounter in an article published in 1866 in a respectable English journal; Walt, maintaining that it was erroneous in parts, nevertheless was pleased with the unexpected attention.)

Conway lent Rossetti John Burroughs' new book, *Notes on Walt Whitman as Poet and Person,* and also the new (fourth, or 1866-67) edition of *Leaves of Grass*. Rossetti wrote an essay on Whitman which was published in the London *Chronicle* in the summer of 1867. In it he outspokenly called Whitman's volume "incomparably the largest poetic work of our period," and declared that in time the American poet would rank with Homer and Shakespeare in reflecting his own time and place. With Whitman's permission, Rossetti prepared a special selection of his poems for English publication. Rossetti's choices were made deliberately to avoid offending new readers, thereby hopefully to increase the American poet's chance for a favorable reception from the English critics and reading public.

When *Poems of Walt Whitman* appeared in England in early 1868, it received far more balanced and fair reviews than Whitman's poetry had ever encountered in his homeland. Rossetti did not wish to be Walt's apostle; he had not accepted Whitman's artistry wholly and uncritically—as his introduction to the collection explicitly stated. He lauded Whitman as "a master of words and sounds," "one of the huge . . . forces of our time," and "the most sonorous poetic voice . . . of actual and prospective democracy." But he tempered these praises with reservations. Whitman spoke occasionally "of gross things in gross, crude, and plain terms"; some of his words were "absurd or ill-constructed"; and his style was often "obscure, fragmentary, and agglomerative." Whitman's apparent egoism also bothered him: "His self-assertion is boundless."

That Whitman's English editor noted possible faults, rather than spouting a fervent, unquestioning adoration, helped to put critics more at ease. They could respond to whatever was unique and good, moving and powerful in Whitman's poetry—instead of feeling compelled to search out a god's clay feet in order to smash them. Though Whitman may have been a bit vexed over Rossetti's selective and somewhat reserved approach, he was admirably served in this English introduction. Rossetti's initial efforts were going to be instrumental in gaining Whitman favorable opinions, ardent attention, and even economic support in England and on the Continent in the coming years.

The English poet Algernon Swinburne added his own eager discovery of Whitman to Rossetti's. (Later, he would rescind this youthful enthusiasm.) In a published essay he compared Whitman favorably with the prophetic English poet William Blake. He called the long Lincoln elegy "the most sweet and sonorous nocturne ever chanted in the church of the world"; "Out of the Cradle Endlessly Rocking" he declared to be "the most lovely and wonderful thing I have read for years and years . . . there is such beautiful skill and subtle power in every word of it." To him Whitman represented the democratic spirit so long dormant in Europe, ever awaiting fulfillment, and needing Whitman's encouragement. Soon Swinburne would write a long ode—"To Walt Whitman in America."

Send but a song oversea for us,
    Heart of their hearts who are free,
Heart of their singer, to be for us
    More than our singing can be;
Ours, in the tempest at error,
With no light but the twilight of terror;
    Send us a song oversea!

This sympathetic interest and intelligent understanding beginning to emanate from the Old World must have cheered Whitman considerably. For long years he had criticized Americans for being subservient to English literary verdicts and writing styles, to the detriment of developing their own national literature. Now, oddly enough, this American tendency to look toward England would start to work in his favor.

Sail forth—steer for the deep waters only,
Reckless O soul, exploring, I with thee,
and thou with me . . .

X

STEER FOR THE DEEP WATERS ONLY

(1869-1879)

By the time Walt Whitman reached his fiftieth year, the meridian of middle age and midway point in a century, he often seemed restlessly eager to be off and away on some long journey, with his soul as a companion:

> Darest thou now O soul,
> Walk out with me toward the unknown region,
> Where neither ground is for the feet nor any path to follow?

> No map there, nor guide,
> Nor voice sounding, nor touch of human hand,
> Nor face with blooming flesh, nor lips, nor eyes, are in that land.

The poems Whitman now wrote increasingly emphasized matters of the spirit rather than the body. He had so often praised the body's physiognomy from "tip to toe"; but now he seldom dwelled upon youth's delights or the vigor of manhood. He himself no longer possessed physical exuberance, and for some years he had looked much older than his actual age—as if the very intensity of his inner and outer lives sped up the aging process.

The symptoms of Walt's malaise today sound like those of chronic hypertension. However calm and relaxed he might appear to others, he had long been overtaxing his nervous system by deliberately projecting a "magnetic personality" to attract and inspire others. Inwardly, too—and of this his poems gave sufficient proof—he was often beset by depressions, unacceptable urges, and thwarted literary ambitions. Above all, the Civil War and its aftermath had taken a heavy toll on Walt's health and spirits—which he himself recognized and admitted. He took frequent leaves from his job, going home to Brooklyn to recuperate, these visits often corresponding conveniently with publishing projects.

As his body faltered, Whitman was becoming a specialist in the soul—whatever that might be. More and more to him one's earthly career seemed only preparatory for an afterlife. "The personality of mortal life is most important with reference to the immortal, the unknown, the spiritual, the only permanently real, which as the ocean waits for and receives the rivers, waits for us each and all," Whitman wrote in *Democratic Vistas*.

The imagery of ocean, ships, and sea voyages appeared in Whitman's prose and predominated his new poetry. Walt's spring fever in "Warble for Lilac-Time" became an escapism of the spirit:

> Thou, soul, unloosen'd—the restlessness after I know not what;
> Come, let us lag here no longer, let us be up and away!
> O if one could but fly like a bird!
> O to escape, to sail forth as in a ship!
> To glide with thee O soul, o'er all, in all, as a ship o'er the
> waters . . .

This new "spiritual" phase in Whitman's life and feeling emerged most notably in "Passage to India," the last poem to rank among his masterworks. Composed in 1868-69, it ostensibly extolled three recent engineering achievements: the finally successful laying of the Atlantic cable which connected Europe and America by a heavily insulated telegraph wire; the meeting of the east and west transcontinental railroads in Utah; and the completion of the Suez Canal, which gave Europe the direct ocean route to India and the Orient sought for centuries.

Whitman praised the modern scientific advances which had made this progress possible; but then he showed that he was really interested in spiritual values behind these accomplishments:

> A worship new I sing,
> You captains, voyagers, explorers, yours,
> You engineers, you architects, machinists, yours,
> You, not for trade or transportation only,
> But in God's name, and for thy sake O soul.

The new passages, new joinings, linked the world now in a close network of mutual concerns. Technology, by reaching out to Asia, had actually led mankind back into its past, to the lands and times where people were absorbed in the needs and quests of the human soul. And so the poet himself now urged his own soul to make a voyage toward the East—"to primal thought," "to realms of budding bibles"—especially to India, home of soul-oriented Hinduism and Buddhism.

> O soul, repressless, I with thee and thou with me,
> Thy circumnavigation of the world begin,
> Of man, the voyage of his mind's return,
> To reason's early paradise,
> Back, back to wisdom's birth, to innocent intuitions,
> Again with fair creation.

He desired to go away with his soul and sail freely and fearlessly across the world's seas—or through the universe:

> Passage, immediate passage! the blood burns in my veins!
> Away O soul! hoist instantly the anchor!
> Cut the hawsers—haul out—shake out every sail!
> Have we not stood here like trees in the ground long enough?
> Have we not grovel'd here long enough, eating and drinking like mere brutes?
> Have we not darken'd and dazed ourselves with books long enough?

Sail forth—steer for the deep waters only,
Reckless O soul, exploring, I with thee, and thou with me,
For we are bound where mariner has not yet dared to go,
And we will risk the ship, ourselves and all.

O brave soul!
O farther farther sail!
O daring joy, but safe! are they not all the seas of God?
O farther, farther, farther sail!

The individual's life-to-death journey, once contained within
the harbor in "Crossing Brooklyn Ferry," was now enacted on the
high seas. A sailing ship with an immortal soul on board left the
safe port for unknown, far-distant shores, outward- and eternity-
bound. No more did the poet take a bird's soaring flights over
solid land to witness and visit the complex realities of nature and
humanity below. Instead, the vast, mystic ocean of the universe
beckoned him, and upon it he intended to float, with the once-
widespread wings of his imagination now become ship's sails.

During the late 1860s and early 1870s Walt Whitman wrote a
number of mariner-type poems which indicated his anticipation
over an impending "voyage":

Now finalè to the shore,
Now land and life finalè and farewell,
Now Voyager depart, (much, much for thee is yet in store,)
Often enough hast thou adventur'd o'er the seas,
Cautiously cruising, studying the charts,
Duly again to port and hawser's tie returning;
But now obey thy cherish'd secret wish,
Embrace thy friends, leave all in order,
To port and hawser's tie no more returning,
Depart upon thy endless cruise old Sailor.

Whitman may have suspected some change for the worse in his
prospects. He made out a will giving all his possessions to his
mother. There wasn't much there, as he admitted in "My Legacy";
the only item in which he took pride was Leaves of Grass.

> The business man the acquirer vast,
> After assiduous years surveying results, preparing for departure,
> Devises houses and lands to his children, bequeaths stocks, goods,
>   funds for a school or hospital,
> Leaves money to certain companions to buy tokens, souvenirs of
>   gems and gold.
>
> But I, my life surveying, closing,
> With nothing to show to devise from its idle years,
> Nor houses nor lands, nor tokens of gems or gold for my friends,
> Yet certain remembrances of the war for you, and after you,
> And little souvenirs of camps and soldiers, with my love,
> I bind together and bequeath in this bundle of songs.

While putting "all in order" in case of an abrupt departure, Whitman busily prepared a fifth edition of *Leaves of Grass*, to be presented in 1871; planned the book version of his essays on American democracy, *Democratic Vistas;* and printed a 120-page booklet containing "Passage to India" and other new poems, among them "Proud Music of the Storm"—all, of course, published at his own expense.

In the latter poem the poet described a succession of sounds and musical passages sweeping through him while he slept at night; they were part of a "new rhythmus" fitted for his soul—

> Poems bridging the way from Life to Death, vaguely wafted in the
>   night air, uncaught, unwritten,
> Which let us go forth in the bold day and write.

Whether consciously or unconsciously, then, Whitman was preparing for a journey toward that region which had always perplexed yet fascinated him: death. Maybe there the poet would find something he had dearly wanted but had never found—though he could not say exactly what it was. The feeling was dramatic enough for him to enclose in a tiny, two-line, nautical poem:

> The untold want by life and land ne'er granted,
> Now voyager sail thou forth to seek and find.

So often in the past Walt had admitted that his emotions went unfulfilled, expressing a deep yearning for some body- or soul-mate who would understand him and return his great love in equal measure. During the war he had roughly sketched these feelings in a notebook-jotting:

> The Soul, reaching, throwing out for love,
> As the spider, from some little promontory, throwing out filament
>   after filament, tirelessly out of itself, that one at
>   least may catch and form a link, a bridge, a
>   connection,
> O I saw one passing alone, saying hardly a word—yet full of love
>   I detected him, by certain signs
> O eyes wishfully turning! O silent eyes! . . .

In the poem's final version published in 1868, the poet's soul, like the spider, labored in a more philosophical way, sublimated beyond mere romantic "adhesiveness":

> A noiseless patient spider,
> I mark'd where on a little promontory it stood isolated,
> Mark'd how to explore the vacant vast surrounding,
> It launch'd forth filament, filament, filament, out of itself,
> Ever unreeling them, ever tirelessly speeding them.
>
> And you O my soul where you stand,
> Surrounded, detached, in measureless oceans of space,
> Ceaselessly musing, venturing, throwing, seeking the spheres to
>   connect them,
> Till the bridge you will need be form'd, till the ductile anchor hold,
> Till the gossamer thread you fling catch somewhere, O my soul.

Those slender yet durable threads which Whitman constantly spun out of himself and sent off were the poems he wrote. In them he expressed what he knew and felt; with them he hoped to bind together life's random experiences into a webbed pattern that would be natural, beautiful, useful, and everlasting.

Occasionally certain readers, caught by Whitman's tenuous filaments, would respond in a personal vein to his pleas for love and understanding. No one ever did so with the same sensitivity and passion as an Englishwoman named Anne Gilchrist. The story of her attachment to Walt provides a few clues to his contradictory character as man and poet while displaying a pathos of a near-tragic dimension. But above all, it shows how Whitman sometimes gained "converts" whose way of life radically changed after reading *Leaves of Grass*.

Of all the praises from England, none had pleased Whitman as much as a few letters which Rossetti had received from a woman friend and then passed on to him. Mrs. Anne Gilchrist was a widow in her late thirties when she read Rossetti's edition of the Whitman poems. Its effect upon her was sudden, dramatic, mesmeric. "Since I have had it," she wrote Rossetti, "I can read no other book; it holds me entirely spell-bound, and I go through it again and again with deepening delight and wonder."

Mrs. Gilchrist was no ordinary reader, so her opinion was especially valuable to Rossetti in confirming his own impression of Whitman's worth. She and her husband, a reputable critic, had lived next door to Thomas Carlyle and through him met many important writers and artists of the age. After Gilchrist's death, Anne finished his ambitious biography of William Blake, proving her own literary competence. She raised her four children with no funds except a small support provided by her mother, while continuing to write, usually articles for magazines and newspapers.

Rossetti lent Mrs. Gilchrist a copy of the complete, unexpurgated *Leaves of Grass*, which she accepted "quite fearlessly." The long letter which she sent to Rossetti after reading it, in July of 1869, contained some of the most sympathetic, intelligent, and provocative considerations of Whitman's poetry ever written during his lifetime. At Rossetti's urging, Mrs. Gilchrist prepared this correspondence for publication in the United States by the Transcendentalist magazine *The Radical*. Called "A Woman's Estimate of Walt Whitman," the article was published anonymously because Rossetti wished to spare Mrs. Gilchrist injurious publicity.

Mrs. Gilchrist openly declared the astounding impact that *Leaves of Grass* had made upon her personally. "I had not dreamed," she wrote, "that words could cease to be words, and become electric streams like these. I do assure you that, strong as I am, I feel sometimes as if I had not bodily strength to read many of these poems." But then, when reading certain other passages, she received "such calm wisdom and strength of thought, such a cheerful breadth of sunshine, that the soul bathes in them renewed and strengthened."

While recognizing that some poems were superior to others, she said, "All are vital. They grew—they were not made." And she likened them to seeds, branches, and leaves, each "growing in strength and beauty its own way, a law to itself, yet, with all this freedom of spontaneous growth, the result inevitable, unalterable. . . ." And she contrasted Whitman's "free verse" with previous poetic masterpieces which were akin to architecture, "planned with subtile art that makes beauty go hand in hand with rule and measure, and knows where the last stone will come, before the first is laid."

There was a new kind of music or melody in Whitman's poetry, said Mrs. Gilchrist. "I see that no counting of syllables will reveal the mechanism of the music," she wrote, "and that this rushing spontaneity could not stay to bind itself with the fetters of metre." The music was there—and nothing could ever make her "change ears with those who cannot hear it."

She also defended Whitman's use of "unexpected" words. "The shorter and more direct, the better," she decided, knowing that "poetic diction"—"pretty, soft, colourless words, laid by in lavender for the special uses of poetry, that have none of the wear and tear of daily life"—would hardly suit Whitman's bold purpose.

But most significantly, this courageous woman publicly defended the "Children of Adam"—"these beautiful, despised poems" —in which Walt Whitman had dared to write about sex as passion or act. "I saw at a glance," she said, "that it was not, as men had supposed, the heights brought down to the depths, but the depths lifted up level with the sunlit heights, that they might become clear and sunlit, too. Always, for a woman, a veil woven out of her own soul—never touched upon even, with a rough hand, by this poet. But, for a man, a daring, fearless pride in himself, not a mock modesty woven out of delusions . . ."

She too struck out at the damaging prudery of the Victorian era. Its sense of shame really demonstrated "a mean distrust of a man's self and of his Creator." It was necessary that "this silence, this evil spell, should for once be broken, and the daylight let in, that the dark cloud lying under might be scattered to the winds." Whitman, who looked bravely at the "beauty of Death," could just as ably "look with fearless, untroubled eyes at the perfect beauty of Love in all its appointed realizations."

Always interested in science—perhaps even more than in the arts—Mrs. Gilchrist, like Whitman, had incorporated the century's scientific outlook and discoveries into her own thinking. She saw no reason for there to be a conflict between scientist and poet. Both knew that "destructibility" did not really exist in nature. "It is only the relationships of things—tangibility, visibility—that are transitory," she said. Both saw body and soul as one, "the great whole imperishable; in life and death continually changing substance, always retaining identity." And she indicated the difference in their roles. "The man of science, with unwearied, self-denying toil, finds the letters and joins them into words. But the poet alone can make complete sentences. The man of science furnishes the premises; but it is the poet who draws the final conclusion."

Mrs. Gilchrist felt confident about humanity's future, especially since a poet like Walt Whitman was "lighting up dark social and political problems, and kindling into a genial glow that great heart of justice which is the life-source of Democracy." And then she exclaimed, "Happy America, that he should be her son! One sees, indeed, that only a young giant of a nation could produce this kind of greatness, so full of the ardour, the elasticity, the inexhaustible vigour and freshness, the joyousness, the audacity of youth." But English as she was, Anne Gilchrist pointed out that the United States was really the offspring of the "old English giant"—so the great English race now renewed itself in a splendid new land.

Whitman felt grateful to this unknown woman across the ocean who had written so effectively to answer his critics at home by pointing out the genuine artistry and moral purity of *Leaves of Grass.* "I realize indeed," he told Rossetti, "of this smiling and emphatic *well done* from the heart and conscience of a true wife and mother, and one, too, whose sense of the poetic . . . must also move through and satisfy science as much as the esthetic, that I had hitherto received no eulogium so magnificent." (In his old age Walt scarcely forgot Mrs. Gilchrist's tribute. "You can imagine," he told a friend, "what such a thing as her 'Estimate' meant to me at that time. Almost everybody was against me—the papers, the preachers, the literary gentlemen—nearly everybody with only here and there a dissenting voice—when it looked on the surface as if my enterprise was bound to fail . . . then this wonderful woman.")

Whitman expressed his gratitude by sending "the lady"— through Rossetti—a photograph of himself and, later, a copy of the new fifth (1871) edition of *Leaves of Grass.* These small, personal attentions seemed sufficient to him. Then in September of 1871 Mrs. Gilchrist shed her anonymity by writing Walt a long, impassioned letter in which she revealed the extent of her attachment to the author of *Leaves of Grass.*

In this intimate and intriguing epistolary confession, Anne Gilchrist told Walt of her early marriage to a kind man whose love she was unable to return fully. She had thought she had little capacity for love; now she realized that it had only been undeveloped. "For, dear Friend," she said, "my soul was so passionately aspiring—it so thirsted & pined for light, it had not power to reach alone and he could not help me on my way. And a woman is so made that she cannot give the tender passionate devotion of her whole nature save to the great conquering soul, stronger in its power, though not in its aspirations, than her own, that can lead her forever & ever up and on."

Nevertheless, she and her husband had lived "a happy and good life" together for ten years. Since they could not afford a servant, Mrs. Gilchrist learned to do all household tasks. The experience was "bracing, healthful, cheering" for her and also helped her understand Walt's depiction of the female role. "I think there is no more beautiful task for a woman," she told him, "than ministering all ways to the health & comfort & enjoyment of the dear bodies of those she loves."

When her husband died suddenly, Anne had felt remorseful that "to the last my soul dwelt apart & unmated & his soul dwelt apart unmated." Without whimpering, she cared for their four children. "I have had much sweet tranquil happiness," she said to Walt, "much strenuous work and endeavour raising my darlings."

Then in May of 1869 "came the voice over the Atlantic to me— O, the voice of my Mate: it must be so—" This was when she first read Whitman's poetry. Above all, she had responded to the mournful cry of the male mockingbird in "Out of the Cradle Endlessly Rocking," who called across the wide ocean:

> *Loud! loud! loud!*
> *Loud I call to you, my love!*
>
> *High and clear I shoot my voice over the waves,*
> *Surely you must know who is here, is here,*
> *You must know who I am, my love.*

She felt that the poet was really crying out for her; she sensed "the divine soul embracing mine." And she said further: "I never before dreamed what love meant: not what life meant. Never was alive before—no words but those of a 'new birth' can hint the meaning of what then happened to me."

Anne literally fell in love with a man whom she had never met. Her womanly instinct, however, had cautioned her to "wait to be sought—not to seek." The letters to Rossetti at least provided a way of expressing her devotion to Whitman. Yet she had not liked being anonymous when her "Estimate" was published. "My nature is proud and as defiant as thine own," she told Walt, "and immeasurably disdains any faintest appearance of being afraid of what I had done." She had expected that the poet would see the truth behind her essay: "O dear Walt, did you not feel in every word the breath of a woman's love? . . . I was so sure you would speak, would send me some sign." At least he had sent her his photograph, which she often gazed at long and lovingly, imagining "in the ineffable tenderness of thy look" that his soul yearned for her too.

Then Mrs. Gilchrist fell seriously ill and thought she was dying. (She later attributed this collapse to the rapture induced by reading *Leaves of Grass*.) Recovering, she had resolved to tell Whitman directly of her feelings; she could no longer hold them within. "Dear love," she told him now, "the sinews of a woman's outer heart are not twisted so strong as a man's; but the heart within is strong & great & loving. So the strain is very terrible." And she avowed, "I can wait—any time, a lifetime, many lifetimes—I can suffer, I can dare, I can learn, grow, toil, but nothing in life or death can tear out of my heart the passionate belief that one day I shall hear that voice say to me, 'My Mate. The one I so much want. Bride, Wife, indissoluble eternal!'"

Such was the tone of the first of many letters which Anne Gilchrist wrote to Walt Whitman during fourteen years: an extraordinary correspondence lopsided emotionally because Walt could not respond in kind, especially at first, and also preponderantly in Mrs. Gilchrist's words since many of Whitman's letters and brief notes to her either have been destroyed or have never been published.

This was not the first time, nor would it be the last, that a woman became infatuated with Walt Whitman while reading *Leaves of Grass*. During his lifetime he received at least several marriage offers and also requests for his participation in eugenic experiments. These incidents attest to the powerful rapport he sometimes achieved with individual readers—exactly what he had hoped to do. But when readers took his pleas for love and understanding and perfect mates quite literally and personally, Walt was perturbed, even shocked. He gave out strong love potions but provided no ready antidotes.

Anne Gilchrist's letter to him, therefore, was both flattering and embarrassing. Appreciative though he was of this sensitive and intelligent Englishwoman who, a total stranger to him, had enthusiastically and bravely endorsed his poetry, he now was alarmed by her confession of love. He did not know how to answer without wounding her by necessarily rejecting her proffered adoration, so he evaded the awkward problem simply by delaying an answer.

Meanwhile, in England, Mrs. Gilchrist anxiously awaited Walt's reply. After two months she wrote again to ask whether Walt had even received her first letter: "Spare me the needless suffering of uncertainty & let me have one line, one word, of assurance that I am no longer hidden from you by a thick cloud—I from thee, not thou from me: for I that have never set eyes upon thee, all the Atlantic flowing between us, yet cleave closer than those that stand nearest & dearest around thee . . ."

Realizing how her forwardness might strike him, she argued that "it is not true thou hast not sought or loved me. For when I read the divine poems I feel all folded round in thy love: I feel often as if thou wast pleading so passionately for the love of the woman that can understand thee—that I know not how to bear the yearning answering tenderness that fills my breast. . . . Try me for this life, my darling—see if I cannot so live, so grow, so learn, so love, that when I die you will say, 'This woman has grown to be a very part of me. My soul must have her loving companionship everywhere & in all things.'" Anne went on to say that she still was young enough to bear children of Walt's, "if God should so bless me."

After this second letter, Walt could no longer put off a reply. "I am not insensible to your love. I too send you my love," he wrote in a brief note intended to discourage Mrs. Gilchrist from her love suit. "My book," he went on, "is my best letter, my response, my truest explanation of all. In it I have put my body and spirit. You understand this better and fuller and clearer than any one else. And I too fully and clearly understand the loving letter it has evoked. Enough that there surely exists so beautiful and a delicate relation, accepted by both of us with joy."

Walt's evasiveness keenly disappointed Anne. His suggestion that their friendship was already sufficient struck her like "a blow on the breast." "The tie between us would not grow less but more beautiful, dear friend, if you knew me *better*: if I could stand as real & near to you as you do to me." Life now held no other meaning than to aspire to be his "dear companion"; indeed, she would welcome death if it meant she could be with him.

Despite further short and noncommittal replies from Walt, Anne continued her wooing. Every morning she looked for letters from him which did not arrive. She longed to have him "come & see if you feel happy beside me: no more this painful struggle to put myself into words, but to let what I am & all my life speak to you." To make her existence more real to him, she described herself, her home, her daily life, and her children, as well as her elderly mother who was the main reason why Anne could not embark at once for America to be with her "Dear Boy."

Again Whitman tried to halt Anne's delusions by writing bluntly: "Let me warn you about myself and yourself also. You must not construct such an unauthorized and imaginary figure and call it W. W., and so devotedly invest your loving nature in it. The actual W. W. is a very plain personage and entirely unworthy such devotion." The poet-personality "W.W.," however, Walt had deliberately created to inspire with words alone an awakening of body and spirit such as Mrs. Gilchrist now experienced—and suffered.

Even if Walt declined to assume any responsibility for his deed, Anne would at least point out the supreme success of his intentions. "If it seems to you there must needs be something unreal, illusive, in a love that has grown up entirely without the basis of personal intercourse, dear Friend," she wrote, "then you do not yourself realize your own power nor understand the full meaning of your own words, 'whoso touches this, touches a man'—'I have put my Soul & Body into these Poems.' Real effects imply real causes." A woman of her age and circumstance simply could not have been affected thus by a figment of her own fancy, she asserted.

Yet Anne began to suspect that she was not alone in loving Whitman. She pictured him "eagerly beset by hundreds like myself whose hearts are so drawn out of their breasts by your Poems that they cannot rest without striving, some way or other, to draw near to you personally." Gradually she became calmer and more sensible, although her great affection for Walt hardly abated. "I will not write any more such letters," she promised. Or if she did, she would not mail them.

She hoped for little bits of news from Walt, "for any thing that helps my eyes to pierce the distance & see you as you live & move to-day." Perhaps if he could not always write to acknowledge the receipt of a letter, he could send her American newspapers from time to time, indirectly informing her that he was well, the post-marks to tell her where he was in his wanderings. This was a request Whitman could and did fill; in subsequent months packets of newspapers and journals, some with articles about Whitman, others containing published works of his, arrived almost regularly to reassure Mrs. Gilchrist. Occasionally she even got a note.

Meanwhile, Anne was making plans. "When we come to America," she told Walt, "I shall not want you to talk to me, shall not be any way importunate. To settle down where there are some that love you & understand your poems, somewhere that you would be sure to come pretty often—to have you sit with me while I worked, you silent, or reading to yourself, I don't mind how: to let my children grow fond of you—to take food with us; if my music pleased you, to let me play & sing to you of an evening. Do your needlework for you—talk freely of all that occupied my thoughts concerning the children's welfare &c—I could be very happy so. But silence with the living presence and silence with all the ocean in between are two different things. Therefore, these years stretch out your hand cordially, trustfully, that I may feel its warm grasp."

Meanwhile, Whitman undertook to write the official opening poem for the National Industrial Exhibition in New York City in 1871. In "Song of the Exposition" he asked the antique muse of poetic song to migrate from the Old World to the New:

> For know a better, fresher, busier sphere, a wide, untried domain
> awaits, demands you.

Then he jauntily imagined her moving easily among the many products of America's invention and industry:

Making directly for this rendezvous, vigorously clearing a path for
     herself, striding through the confusion,
By thud of machinery and shrill steam-whistle undismay'd,
Bluff'd not a bit by drain-pipe, gasometers, artificial fertilizers,
Smiling and pleas'd with palpable intent to stay,
She's here, install'd amid the kitchen ware!

(Whitman's novel suggestion that the muse might be thoroughly at home among everyday artifacts and matters was to be fulfilled by many twentieth-century poets.)

Whitman distributed copies of his poem to the press, and some newspapers published it. Inescapably, Walt was ridiculed for both his bombastic style and his high-flown visions. Among other things, he had proposed building museums to display science, industry, history, and the arts, which would be America's own great and enduring "pyramids and obelisks":

Somewhere within their walls shall all that forwards perfect human
     life be started,
Tried, taught, advanced, visibly exhibited.

Not long afterward, New York City erected several museums which admirably realized Whitman's dreams.

Early in 1872 Whitman composed another long poem, "As a Strong Bird on Pinions Free" (later called "Thou Mother with Thy Equal Brood"), which likened America to a mother-eagle, the states to her eaglet-brood.

As a strong bird on pinions free,
Joyous, the amplest spaces heavenward cleaving,
Such be the thought I'd think of thee America,
Such be the recitative I'd bring for thee.

The long, rhetorical poem—Whitman's last big poem on the whole subject of American democracy—expressed some of Walt's ideas and attitudes recently published in *Democratic Vistas*. The poet, however, seemed more confident that his nation would admirably survive and overcome all present and future perils:

The storm shall dash thy face, the murk of war and worse than
 war shall cover thee all over,
(Wert capable of war, its tug and trials? be capable of peace, its
 trials,
For the tug and mortal strain of nations come at last in prosperous
 peace, not war;)
In many a smiling mask death shall approach beguiling thee, thou
 in disease shalt swelter,
The livid cancer spread its hideous claws, clinging upon thy
 breasts, seeking to strike thee deep within,
Consumption of the worst, moral consumption, shall rouge thy
 face with hectic,
But thou shalt face thy fortunes, thy diseases, and surmount them
 all,
Whatever they are to-day and whatever through time they may be,
They each and all shall lift and pass away and cease from thee . . .

Whitman had written the lengthy poem at the request of the
Dartmouth senior class. It turned out to be something of a students' prank upon the faculty; nevertheless, the college elders
received Walt graciously when he arrived on campus in June to
recite his poem at their commencement ceremony. Then, since he
was so far north, Whitman went off to Vermont to visit his sister
Hannah for a few days before returning to Washington.

One evening in late 1872 Whitman and his great friend William
O'Connor were discussing whether all ex-slaves should be given
the right to vote. O'Connor, a long-time Abolitionist, ardently
supported Negro suffrage, whereas Whitman felt more cautious,
believing that voters should have at least a rudimentary education. Usually Walt spoke mildly, avoiding the hot verbal debates
that frequently went on around him, especially when O'Connor
was involved. This night, however, he shocked and offended
William by becoming vehement, even insulting, while expressing
his opinions. The bitter argument ended only when Walt walked
out of the O'Connor house.
Whitman deeply regretted the unpleasant episode, and on the
following day, seeing his friend on the street, he went up and

put out his hand in a conciliatory gesture. But O'Connor refused to take it; he was unwilling and unable to accept misbehavior and an illiberal, unidealistic attitude from the author of *Leaves of Grass,* whom for some years he had nearly deified.

The sudden deprivation of O'Connor's fellowship hurt Whitman badly. He had depended upon the Irishman's constant moral support and admiration and always enjoyed the stimulating social life provided by the bustling O'Connor household, where he came and went as he liked. Nelly O'Connor, however, did not take part in her husband's feud and remained as friendly as ever toward Walt.

Soon, too, another important association was disrupted. John Burroughs accepted a job as a bank inspector in New York state, enabling him to live once again in the real country. Although Walt might look forward to visits to the new Burroughs farm, the near-daily, highly satisfying contact with his naturalist and writer friend was over. Walt was now deprived of the two households where he had been warmly welcomed as a family member.

On a cold and wet evening in January of 1873, Walt was reading in his office at the Treasury Building. But he did not feel well, and when he left the building he obviously looked sick, for the night watchman wanted to escort him to his nearby boarding-house. Walt, declining assistance, plodded heavily homeward alone through the sharp wind and icy sleet, while the faithful guard stood outside, holding up his lantern and watching Whitman until he saw him arrive safely at his own doorstep.

In the middle of the night Walt awoke to find that he could not move his left arm. Drowsy, and feeling sure that the trouble would pass, he went back to sleep. But when he awakened at dawn the condition remained, now affecting his left leg too. He could not even get out of bed to summon help. Fortunately, several friends came in a few hours and sent at once for a doctor.

Walt Whitman had suffered a stroke which had paralyzed one side of his body. He who had praised and cultivated bodily health and vigor now felt betrayed. Yet he believed that he would fully recover in time, through persistent effort and sheer force of will. His doctor seemed optimistic too.

Walt's friends rallied around to help him out. They took turns staying with him and tending to his every need. When he improved, they assisted him in getting back on his feet—though at first the effort of walking, especially down the long stairs, exhausted him and even set back his recovery. Walt was very upset too to learn of the death of Jeff's wife "Matt," of whom he had been so fond. (For several years Jeff and his family had been living in St. Louis.)

Especially attentive to Walt were Charles Eldridge and Peter Doyle. Nelly O'Connor came regularly with food and good cheer. Ursula Burroughs—still in Washington trying to sell the little "farm" on Capitol Hill—visited often, and a month after Walt's stroke she took him out for a ride in her carriage. Never had she seen anyone enjoy himself so much, she wrote to John.

J. H. Ashton, who had arranged Walt's job in the Attorney General's department, wanted Walt to come and stay with his own family. But Walt, hopeful of a quick recovery, refused his kind offer; he wished to remain independent. "They live in a grand style & I should be more bothered than benefitted by their refinements & luxuries, servants, &c.," Walt remarked in a scrawling note to his mother. Every few days he faithfully wrote to her from his sickbed.

Mrs. Whitman had recently given up her residence in Brooklyn to go and live, at their insistence, with George and his wife Lou in Camden, New Jersey, where her son worked as an inspector of gas pipes. Although Walt's mother was very concerned about his stroke, she too had her problems, which she did not spare him now. She felt disoriented and neglected in a household managed by another woman. And fretting over this new circumstance, she detailed to Walt her troubles and recent illnesses.

Walt assured his mother that he would soon recover and return to work: then he would buy a little house in which he and she and Eddie could all live happily together again. As it was, Walt employed a substitute to do his office work for him, so he continued to receive a portion of his salary.

By May Walt was well enough to spend several hours a day on the job. Then he heard that his mother's health had suddenly and seriously failed. Alarmed, he left right away for Camden. Three days later, on May 23, Mrs. Whitman died, at the age of seventy-eight. Her death was the hardest blow that Walt had ever had to bear. "It is the great cloud of my life," he wrote in anguish to Peter Doyle. He would never really get over his mother's departure, and for a long while he expected to join her soon. As with all else that touched and preoccupied him, Walt would write a poem for his *Leaves:*

> As at thy portals also death,
> Entering thy sovereign, dim, illimitable grounds,
> To memories of my mother, to the divine blending, maternity,
> To her, buried and gone, yet buried not, gone not from me,
>
> .   .   .
>
> To her, the ideal woman, practical, spiritual, of all of earth, life,
>   love, to me the best,
> I grave a monumental line, before I go, amid these songs,
> And set a tombstone here.

His mother's death coming on top of his own illness proved too much for Walt. He returned to Washington a week after the funeral. Extremely depressed and debilitated, he now accepted the Ashtons' hospitality, for he did not want to be alone. His friends were quite concerned about his condition. "I begin to doubt whether Walt is going to recover," Eldridge wrote to Burroughs, "and I am very apprehensive of another attack. . . . He is a mere physical wreck to what he was. . . . It is a terrible misfortune, one of the saddest spectacles I have ever seen. His mental powers seem to be as vigorous as ever, which is the brightest part of his case, but to be stricken with such physical weakness that he cannot walk a block without resting—it is very pitiful. Such vigor, health, and endurance to be so changed, is a melancholy thing. . . . Walt himself believes that he is going to get well, and we all do as much as possible to encourage that belief." Eldridge feared, however, that if Walt continued for long in this state, he would become "hypochondriacal."

Realistically considering his situation, Walt knew that he needed a prolonged rest; he obtained a leave of absence. Peter Doyle helped him pack up his belongings, and Walt went to Camden to stay with George and Lou. George's wife, who adored Walt, fussed over him and cooked his favorite dishes, just as his mother would have done. But there in Camden Walt felt sick, weak, old, isolated, and frustrated. He needed the company and stimulation of his friends, of people alive with ideas and projects. Like his mother, Walt also fretted in his dependency upon George, who had little in common with him. ("George," Walt once remarked, "is interested in pipes not poems.")

The most satisfying experience Camden offered Walt at this dismal time in his life was the nearby railroad depot and yard. The bells, whistles, and clanging from the trains coming and going every hour of the night and day in a resounding noise of steam and locomotion made bright events in Whitman's tedious invalidism—instead of terrible annoyances as they might have been to somebody else. Trains, after all, meant movement, progress, excitement, hope: things then in short supply in Walt's life.

In "To a Locomotive in Winter" Whitman would soon praise the vigorous thrust of a train engine, no doubt inwardly contrasting it with his own complete standstill. (And who else but Whitman in that era would have found suitable poetic material in a machine?)

> Fierce-throated beauty!
> Roll through my chant with all thy lawless music, thy swinging
> lamps at night,
> Thy madly-whistled laughter, echoing, rumbling like an earth-
> quake, rousing all,
> Law of thyself complete, thine own track firmly holding,
> (No sweetness debonair of tearful harp or glib piano thine,)
> Thy trills of shrieks by rocks and hills return'd,
> Launch'd o'er the prairies wide, across the lakes,
> To the free skies unpent and glad and strong.

Largely confined to his upstairs room, Walt distracted himself by planning future trips with Pete all over the country, on trains like these and on steamboats. Living now with George, Walt felt trapped by middle-class notions and concern over status and possessions. He sorely missed his contacts with the artists and intellectuals he knew in the capital and the free and easy associations with Doyle and his working-class friends.

During the first months of his illness, Walt neglected Anne Gilchrist. Learning of his collapse, she had written of her desire to be with him: "You see dear Friend, a woman who is a mother has thenceforth something of that feeling toward other men who are dear to her—a cherishing, fostering instinct that rejoices so in tending, nursing, caretaking . . ."

In the summer of 1873 Walt finally wrote to Anne from Camden, telling not only of his current condition but of the deaths of his mother and sister-in-law, which had slowed his recovery. "I am still feeble, palsied & have spells of great distress in the head," he reported. "But there are points more favourable. I am up & dressed every day, sleep & eat middling well & do not change much yet, in flesh & face, only look very old. . . . As I write to-day, I feel that I shall probably get well—though I may not." He had thought many times of Anne and her children, but had simply been unable to reply to her letters. "Do not think hard of me," he said. "If you could look into my spirit & emotion you would be entirely satisfied & at peace."

With Walt's note went something else: "The enclosed ring I have just taken from my finger, & send to you, with my love." Both letter and ring were received joyfully in England; as any woman might, Mrs. Gilchrist seemed to regard this gift of Walt's ring as the token of a spiritual, if not actual, engagement to wed. "My Darling!" she exclaimed, "take comfort & strength & joy from me that you have made so rich & strong. Perhaps it will yet be given us to see each other, to travel the last stage of this journey side by side, hand in hand—so completing the preparation for the fresh start on the greater journey. . . ."

After a while, Walt began to hobble around town, leaning on a cane. Fastening his eyes upon sights other than his bedroom walls made him more cheerful. He soon ventured farther afield, going by streetcar to Camden's ferry landing, thence across the

Delaware River to Philadelphia, where he spent many hours contentedly reading in a library. His ready fellowships with the people he encountered en route—postmen, railroad workers, streetcar conductors, ferryboat pilots and deck hands—gave him contact again with the out-of-doors city people he had always enjoyed. He also began to cultivate friendships with professional people—doctors, lawyers, publishers, journalists—in Camden and Philadelphia, who liked Walt if not all of them appreciated his poetry.

As his irritation over a strict confinement dissipated, Walt's creative spirit revived and he returned to writing. Journalism seemed more immediately promising as a way to add to his small income. Walt wrote reminiscences of the capital's political scenery and also put together a group of articles and notes he had written during the Civil War. Both series were published in installments in the New York *Daily Graphic.*

The editor of the Camden *New Republic* let Walt use his printing facilities to set up and make copies of the new poems he was writing. Two of them, to Walt's gratified surprise, were accepted for publication by the much-respected *Harper's Monthly.* "Song of the Redwood-Tree" and "Prayer of Columbus" were both obvious products of Whitman's convalescence; they signaled his rising spirits within an acceptance of his physical condition.

Whitman had recently read about the forests of gigantic redwoods in California. The sequoias were being felled by the western pioneers to make buildings, homes, and bridges for their new settlements. Walt imagined how "a mighty dying tree" might sing out while woodcutters hacked away. His redwood giant actually welcomed its untimely demise, for it thereby contributed to progress, in which humanity's needs took precedence over nature's most spectacular growths—an attitude surely dismaying to conservationists.

Whitman had not yet abdicated his chosen role as the bard of democratic America, but in *Democratic Vistas* and in recent poems he seemed to consider himself a spiritual progenitor of a whole new species of poets to come. Now, sick in body and devitalized in spirit, he took strength from the notion that he, like the redwood tree, would be absorbed into his country's future. "Song of the Redwood-Tree" therefore was no wail or dirge, but a song of happy anticipation. Tree and poet both acceded to their fates, knowing they were the noble forebears of an even nobler type to come:

> Fresh come, to a new world indeed, yet long prepared,
> I see the genius of the modern, child of the real and ideal,
> Clearing the ground for broad humanity, the true America, heir of
>   the past so grand,
> To build a grander future.

"Prayer of Columbus" also paralleled Whitman's situation after his stroke. In it he identified with the historical figure who had discovered and opened up the Americas to European colonization, yet spent his last years in bodily suffering and public disgrace. (In "Passage to India" Whitman had already expressed his kinship-feeling toward Columbus.) The poet too had been rejected by society and denied recognition as a prophetic hero. In *Leaves of Grass* Whitman had launched his own "fleet" of poems which offered whole new vistas for mankind, reporting them in a bold way which brought him derision, criticism, ostracism.

Now Walt felt sick and old, already approaching death's door. Into his new portrayal of Columbus, Walt put all his own grievances, depressions, disappointments, and sense of isolation:

> A batter'd, wreck'd old man,
> Thrown on this savage shore, far, far from home,
> Pent by the sea and dark rebellious brows, twelve dreary months,
> Sore, stiff with many toils, sicken'd and nigh to death,
> I take my way along the island's edge,
> Venting a heavy heart.

But despite all rebuffs and pains, the poet-mariner daily struggled to send messages to the God who had ordered his very life yet now seemed to have forgotten him:

> Thou knowest my years entire, my life,
> My long and crowded life of active work, not adoration merely;

Thou knowest the prayers and vigils of my youth,
Thou knowest how before I commenced I devoted all to come to
Thee,
Thou knowest I have in age ratified all those vows and strictly kept
them,
Thou knowest I have not once lost nor faith nor ecstasy in Thee,
In shackles, prison'd, in disgrace, repining not,
Accepting all from Thee, as duly come from Thee.

This God to whom the poet, as Columbus, addressed himself had initially inspired his creative ventures through a mystical communication:

O I am sure they really came from Thee,
The urge, the ardor, the unconquerable will,
The potent, felt, interior command, stronger than words,
A message from the Heavens whispering to me even in sleep,
These sped me on.

As dark clouds gathered above Columbus and death approached, he trustingly held fast to God; though a failure in his missions and doubtful of his own sanity, he was still sure of Him:

My hands, my limbs grow nerveless,
My brain feels rack'd, bewilder'd,
Let the old timbers part, I will not part,
I will cling fast to Thee, O God, though the waves buffet me,
Thee, Thee at least I know.

Is it the prophet's thought I speak, or am I raving?
What do I know of life? what of myself?
I know not even my own work past or present . . .

Suddenly Columbus was granted a prophetic vision of glorious things to come, which justified his own sacrifices and hardships:

And these things I see suddenly, what mean they?
As if some miracle, some hand divine unseal'd my eyes,
Shadowy vast shapes smile through the air and sky,

And on the distant waves sail countless ships,
And anthems in new tongues I hear saluting me.

The connection between Whitman and Columbus was certainly
not lost on perceptive readers like Anne Gilchrist. After reading
Walt's "sacred Poem," she told him, "You too have sailed over
stormy seas to your goal—surrounded with mocking disbelievers—
you too have paid the great price of health—our Columbus."

During his convalescence Whitman wrote two other "key"
poems, these essentially philosophical, and which reflected his
prevailing mood. Asked to provide a poem for the graduation
ceremony at Tufts College, Whitman composed "Song of the
Universal." For some while he had studied and admired the
German philosopher Hegel's concept of the "dialectic" process in
history, in which events in time proceeded on a spiral course
upward, each new turn or "thesis" passing through an antithetical
area that was dark and turbulent, then emerging from it to reach
a "synthesis" in a higher stage of development. Civilization in
this way would slowly approach a state of perfection in which the
real finally would approximate the ideal.

"Song of the Universal" expressed Whitman's own Hegelian-
style belief in the perfectibility of all things and the denial of
"evil" except as a negative force contributing its parts to the
evolution of democracy. Whitman thereby soothed his dismay
over the Reconstruction Era by regarding its manifestations as an
unpleasant but necessary part of his nation's progression:

Out of the bulk, the morbid and the shallow,
Out of the bad majority, the varied countless frauds of men and
states,
Electric, antiseptic yet, cleaving, suffusing all,
Only the good is universal.

The rhythmic "Eidólons," written in regular four-line stanzas,
made a companion piece. The title was the Greek word for
"phantom" or "image"—by which Whitman meant the shadowy
spirit or ideal behind every material or "real" object, body, nation,
or experience, in the Platonic tradition. The function of prophets

and bards was to interpret to modern democracy "God and eidólons." Walt was still looking forward to the wholly perfect spiritual encounter that lay ahead of him:

> And thee my soul,
> Joys, ceaseless exercises, exaltations,
> Thy yearning amply fed at last, prepared to meet,
> Thy mates, eidólons.
>
> Thy body permanent,
> The body lurking there within thy body,
> The only purport of the form thou art, the real I myself,
> An image, an eidólon.

Having successfully raised his mind often to dwell above the subsistence-level concerns of the invalid, Walt was definitely on the mend. He planned on eventually returning to his clerkship in Washington; in the meantime he continued to employ a substitute, and made enough money in the transaction to pay George for his board and also help to support Eddie, now living with a family in the country. Walt was quite shaken, then, when he received notice that his job with the government would be terminated in July of 1874. His increasing dependence upon George's generosity chafed at him, and he became more anxious than ever to earn money from his writing.

Whitman rather expected to be asked to compose the opening poem for Philadelphia's Centennial Exposition celebrating the Republic's one hundredth birthday. But Camden's resident poet was ignored. Nevertheless, he ambitiously prepared a two-volume "Centennial" edition of his own works, the first to contain *Leaves of Grass* (its sixth version, substantially as presented in its 1871 edition), the second—*Two Rivulets*—to be a heterogeneous collection of his prose and recent poems.

In November of 1875 Walt was delighted when George and Lou had a baby boy, whom they named after him. (Unfortunately, the infant—the only child they were to have—was sickly and died in less than a year.) Later in the month Walt felt well enough to go to Washington, where he stayed for several weeks, noting with interest the changes that had taken place since his departure. But no longer was Walt up to making his poetic national surveys or prose critiques of present-day American democracy; from now on he would be on the sidelines of current events and issues—briefly commenting upon them just when he felt like it. His illness and comparative isolation caused him to concentrate upon his own private world, and the poems of his later years reflect the narrowing of his focus and the diminished vigor of his muse.

Despite his improvement in health and his busy application to literary projects, Whitman often felt sorry for himself. He probably wrote the article published in the *West Jersey Press.* "Walt Whitman's Actual American Position" revealed "the real truth": that "with the exception of a very few readers (women equally with men), Whitman's poems in their public reception have fallen stillborn in this country. They have been met, and are met today, with the determined denial, disgust and scorn of orthodox American authors, publishers and editors, and in a pecuniary and worldly sense, have certainly wrecked the life of their author."

In the twenty years since *Leaves of Grass* had first appeared, the poet had made little headway: "Still he stands alone. No established publishing house will yet print his books. Most of the stores will not even sell them. In fact, his works have never been really published at all." Whitman now found that, after the first flush of success in publishing some of the poetry and prose of his early convalescent period, almost all doors of magazine and newspaper editors were closed to him. To disturb him further, an unscrupulous publisher, who possessed the plates for the third edition of *Leaves of Grass* put out by Thayer & Eldridge, was selling a pirated edition of the work, for which the author himself received no royalties.

Whitman sent the newspaper article about himself to Rossetti, with the comment that his situation was "even worse than described" therein. He must have hoped that Rossetti would circulate it—and indeed he did. Reprinted in a London paper, the article stirred up vituperative attacks by literary Englishmen upon the Americans, who were either stupidly or intentionally neglecting their greatest writer. Naturally these protests were read in the United States, where editors—particularly Bayard Taylor of the New York *Tribune,* once a friend of Whitman but now a determined detractor—intemperately attacked Whitman and his poems in order to defend themselves from the English assault.

The few American voices raised in Whitman's behalf came notably from John Burroughs and William O'Connor, who encountered trouble just in getting their letters printed. (Walt's estranged friend never stayed silent whenever *Leaves of Grass* was criticized.) The publicity aroused by the episode may have done Whitman's American reputation more harm than good— although people were undeniably impressed with the roster of renowned English names gathered in his support. Also, English sympathy for the poet resulted in a heavy subscription for his new "Centennial" edition, so that after paying the printing expenses, Walt even made a small profit.

In the late autumn of 1875 Walt's friend Harry Stafford, a young printers' assistant, took Whitman to meet his parents, who owned a farm about twelve miles from Camden. The Staffords liked Walt, and Mrs. Stafford, showing maternal concern over his feeble physique, invited him to come and stay with them at Timber Creek whenever he wished.

In the spring of 1876 Walt began to take frequent advantage of the Staffords' kind hospitality. He enjoyed the family atmosphere but, even more, the fields and woods surrounding the farm. Finding that this rapport with nature regenerated both body and spirit, Walt sometimes stayed at Timber Creek for several weeks at a time. He was given a room of his own, the only drawback being Mrs. Stafford's insistence that it be kept neat. She was aghast at Walt's habit of strewing manuscripts, papers, and books all over table, chairs, and floor. After a few temperamental outbursts, Walt learned to take his hostess's bossy "mothering" with good humor, doubtless drawing some needed filial sustenance from this new relationship.

At first Walt only felt up to taking short walks close to the house. One of the Stafford children would accompany him, carrying a chair for him to sit upon whenever he grew tired. He soaked up the spring sunshine, watched and listened to the nesting birds, admired the profusion of wildflowers along the country lane, observed the stars at night, and smelled the odors of moist soil and growing things in the spring-resurrected world. Almost always Walt took a little notebook with him, and in it he jotted down the vivid impressions and observations which would eventually occupy much of the last section of *Specimen Days*.

Nature, as ever, proved the best tonic for Walt. He said that overcivilized man needed an affinity with open air, sun and stars, and the changing seasons. "Away then to loosen, to unstring the divine bow, so tense, so long," Whitman exclaimed. "Away, from curtain, carpet, sofa, book—from society . . . away from ligatures, tight boots, buttons, and the whole cast-iron civilized life . . . returning to the naked source-life of us all—to the breast of the great silent savage all-acceptive Mother."

Walt made companions of the trees at Timber Creek; each seemed to possess its own special identity. "How strong, vital, enduring! how dumbly eloquent!" he said of them. Always in conflict within—who was he really and what did he wish to be?—he much admired that quality in nature, especially manifest in the tree, which simply *was*, making no pretense about being anything else, saying nothing, and unconcerned about the opinions of others. Neither in the society of men nor in the company of the books they wrote, but only in nature had Walt ever thoroughly relaxed. Now he returned to the fresh wonder and oneness with the world that he had felt as a child.

In this renewed communion with the outdoors, Walt took therapeutic joy in sheer physical contact with a tree that possessed those qualities he sorely needed: youthfulness, vigor, purpose, hope, futurity. "A solitary and pleasant sundown hour at the pond," he recorded, "exercising arms, chest, my whole body, by a tough oak sapling thick as my wrist, twelve feet high—pulling and pushing, inspiring the good air. After I wrestle with the tree awhile, I can feel its young sap and virtue welling up out of the ground and tingling through me from crown to toe, like health's wine." Then Walt made the woods resound with his "vocalism"

as he shouted some favored declamatory Shakespearean lines or
sang operatic arias, folk tunes, and patriotic songs.

Walt Whitman's fundamental health was returning—just in
time. Anne Gilchrist, who had long and faithfully fussed over him
by mail, was actually coming to America now, after seven years
of delay. "Soon, very soon, I come, my darling," she wrote to Walt
in February of 1876. "This is the last spring we shall be asunder—
O I passionately believe there are years in store for us, years of
tranquil, tender happiness. . . . Hold on but a little longer for me,
my Walt . . ."

Anne's mother's death had finally released her from any obli-
gation to remain in England. Her oldest son, Percy, now had a
good job; he was getting married and starting his own home.
Anne's three other children—Herbert, an aspiring artist; Beatrice,
who wanted to become a doctor but as a woman could get no
training in England; and the youngest, Grace—would all be
coming with her. Apparently Anne intended to stay, for she was
bringing her household furnishings too. And she was going to
share with Walt her worldly possessions, to help ease his life of
poverty, sickness, and neglect.

Especially since his illness, Walt had appreciated Mrs. Gilchrist's flattery and loving attentions. Sometimes he had written
his own sweet encouragements, feeling safe from any real com-
mitment to her because she was on the far side of the ocean. Now
the prospect of having her physically close alarmed him; naturally
he balked at any suggestion of dependency upon her—or she on
him. "My dearest friend," he hurriedly wrote, "I do not approve
your American trans-settlement. I see so many things here you
have no idea of—the social, and almost every other kind of crudeness, meagerness, here . . ." He virtually ordered her not to make
a move without further advice from him.

But Anne had made her decision, and Walt's criticisms of his
own country would not stop her from coming. "I have not shut
my eyes to the difficulties and trials & responsibilities (for the
children's sake) of the enterprise," she wrote. But Whitman's
poems urged her to cross the ocean: "They teach me to look be-

neath the surface & get hints of the great future that is shaping itself out of the crude present."

So she told Walt, "Do not dissuade me from coming this autumn, my dearest Friend . . . I cannot wait any longer." She was also coming, she said, for practical reasons: furthering Herbert's and Beatrice's educations. They would stay in Philadelphia, close to Walt. But realizing that Walt now shrank back from her bold move, she tried to reassure him: "Have no anxiety or misgivings for us. Let us come & be near you—& see if we are made of the right sort of stuff for transplanting to American soil." She also made it clear that she expected nothing from him, really. "We shall light on our feet & do very well," she confidently predicted.

In early September Mrs. Gilchrist and children arrived in Philadelphia. Shortly thereafter Walt met them, either at their hotel or at his home with George. Nobody recorded for posterity the scene that took place between Walt Whitman and this gracious, intelligent, and high-strung woman who had fallen in love with him through his poetry and whose durable attraction to him had now brought her to the United States.

If Walt anticipated the initial encounter with guarded feelings or even dread, he quickly eased his mind about his "dear friend" from England. Anne was tall, lithe, lively. Beneath brown hair and a high brow her hazel eyes held a brightly lit, penetrating gaze. When she conversed, her face became radiantly expressive. Although she was a gifted writer, she particularly shined in conversations, Walt saw; she displayed an intelligence that was wideranging, facile, deep, and unaffected. She was realistic and drew upon the sciences for much of her wisdom; yet essentially she was profoundly religious—just as Walt was. She could be as intense and as passionate as her letters, with a difference: the living woman, though warm, seemed controlled and serene. And she laughed often, humor being an important part of her nature. Walt especially liked her voice. "The voice indicates the soul," he said; he was to remember hers as "the tenderest, most musical voice ever to bless our ears."

Probably to his great surprise, then, Walt liked Anne Gilchrist immediately. He felt both relaxed and buoyant in her company. He and her children liked each other too: for years, of course, they had been schooled to appreciate *Leaves of Grass,* and he had heard much about them from Anne's letters.

Once again Walt belonged to a congenial family. When John Burroughs came down to visit Walt in Camden that autumn, Walt took him right away across the river to meet Mrs. Gilchrist. John, finding Anne delightful, could well understand Walt's admiration.

Anne reserved one room in her rented home for Walt, so that he could come and stay for a night, or even a week at a time— which he often did. And when he did not, almost every afternoon he would take the ferry across the Delaware River, then board a horse-car, and arrive at Anne's house in time for tea, frequently staying for supper too. She played the piano and sang; he often recited poetry—his own, or other people's; and the children and anybody else who was there joined in the ever-lively talk. It was just as Anne had always imagined it would be—almost.

If Anne Gilchrist had expected to marry Whitman, she probably altered her feelings and expectations at their first meeting. A close friendship was thoroughly possible, but not marriage: and on this point Walt may have been explicit from the start, not wanting to encourage her hopes further. When finally seeing Walt in person, too, Anne's female instincts surely alerted her to a celibate, solitary element in his nature. He was neither an ordinary man with normal emotions and urges, nor the vigorously sensuous superman of the "Children of Adam." He had been right: the mythical "W.W." in his poetry was hardly identical with the actual poet—who was now old, enfeebled, partially paralyzed. Moreover, Walt possessed an innate pride that would never permit him to become dependent, emotionally and economically, upon a generous woman—however much he might love her.

Anne's romantic feelings toward Whitman were swiftly altered to fit into a remarkable Platonic relationship. Rossetti had never guessed the extent of Mrs. Gilchrist's admiration for Whitman, and when she wrote she indicated no disappointment at all in the poet. "Our greatest pleasure," she reported early during her stay, "is the society of Mr. Whitman, who fully realizes the ideal I had formed from his poems, and brings such an atmosphere of cordiality and geniality with him as is indescribable."

A year later she was telling Rossetti, "We are having delightful evenings this winter; how often do I wish you could make one in the circle around our tea table where sits on my right hand every evening but Sunday Walt Whitman. He has made great progress in health and recovered powers of getting about during the year we have been here: nevertheless the lameness—the dragging instead of lifting the left leg continues; and this together with his white hair and beard give him a look of age curiously contradicted by his face, which has not only the ruddy freshness but the full, rounded contours of youth, nowhere wrinkled or sunk; it is a face as indicative of serenity and goodness and of mental and bodily health as the brow is of intellectual power. But I notice he occasionally speaks of himself as having a 'wounded brain,' and of being still quite altered from his former self."

Altogether, 1876 made a busy and sociable year for Walt. During the autumn his brother Jeff came to visit and brought his two daughters, making a family reunion. They all took a trip down to the New Jersey seashore and drove around in a carriage. In the evening Walt wandered off by himself to absorb the smells and sights and sounds of the ocean and sand, which he had sorely missed during his invalidism: they struck "emotional, impalpable depths, subtler than all the poems, paintings, music, I have ever read, seen, heard."

Walt's stays at Timber Creek had given him new contacts with nature. Mrs. Gilchrist gave him intelligent and affectionate companionship while stirring the philosophic bent of his mind. Then, Whitman's almost daily (and nightly) trips on the Camden ferry rekindled his childhood love for the river-crossing with its associative contact with humanity. Once more he noticed details of the "human comedy" enacted aboard ship; he found excitement too in watching the traffic of the myriad ships—steam and sail, domestic and foreign—in the port of Philadelphia.

The vista of the night sky afforded by the ferry deck provided one of Walt's favorite scenes. During the day there had been constant "exhilaration, change, people, business." But now, usually alone, he held a soothing and silent communion with water, air, sky, and stars "that speak no word, nothing to the intellect, yet so eloquent, so communicative to the soul." Sometimes a friendly astronomer on shipboard delivered little lectures on the heavenly displays, but most of the time Walt, who had long written familiarly of the science of space and stars, made his own solitary studies—possible too on clear nights down at Timber Creek. "Never did I realize more latent sentiment, almost *passion*, in those silent, interminable stars up there," he said in *Specimen Days*. "One can understand, such a night, why, from the days of the Pharaohs or Job, the dome of heaven, sprinkled with planets, has supplied the subtlest, deepest criticism on human pride, glory, ambition."

Mrs. Gilchrist terminated her Philadelphia residence in the spring of 1878 and went to stay in Boston, where Beatrice was working in a hospital to prepare for her career as a doctor. Certainly Walt missed Anne and her convivial household. She wrote often to him, among other things describing her visit to Concord, when she had met the elderly Emerson and others whom Walt knew and liked. She spent the winter in New York, and Walt joined her there for some weeks, staying with his friend J. H. Johnston, whom he had visited in the previous year. During the days he usually went off on his own, reacquainting himself with Manhattan's sights—and its people, who now numbered a million.

Still fascinated by New York City, Walt happily watched the crowds shopping along Broadway, the many carriages taking elegantly dressed people on outings through Central Park, the comings and goings of the vessels in the harbor, the work of building crews. Walt considered what the whole metropolitan display meant both to him and to his country. After his dismal mood the decade before in *Democratic Vistas*, his overall outlook was now optimistic. "The brief total of the impressions, the human qualities of these vast cities," he wrote, "is to me comforting, even heroic, beyond statement." He asserted that "an appreciative and perceptive study of the current humanity of New York gives the directest proof yet of successful Democracy, and of the solution of that paradox, the eligibility of the free and fully developed individual with the paramount aggregate." At this time—"lame and sick, pondering for years on many a doubt and danger for this republic of ours"—Walt found in this visit to New York "the best, most effective medicine my soul has yet partaken."

Some of Whitman's New York friends arranged for him to read in a public hall his already prepared lecture on the assassination of Abraham Lincoln. (In years to come, in various cities, this talk would be a standard Whitman offering on the anniversary of Lincoln's death. Whitman's friends always promoted attendance, knowing that the several hundred dollars he might earn as his fee would add appreciably to his small income.) Whitman sat on stage and read from his manuscript. A friend who heard him remarked afterwards that his voice changed under the strain of public speaking; apparently his throat muscles tightened, making his voice higher and unnatural-sounding. Although Walt had often considered becoming a poet-orator, he was probably unsuited for such a vocation.

That spring Walt also visited the Burroughs at their sturdy stone farmhouse "Riverby" at Esopus, eighty miles north of New York City and close to the Hudson River's west bank. Many a pleasant day Walt and John spent together, roaming the countryside by foot or by cart, bird-watching, woods-exploring, chatting with the country people. Walt's greatest treat was picking the profuse currants and raspberries and then eating them, sugared, for breakfast. He also loved to watch and listen to the trains which chugged and whistled across the Hudson; rather than resenting this intrusion by man and mechanism into nature, he welcomed it.

At the Burroughs' place, then and on later visits, Walt as usual took notes on especially interesting sights—his own observations often supplemented by John's. He often saw a bird making "the very grandest" appearance by the Hudson. "Sometimes in the fiercest driving storm of wind, rain, hail, or snow a great eagle will appear over the river," he wrote, "now soaring with steady and now overbended wings—always confronting the gale, or perhaps cleaving into, or at times literally *sitting* upon it. . . . The splendid bird enjoys the hubbub—is adjusted and equal to it—

finishes it so artistically. His pinions just oscillating—the position of his head and neck—his resistless, occasionally varied flight— now a swirl, now an upward movement—the black clouds driving—the angry wash below—the hiss of rain, the wind's piping (perhaps the ice colliding, grunting)—he tacking or jibing—now, as it were, for a change, abandoning himself to the gale, moving with it with such velocity—and now, resuming control, he comes up against it, lord of the situation and the storm—lord, amid it, of power and savage joy."

Surely, as Whitman wrote this tribute to the majestic eagle who sought out the tempest to defy or ride with it, he remembered that this bird was his country's chosen emblem. He must also have thought of what he himself had tried to be and do as a poet. Age and illness had halted his own high-soaring flights; earthbound now, he judged those wonderful aerial journeys of his imagination more appealing and vital than a talent for singing— as he revealed in a posthumously published poem.

> I have not so much emulated the birds that musically sing,
> I have abandon'd myself to flights, broad circles,
> The hawk, the seagull, have far more possess'd me than the canary
> or mocking-bird,
> I have not felt to warble and trill, however sweetly,
> I have felt to soar in freedom and in the fullness of power, joy,
> volition.

In the spring of 1879 Mrs. Gilchrist decided to return to England. Beatrice wanted to study medicine in Switzerland, and Anne herself longed to see her first grandchild, born in the previous autumn. Although she spoke of returning to try the "transplanting" again, she recognized that proximity to Whitman must no longer determine her life's course.

During Anne's last weeks in the United States both she and Walt were guests in the Johnstons' New York home. The night before her departure, Anne and Walt talked for a long time just by themselves in the parlor. When they emerged, their host saw that they were both quite moved. No one, apparently, was ever to know exactly what was said between them. But whatever Walt's words, he could not possibly have expressed himself better than he already had in a poem written some years before to another woman (perhaps Mrs. Juliette Beach) who, like Anne Gilchrist at first, wished to hold him permanently and exclusively.

Although the poet had not denied his love, he showed that his loving impulse was too vast and pervasive ever to be confined in a single relationship. In its oceanic imagery, the poem peculiarly anticipated Mrs. Gilchrist. Surely its aptness had sometimes struck Anne poignantly—especially now.

> Out of the rolling ocean the crowd came a drop gently to me,
> Whispering *I love you, before long I die,*
> *I have travel'd a long way merely to look on you to touch you,*
> *For I could not die till I once look'd on you,*
> *For I fear'd I might afterward lose you.*
>
> Now we have met, we have look'd, we are safe,
> Return in peace to the ocean my love,
> I too am part of that ocean my love, we are not so much separated,
> Behold the great rondure, the cohesion of all, how perfect!
>
> But as for me, for you, the irresistible sea is to separate us,
> As for an hour carrying us diverse, yet cannot carry us diverse
>   forever;
> Be not impatient—a little space—know you I salute the air, the
>   ocean and the land,
> Every day at sundown for your dear sake my love.

When Mrs. Gilchrist departed for England, she did not feel that her American mission had totally failed. She had at least become a close friend, even a soul-mate, to the poet whom she had long loved from the distance. She survived, then triumphed over her inability to form a lasting, conventional tie with Whitman. But, after all, she had her own responsibilities and needs, and in the end her desire to live close to all her children outweighed her satisfying companionship with Walt.

As for Whitman, he always acknowledged that Anne Gilchrist had been a unique element in his life. "She was a wonderful woman—a sort of human miracle to me," he said in his old age. "She was near to me: she was subtle: her grasp on my work was tremendous—so sure, so all around, so adequate." At another time, trying to describe Anne, he said: "Oh! she was strangely different from the average; entirely herself; as simple as nature; true, honest; beautiful as a tree is tall, leafy, rich, full, free—*is* a tree. Yet, free as she was by nature, bound by no conventionalisms, she was the most courageous of women; more than queenly; of high aspect in the best sense. She was not cold; she had her passions; I have known her to warm up—to resent something that was said; some impeachment of good things—great things; of a person sometimes; she had the largest charity, the sweetest fondest optimism. . . . She was a radical of radicals; enjoyed all sorts of high enthusiams; was exquisitively sensitized; belonged to the times yet to come; her vision went on and on."

Of all women, Anne Gilchrist was probably most eligible to be Walt Whitman's wife—late though she came into his life. Regrettably for her, and perhaps in some ways for him as well, he did not want it so.

Across the Atlantic, Mrs. Gilchrist would remain Walt's devoted friend. Sometimes she wistfully spoke of returning to him and America, "for the sake of being near you in body as I am in heart & soul," but she recognized now that she and her children belonged where they were. She kept hoping that one day Walt would come and visit them in his "English home."

As ardent and intelligent a disciple as Whitman could ever have hoped to inspire and teach, Anne believed that an eternity lay ahead that was far more alluring and profound—and spiritually conjugal—than any brief earthly attachment. Within their idealistic philosophies of life and death, both she and Walt felt certain that kindred souls, as they assuredly were, would meet again to love forever, in a far different way than mortal existence allowed. "Time has good things in store for us sooner or later, I doubt not," she wrote to Walt. "I could hardly express to you how welcome is the thought of death to me—not in the sense of any discontent with life—but as life with fresh energies & wider horizon & hand in hand again with those that are gone on first."

Yet only human, and a woman as well, Anne Gilchrist often remembered back to those days in Philadelphia—when Walt would tap on her door, take her hand warmly in his, then sit down for tea and a good long chat.

Farewell dear mate, dear love!
I'm going away, I know not where,
Or to what fortune, or whether I may
ever see you again,
So Good-bye my Fancy.

XI

I'M GOING AWAY, I KNOW NOT WHERE

(1879-1892)

At Timber Creek Walt Whitman restored some of his lost health and vitality. He had first awakened to life in the natural world, and now he returned to it regularly and religiously for bodily and spiritual sustenance. The trees offered him company; birds entertained him with their songs, flights, and flirtations; wildflowers assured him of the eternal beauty and fecundity of nature.

But probably nothing helped Walt so much as simply basking in the sunshine. On warm mornings, in his retreat in a secluded dell by the creek—Mrs. Stafford had instructed her children to leave him alone at such times—Walt shed his clothes and reveled in mud baths. Then he scrubbed his body with an abrasive brush and exposed his skin to the sun. By this "Adamic air-bath" he achieved an intimate contact with nature which surprised even him. "Never before did I get so close to Nature," he said; "never before did she come so close to me."

After the vigorous workout at the creek and moments of relaxation under the sun, Walt felt ready to roam about—still without his clothes. In *Specimen Days* he wrote a paean to nudity which harmonized with his attitude toward the human body, expressed throughout *Leaves of Grass* and "Children of Adam" in particular. "Somehow I seem'd to get identity with each and every thing around me, in its condition," he remarked. "Nature was naked, and I was also. . . . Perhaps the inner never lost rapport we hold with earth, light, air, trees, etc., is not to be realized through eyes and mind only, but through the whole corporeal body, which I will not have blinded or bandaged any more than the eyes. Sweet, sane, still Nakedness in Nature!—ah if poor, sick, prurient humanity in cities might really know you once more! Is not nakedness then indecent? No, not inherently. It is your thought, your sophistication, your fear, your respectability, that is indecent." Walt went on to attribute the great accomplishments of the Greeks in the arts, philosophy, and heroism to "their natural and religious idea of Nakedness."

About his own nudism Walt acknowledged, "Some good people may think it a feeble or half-crack'd way of spending one's time and thinking," and then admitted, "Maybe it is." Nevertheless, he credited his "partial rehabilitation" largely to these therapeutic sessions at Timber Creek. As a child, then an energetic man, he had mentally "absorbed" the external world. Now, with almost single-minded attention, Walt let his skin take in the sun's rays— as though storing up their bright warmth for the gray and chilly years ahead. Whenever and wherever it shone above him, the sun had become a friendly deity to whom Walt could address a poem of both praise and earnest request, as in "Thou Orb Aloft Full-Dazzling":

Hear me illustrious!
Thy lover me, for always I have loved thee,
Even as basking babe, then happy boy alone by some wood edge,
        thy touching-distant beams enough,
Or man matured, or young or old, as now to thee I launch my
        invocation.

      •   •   •

Shed, shed thyself on mine and me, with but a fleeting ray out of
        thy million millions,
Strike through these chants.

> Nor only launch thy subtle dazzle and thy strength for these,
> Prepare the later afternoon of me myself—prepare my lengthening
>   shadows,
> Prepare my starry nights.

Walt had reached the afternoon of his life. He might now regret
the passing of ebullient youth and hearty manhood, but years before, in the first edition of *Leaves of Grass,* he had welcomed
their inevitable successor.

> Youth, large, lusty, loving—youth full of grace, force, fascination,
> Do you know that Old Age may come after you with equal grace,
>   force, fascination?
>
> Day full-blown and splendid—day of the immense sun, action,
>   ambition, laughter,
> The Night follows close with millions of suns, and sleep and
>   restoring darkness.

Now in Walt's life a circle was being rounded. In old age, life's
evening, he would surely be compensated when viewing the vast
splendor of the soul-proclaiming heavens with their myriad faraway suns—to be seen only when the earthly sun had journeyed
to the other side of the sphere. "A Clear Midnight" was the time
for spiritual expansion:

> This is thy hour O Soul, thy free flight into the wordless,
> Away from books, away from art, the day erased, the lesson done,
> Thee fully forth emerging, silent, gazing, pondering the themes
>   thou lovest best,
> Night, sleep, death and the stars.

With his improved health, Walt could do more than sit with
his memories, looking back over the long road he had traveled for
sixty years, or scan the short span which lay ahead.

In the past for his poems' geography he had frequently relied
upon his own imagination and secondhand reports describing
much of the American continent. During his Mississippi boat trip
in 1848, coming north from New Orleans, he had only glimpsed

the start of the vast prairie land. Three decades later, in the autumn of 1879, Walt was invited westward as the "guest-poet" at Kansas's Quarter-Centennial celebration. Whitman's friend Colonel Forney, publisher of the Philadelphia *Press*, had reserved berths on the newly-designed Pullman car for members of his staff, and he wanted to take Whitman too on the train trip. Walt gladly accepted this offer of a free ride, along with food and bed, across midwestern America. He also planned to visit his brother Jeff in St. Louis before returning to Camden.

At the ceremony in Topeka, the poet failed to recite a poem because nobody had asked him beforehand to compose one for the occasion. And as for the speech he had hastily written instead, he did not deliver it either; he was forgetful of the time while busily socializing. The Westerners he met thoroughly delighted him; almost to a man they fitted his long-cherished conceptions of the new American breed spawned in the West. He was disappointed, however, in their womenfolk, who were not shaping themselves into brave new forms, but still relied upon the fashions, frills, and manners of their Eastern counterparts.

From Kansas, by himself, Walt took the train farther west to Colorado, for he wished to see the Rocky Mountains. Visiting Platte Canyon, he was struck by its uncanny resemblance to his own artistry. "I have found the law of my own poems," he announced, and then wrote a short poem to demonstrate what he meant.

Spirit that form'd this scene,
These tumbled rock-piles grim and red,
These reckless heaven-ambitious peaks,
These gorges, turbulent-clear streams, this naked freshness,
These formless wild arrays, for reasons of their own,
I know thee, savage spirit—we have communed together,
Mine too such wild arrays, for reasons of their own;
Was't charged against my chants they had forgotten art?
To fuse within themselves its rules precise and delicatesse?
The lyrist's measur'd beat, the wrought-out temple's grace—column
      and polish'd arch forgot?

But thou that revelest here—spirit that form'd this scene,
They have remember'd thee.

Returning eastward then, Walt was thrilled with the vistas provided by the moving train: of wild animals staring in disbelief as the man-made monster roared by; of the wide, flat, seemingly endless prairie land, tawny beneath the autumnal sun, whose promised fertility might someday support millions of "average" Americans.

Settling down in St. Louis for a long stay with Jeff and his two daughters, Walt spent a lot of time wandering around town, taking stock of its denizens. His visit, however, turned out to be far too prolonged for his liking. Colonel Forney had neglected to provide Walt with the wherewithal to return home, and the stranded poet apparently could not bring himself to ask Jeff for his fare. Walt's friends in the East learned of his predicament, and at Christmas he received a hundred dollars from an anonymous benefactor. Soon after the new year had begun, Walt was back home in Camden, ready for a rest after the trip that had taken him more than 5,000 miles and shown him a good part of western America.

In the summer of 1880 Whitman went traveling again. He left by train for Ontario, Canada, to visit Dr. Richard Maurice Bucke, an "alienist" or psychiatrist who headed the staff of a mental asylum there. Several years before, when Dr. Bucke was visiting Philadelphia, he crossed the river to Camden, hoping to meet the poet of *Leaves of Grass,* a book he had long cherished primarily because of its mysticism—a state of mind that intrigued him. When he first beheld Walt, Dr. Bucke experienced a "spiritual intoxication" which caused, he later claimed, a transformation in his life. His initial impression of Whitman was quite overwhelming: "It seemed to me at that time certain that he was either actually a god or in some sense clearly preterhuman." In his own way Dr. Bucke expressed what others often felt of a strangely magnetic, affecting, essentially unanalyzable aspect in Walt's very appearance. His long white hair and beard added to a Jehovahlike look and demeanor. He was not just another old man: he was somehow a creature apart and above mere mortals.

Dr. Bucke became a close friend of Whitman, who doubtless was flattered to receive the ardent attentions of this scientist-philosopher. He would prove to be one of Walt's most helpful and articulate supporters. Dr. Bucke had lost a foot from frostbite years before, while crossing the Rockies in the wintertime; and Walt, try as he might, could never fully get rid of the drag in his left leg. Now, in Ontario, the two companions limped about the spacious grounds of the institution, all the while deep in conversation. Walt found the hospital's atmosphere pleasant rather than depressing; his friend was using new, humane techniques in treating the mentally ill and was also giving them attractive surroundings.

Later the two men set off on a long journey around the Great Lakes, down the St. Lawrence River, and about Montreal. Ever the journalist, Walt took notes on their adventures, recording the statistics he invariably sought as well as his own impressions of people and places.

In April of 1881 Walt gave his Lincoln lecture in Boston, where he had caused a minor sensation twenty years before. On this visit, many of the area's artists and intellectuals invited him into their own homes and generally made him feel welcome and admired—though a few of the entrenched literati, like Holmes and Lowell, still kept a careful distance from the barbaric bard.

As an important aftermath of Whitman's visit, one of Boston's reputable publishers, James R. Osgood, wrote and proposed to publish a new edition of *Leaves of Grass*. For long and discouraging years Walt had privately issued his works; once more his poetry could appear under a regular publisher's imprint and earn a royalty. Whitman, however, did not want to become so respectable that he would have to slough off any of his notorious "sex odes," so his contract with Osgood explicitly called for the inclusion of all poems in the new edition.

The year 1881 kept Whitman busy. He revised *Leaves of Grass* for its seventh edition. Then, Dr. Bucke had declared his intention to write a biography of Whitman, and instead of dissuading him,

Walt looked upon the project as a chance to get certain facts (or his own interpretations of them) on the official record. "You ask for items, details of my early life," he wrote to Bucke. "You say you want to get at these details mainly as the go-befores and embryons of *Leaves of Grass.* Very good; you shall have at least some specimens of them all." In the process of recollecting his earlier years, Whitman wrote much of the background material for Dr. Bucke's biography-to-be; at the same time he began preparing passages for the first section in his informally autobiographical *Specimen Days.*

Since the real places, even if changed by time, might be more effectively remembered and rendered if actually seen again, Walt and Dr. Bucke took a nostalgic trip together through the various locales of Whitman's Long Island youth. They visited "Paumanok's" seashore and harbors, the countryside around West Hills and Huntington, his grandparents' old homesites, and even the Whitman and Van Velsor graveyards. "My whole family history, with its succession of links, from the first settlement down to date, told here—" Walt wrote in his notebook while sitting upon a grave at the Whitman burial hill; "three centuries concentrate on this sterile acre."

In August Walt returned to Boston to oversee the printing of the perennially growing *Leaves.* He had added, of course, a number of new poems to the volume—many of which had previously been published in newspapers or magazines. But this edition was especially notable because of Whitman's rearrangement of the existing poems; most of them were placed in "final" groups or clusters according to the poet's scheme of gathering poems together by similarities in subject or mood, instead of a sequence according to dates of composition or focus on particular stages in his external and internal lives. The book's table of contents displays the basic design: a first section called "Inscriptions"—mainly poems announcing the poet's intentions and perspective—followed by large groups of poems collected together, interspersed with a number of separate poems, usually fairly long. Whitman planned that any future poems he wrote could be added later as "annexes."

(Thus, in reading through *Leaves of Grass* as Walt Whitman prepared it, the novice reader will not know when a poem was first composed or published unless the date has been supplied by an editor. Poems that appeared in the first edition of the book may be found alongside some written several decades later. *Leaves of Grass* does not present a neat chronological record of Whitman's development either as a man or as a poet, although certain groups —such as "Calamus" and "Drum-Taps" and "Memories of President Lincoln," and the two annexes—relate to definite periods in his life. Yet certain poems even within these groups were composed before or after the rest and were inserted later; others deriving from that particular time-period were taken out, to be moved elsewhere or eliminated altogether from the later editions. Whitman's chronic revisions of his volume—in which he changed titles, altered words and phrases, added or subtracted lines, and generally shifted his poems around—have considerable fascination for some literary scholars, who compare an original composition with its eventual "final" form and note all the stages in between, providing explanations for every change, whether apparently for personal reasons or artistic improvement. In several anthologies of Whitman's writings their editors may give the first version (with the "final" title), preferring it to the long-worked-over poem awarded Whitman's ultimate authorization. Sometimes, then, a Whitman poem in one collection can have the same title as a poem in another book, but they may be quite different from each other.)

The respectful and generous attention given by his new publisher greatly pleased Whitman. Equally pleasant was his visit in mid-September to nearby Concord, where he stayed with an old Abolitionist friend, Frank B. Sanborn. Walt chatted with philosopher Bronson Alcott and his daughter, the writer Louisa May— now more famous and certainly far wealthier than her abstracted father.

Best of all, Walt saw Emerson again. In this last year of his life, the Concord Sage's memory was clouded over by age, but he was still genial—warm like the sun in his smiling benevolence. Walt silently and happily basked in Emerson's presence, gazing perpetually at him while the others around them talked, mainly about Thoreau—whose name Emerson had trouble even remembering, although Thoreau had been almost like a son.

In the past, people had sometimes told Walt some of Emerson's remarks about him; he always seemed more amused than offended by them. Emerson rather acutely had summed up *Leaves of Grass* as a "mixture of the New York *Herald* and the *Bhagavad-Gita*." Another time, he had called Whitman "half song-thrush, half alligator." And he had told a mutual acquaintance, "Yes, Walt sends me all his books. But tell Walt I am not satisfied—not satisfied. I expect him to make the songs of the Nation, but he seems to be contented to make the inventories." Then, in his Journal, Emerson enjoyed recording somebody's quip (probably Wendell Phillips's) that *Leaves of Grass* contained "every leaf but the fig-leaf."

Through the years Emerson's enthusiastic response to Whitman's poetry had definitely cooled—probably in part out of a self-protective caution. Emerson's gradual retreat from the awkward position of being an active Whitman advocate certainly had wounded Walt. Yet Walt himself had increasingly denied—sometimes rather belligerently—Emerson's important impact upon him when first creating his *Leaves*.

In the early years of their relationship, Emerson and Whitman had often dined together whenever Emerson came to New York. But Walt's relish for noisy, low-brow places had annoyed the quiet-living intellectual, and after a while he no longer sought Walt out as a suitable social companion. To his credit, however, whatever his opinion of Walt as person or poet, Emerson always refused to join the ranks of Whitman's fiercely snobbish detractors. He continued to do many helpful things for Walt in both literary and personal matters, such as collecting funds for Walt's war-hospital work and arranging for magazine publication of certain new poems that he liked. Probably Whitman's feelings were most injured when Emerson ignored him completely while editing an anthology of American poetry; however, this was late in Emerson's life and the work was done mainly by his daughter, who disapproved of Whitman.

And now in Concord, Walt looked upon the special invitation to dine with Emerson, his family and friends at "the Manse" as a dumb yet eloquent gesture of Emerson's deep-down belief in him—despite everything that had passed, or failed to pass, between them through the years. It seemed to him a "victor event"—given as an "apology, peace-offering, justification of so much that the world knows not of." And recalling Emerson later on, Walt said, "The world does not know what our relations really were—they think of our friendship always as a literary friendship: it was a bit that but it was mostly something else—it was certainly more than that—for I loved Emerson for his personality and I always felt that he loved me for something I brought him from the rush of the big cities and the mass of men."

While in Concord, Walt visited the Concord battlefield and "Sleepy Hollow" cemetery where both Hawthorne and Thoreau were interred. He also spent an hour at Walden Pond—"that beautifully embower'd sheet of water"—and saw the site of the small rustic cabin which Thoreau had built in the woods in 1845. There visitors customarily placed stones, gradually building up a sort of cairn as a monument to the author of *Walden*. Walt added his own offering to the pile. Thoreau had died years before, in 1862, mourned at first only by a handful of friends and admirers. Yet now his reputation, based on his books and essays, was slowly and steadily growing; in his quiet way Thoreau had managed to become a strong and durable American voice by preaching independent thinking and living, describing the delights of nature, and expounding upon one's right, and indeed duty, to protest social injustices.

When later asked to predict whether Emerson would eventually stand "bigger" than Thoreau by reputation, Whitman admitted that his own "prejudices" favored Emerson because he had liked him so much personally. But then Walt made an astute observation. "Thoreau was a surprising fellow—he is not easily grasped—is elusive: yet he is one of the native forces—stands for a fact, a movement, an upheaval: Thoreau belongs to America, to the transcendental, to the protesters: then he is an outdoor man: all outdoor men, everything else being equal, appeal to me. Thoreau was not so precious, tender, a personality as Emerson: but he was a force—he looms up bigger and bigger: his dying does not seem to have hurt him a bit: every year has added to his fame. One thing about Thoreau keeps him very near to me: I refer to his lawlessness—his dissent—his going down his own absolute road, let hell blaze all it chooses." Thoreau's essay on "Civil Disobedience" alone had guaranteed his survival, indeed prevalence, a century later, not only in his own country but throughout the world—when the once-influential words of the gracefully and profoundly speculative Emerson would seldom be read or recognized except in academic quarters.

On his return to Boston, Whitman heard at night of the death of President Garfield, who had been shot by an assassin in July but had lingered for several months. Garfield's death did not assume for Whitman the tragic dimensions of Lincoln's, but it too affected him—particularly because he had known Garfield personally during his Washington years, when Garfield, a Congressman then, always called out greetings to the poet by quoting Walt's own lines. So now, as Walt heard the city church bells tolling the death of the country's president, he composed a dirge, which he inserted in the forthcoming edition of *Leaves of Grass*.

> The sobbing of the bells, the sudden death-news everywhere,
> The slumbers rouse, the rapport of the People,
> (Full well return, respond within their breasts, their brains, the sad
> reverberations,)
> The passionate toll and clang—city to city, joining, sounding,
> passing,
> Those heart-beats of a Nation in the night.

The new *Leaves of Grass* came out late in 1881; generally it received cordial, even favorable notices. Since the book was selling far better than it ever had before, Walt naturally hoped that his literary offspring would now assist him financially in his old age, paying him back for the quarter-century in which he had subsidized its growth.

But Walt's optimistic outlook, his feeling of having at last "arrived," soon dimmed. Someone complained to Boston's district attorney, and the civil authorities, alerted to a possible contamination of public morals, declared *Leaves of Grass* "obscene literature" and banned it from the mails—and, consequently, distribution.

The situation could be remedied, the publisher was informed, if the author made a number of changes: some in specific lines, but significantly by removing two whole poems, "A Woman Waits for Me" and "To a Common Prostitute." This, of course, the ever-intransigent Whitman refused to do. He always stuck stubbornly by his principles; but also he would never admit—as his excision of these poems would virtually cause him to do—that any of his poems should be shamed, abandoned, or denied an equal place with the others.

James Osgood was a businessman, not a literary crusader. He declined to back Whitman in any legal proceedings or to risk incurring penalties by continuing to publish and sell *Leaves of Grass.* Therefore the arrangement between publisher and poet, begun so amicably, terminated. To compensate for unpaid royalties, Osgood gave Whitman the printing plates for his book, a few hundred unbound copies remaining in stock, and a hundred dollars.

So now Whitman returned to being his own publisher and distributor, a task increasingly burdensome to him. Orders for the book came in heavily for a while, largely because of the notoriety of its being "banned in Boston." This time, mercifully, Walt's period as private publisher was brief. The Philadelphia textbook publisher Rees Welsh took over the business of handling *Leaves of Grass.* Shortly thereafter one of the firm's employees founded his own publishing house; among David McKay's first offerings was the controversial seventh edition of *Leaves of Grass.*

The whole Boston skirmish had made news everywhere, becoming a main topic for dispute among editors, critics, and correspondents, especially in the New York papers. Into the fracas with furious energy charged Walt's erstwhile friend William D. O'Connor—still the fire-breathing defender of *Leaves of Grass* and its author's artistic genius. Though Walt had lost a publisher, he now regained a good friend, for the two men began a cor-

respondence which led to their meeting and complete reconciliation. Already ailing from a progessive muscular disease, O'Connor
realized that the unhappy ten-year hiatus in their relations had
been foolish. In the few years remaining to him, he gratefully
welcomed Whitman's concerned attention.

Whitman's friendship with John Burroughs too was revitalized
after John returned from his first trip to Europe, where he had
visited many Whitman admirers, including Anne Gilchrist. In the
autumn of 1882 John came down to spend a week with Walt at
the New Jersey seashore. The two friends tramped companionably
upon the near-deserted beach, observing every detail of landscape
and seascape and sky while they resumed their easy ability to
communicate their thoughts and feelings.

John, now older and more mature—less dazzled, perhaps, than
other Whitman disciples in the company of the master—nonetheless felt the same old fond adulation. "Much and copious talk,"
he reported in his diary. "His presence loosens my tongue. . . . I
feel as if under the effects of some rare tonic or cordial all the
time. There is something grainy and saline in him, as in the voice
of the sea. Sometimes his talk is choppy and confused, or elliptical
and unfinished; again there comes a long splendid roll of thought
that bathes one from head to foot, or swings you quite free from
your moorings."

After Burroughs went home, Walt remained at the hotel for a
few days, absorbing alone the ocean's scenery and gathering material for new poems. "Sometimes if the temperature allows," he
noted in his own diary, "go down and walk or sit till quite late—
have the whole performance to myself—beyond all operas or finest
vocalism or band. Ever that ceaseless, sulking, guttural of the sea
as if to me its wrongs and toils in confidence—ever those muffled
distant lion roars—. . . . Some vast soul like a planet stopt, arrested,
tied—some mighty freedom pent denied—some cosmic right with-
held."

In "With Husky-Haughty Lips, O Sea!"—a notable poem of his
later years—Whitman used some of the same images and phrases
of his diary notations. Obviously he identified with the sea to
which he had raptly listened hour after hour, finding in it a giant-

sized portrait of himself. He too felt sorrow, anger, and frustration: he was denied understanding and recognition and distressed by the increasing frailty of his years.

> Thy ample, smiling face, dash'd with the sparkling dimples of the
> sun,
> Thy brooding scowl and murk—thy unloos'd hurricanes,
> Thy unsubduedness, caprices, wilfulness;
> Great as thou art above the rest, thy many tears—a lack from all
> eternity in thy content,
> (Naught but the greatest struggles, wrongs, defeats, could make
> thee greatest—no less could make thee,)
> Thy lonely state—something thou ever seek'st and seek'st, yet never
> gain'st,
> Surely some right withheld—some voice, in huge monotonous rage,
> of freedom-lover pent,
> Some vast heart, like a planet's, chain'd and chafing in those
> breakers,
> By lengthen'd swell, and spasm, and panting breath,
> And rhythmic rasping of thy sands and waves,
> And serpent hiss, and savage peals of laughter,
> And undertones of distant lion roar,
>
>   •   •   •
>
> The first and last confession of the globe,
> Outsurging, muttering from thy soul's abysms,
> The tale of cosmic elemental passion,
> Thou tellest to a kindred soul.

When David McKay assumed the publication of *Leaves of Grass*, he agreed to publish a new collection of Whitman's prose, which Walt began preparing for publication in 1882. *Specimen Days and Collect* would be a miscellaneous collection of Walt's reminiscences of his childhood and early manhood, his "memoranda" of the Civil War years (previously published but publicly ignored), impressions jotted down at Timber Creek and after rides on the Camden ferry, notes taken during recent travels, plus various essays and recollections.

In his introduction to this new volume, Walt said that he had felt a "curiously imperative" command to assemble these pieces.

"We give long preparations for some object, planning and delving and fashioning," said Whitman to apologize for this hodge-podge of prose material; "and then, when the actual hour for doing arrives, find ourselves still quite unprepared, and tumble the thing together, letting hurry and crudeness tell the story better than fine work." And he ventured, "Maybe, if I don't do anything else, I shall send out the most wayward, spontaneous, fragmentary work ever printed."

Taking a more serious vein in a footnote, Walt explained himself further. "I suppose I publish and leave the whole gathering, first from that eternal tendency to perpetuate and preserve which is behind all Nature, authors included; second, to symbolize two or three specimen interiors, personal and other, out of the myriads of my time, the middle range of the nineteenth century in the New World; a strange, unloosen'd, wondrous time."

Whatever its lack of framework, its many digressions, and its indefinite intentions, *Specimen Days* is the best prose source for Whitman's autobiographical materials. It has special merit too because it contains his detailed descriptions of the Civil War, provides many delightfully informal pieces which show the poet's love for nature in its particulars, and offers pensive little excursions and diversions.

As Whitman's now-official publisher, McKay in 1883 also published Dr. Richard Maurice Bucke's "authorized" biography of Walt Whitman. It too was a miscellany: the poet's remembrances of earlier years (sometimes erroneous, whether by memory lapse or intention); Bucke's own idealized portrait of Whitman; his interpretation and defense of Whitman's poetry; a sizable appendix which, among other things, reprinted O'Connor's *The Good Gray Poet;* and an attempt to counterbalance praise of Whitman with the reservations of others regarding his versification.

Walt always expressed his satisfaction with Bucke's book; he also voiced the hope that it would be the only biography ever written about him. No doubt he felt uncomfortable when thinking that other writers might probe deeper into their subject, to come up with facts and speculations that would not tally with Whitman's own notion of the proper way of regarding or presenting himself—which his friend Dr. Bucke had seemingly accepted without question.

More than a dozen years before, Walt had recorded these suspicions—indeed, perhaps fears—of his future biographers.

> When I read the book, the biography famous,
> And is this then (said I) what the author calls a man's life?
> And so will some one when I am dead and gone write my life?
> (As if any man really knew aught of my life,
> Why even I myself I often think know little or nothing of my real life,
> Only a few hints, a few diffused faint clews and indirections
> I seek for my own use to trace out here.)

Walt was saying that his own inner life was best revealed in the "hints" within *Leaves of Grass* written primarily for his own benefit and barely understood even by himself. The job of Whitman's near-innumerable biographers—much as he wished to discourage them—has always involved culling and interpreting these "faint clews and indirections" given in his poems.

In his younger years Whitman actually thought well of the art and intentions of biography. While editor of the Brooklyn *Eagle* he had proclaimed: "What a gain it would be, if we could forego some of the heavy tomes, the fruit of an age of toil and scientific study, for the simple easy *truthful* narrative of the existence and experience of a man of genius,—how his mind unfolded in his earliest years—the impressions things made upon him—how and where and when the religious sentiment dawned in him . . . the development of his soul—when he first loved—the way circumstances imbued his nature, and did him good, and worked him ill,—with all the long train of occurrences, adventures, mental processes, exercises within, and trials without, which go to make up the man. . . ."

These have really been the aims of Whitman's own biographers in delineating his developing character and tracing the evolution of his poetry. But, like most other "men of genius," Whitman was a complex and often contradictory person who does not readily lend himself to simple narrative; nor is the "truth" about him easily ascertained. Whatever shaped Walt Whitman and caused him to become a poet may always remain beyond the grasp of analytical scholars—just as he had willed it in "Song of Myself":

> My final merit I refuse you, I refuse putting from me what I really am,
> Encompass worlds, but never try to encompass me . . .

Whitman at last had found a secure situation with a book publisher who could tend to the details of printing and marketing his books. He also had the satisfaction of knowing that both at home and abroad he was steadily gaining a wider readership and new admirers. Many visitors found their way to his door. To Walt's surprise, Henry Wadsworth Longfellow came calling. But a large portion of his guests were Englishmen, like the author-aesthete Oscar Wilde, famed actor Henry Irving, and the literary-minded Lord Houghton.

The English writer Edward Carpenter's meticulous observations of Walt and his surroundings during several long visits gave clear and fascinating pictures of the aging poet. He looked at first "quite an old man with long grey, almost white, beard and shaggy head and neck, grey dress too; but tall, erect, and at closer sight not so old—a florid fresh complexion, pure grey-blue eye (no sign of age there) and full, strong, well-formed hands." Carpenter soon became aware of a "certain radiant power" his host possessed—"a large benign effluence and inclusiveness, as of the sun, which filled out the place where he was—yet with something of reserve and sadness in it too, and a sense of remoteness and inaccessibility." He noticed the similarity between poet and his poetry: "There were clearly enough visible the same strong and contrary moods, the same strange omnivorous egotism, controlled and restrained by that wonderful genius of his for human affection and love."

In 1884 George Whitman built a farmhouse about a dozen miles from Camden. Knowing Walt's fondness for the countryside, he naturally expected his older brother to be overjoyed at the prospect of living closer to nature. For a decade George had given

Walt a home, with freedom to come and go as he liked; but he had never really understood him—and never would. Walt now adamantly refused to move away from Camden to live with George and Lou. His stubborn attitude wounded George deeply; he could not comprehend Walt's desire to stay in noisy, smoke-filled Camden.

But Walt would not wholly abandon the city. His social and intellectual life depended upon the proximity of the ferry to Philadelphia; pure nature simply could not compensate him enough for being cut off from friends and visitors. Bitter words passed between the brothers. For several years George refused to see Walt, although Lou came often into Camden to bring Walt fresh eggs and produce from their farm, along with treats she had baked specially for him.

So now Walt had to shift for himself. A wealthy friend offered a house rent-free in Philadelphia, but Walt declined, wishing to steer clear of any indebtedness. With his own small savings he bought a little house at 328 Mickle Street in Camden. A six-room, two-story frame cottage set on a tiny lot, it was just a block from the stop for the streetcar which would take him to the ferry.

Except for his mother's old bed, which he now used, Walt had no household furnishings of his own. He did not think that he needed any more than the simplest essentials. He began to live as he had in Washington during the war, buying an old oil stove for cooking and heating, and using wooden crates for his tables and chairs.

Having exhausted all his funds and earning little or nothing now from his published writings, Walt spent the winter of 1884-85 suffering from the cold and malnutrition. He did not alert his friends to his grim predicament, first out of unawareness of need, then probably out of sheer pride. When they finally learned of his impoverishment, they did all they could to take care of his immediate needs.

In the meantime, a widow named Mary Oakes Davis watched the lame old poet hobbling along the Camden streets that winter. Taking pity on him, Mrs. Davis began to come to his home once a day to fix him a hot meal and to wash and mend his clothes. A habitual altruist, she had spent her lifetime caring for the help-less or homeless: a blind aunt, an ancient sea captain, orphans, injured birds. She did not understand poetry, but she did understand human misery—and whenever and however she could, she allayed it.

By the spring of 1885, Mrs. Davis had become Walt's official, live-in housekeeper. They had made an odd sort of arrangement between them: he would provide the house and she would furnish it; she would shop for the food and prepare it, and he would pay for it. The once-bare downstairs rooms at Mickle Street were now filled to overflowing with knickknacks, vases, nautical mementoes, overstuffed chairs, caged birds, a cat, and a dog. An orphan girl slept in the kitchen; chickens roosted in the back yard.

Whitman occupied the large second-floor bedroom, to which his visitors usually ascended, since the parlor was small, crowded—and hardly Walt's style. The English writer Edmund Gosse recalled that his opening impression was of extreme simplicity: "A large room, without carpet on the scrubbed planks, a small bedstead, a little round stove with a stackpipe in the center of the room, one chair—that was all the furniture. . . . Various boxes lay about, and one huge clamped trunk, and heaps, mountains of papers in a wild confusion, swept up here and there into stacks and peaks; but all the room, and the old man himself, clean in the highest degree, raised to the *nth* power of stainlessness, scoured and scrubbed to such a pitch that dirt seemed defied for all remaining time. Whitman, in particular, in his suit of hodden grey and shirt thrown wide open at the throat, his grey hair and whiter beard voluminously flowing, seemed positively blanched with cleanliness; the whole man sand-white with spotlessness, like a deal table that has grown old under the scrubbing-brush."

This room, Mrs. Davis, and the Mickle Street house would remain stable features in Whitman's declining years. Mrs. Davis's dedication to the job of tending the aging poet was admirable to the point of heroism. She received little spoken gratitude from Walt himself; he took her beneficent presence in his life for granted. And as he grew older, Walt became almost miserly, so that Mrs. Davis often had to pay the household expenses from her own purse. To make her situation even more difficult, many Camden citizens looked askance at her for living thus with a notorious "libertine"—although obviously there was nothing lascivious in their simple association.

Mrs. Davis seemed to regard Whitman as a maimed, elderly bird who needed her kindly ministrations. She gradually learned that through the years this poet had sung out wondrous songs which other people admired so much that they made pilgrimages to Mickle Street, even from faraway lands, just to look upon him. Walt's importance at least may have made Mrs. Davis feel that her selfless loyalty to him was worthwhile. Certainly someone had to look after him—so why not she?

As for the poet whose ecstatic spirit in younger years had flown like a bird over continents and oceans or soared among the wheeling stars, he was increasingly beset by old age's infirmities —and no longer projected himself into the high-flying eagle or the spellbinding, richly melodic thrush or mockingbird. Like a domesticated pet—"My Canary Bird"—he sang out steadily and clearly yet from a cage.

> Did we count great, O soul, to penetrate the themes of mighty books,
> Absorbing deep and full from thoughts, plays, speculations?
> But now from thee to me, caged bird, to feel thy joyous warble,
> Filling the air, the lonesome room, the long forenoon,
> Is it not just as great, O soul?

Walt still had a few good years ahead of him. As his financial troubles became known, his friends in America and England rallied to find various ways to add to his income, comforts, and conveniences. When growing lameness halted Whitman's pedestrian tours around town, donations were sought from well-to-do notables to provide Walt with his own horse and buggy. The first gift horse was not fast enough to suit him, so he traded it in for another. For several years he drove at a rapid pace around Camden and down country lanes. He liked to get out into nature often, and no longer could visit Timber Creek after the Staffords sold their farm.

Several funds were started in Whitman's behalf—one so that he might eventually buy his own little place in the country. Benefit performances of his Lincoln reading and other talks were scheduled in various cities—when he felt up to giving them. Birthday gatherings to shower praises upon him became regular events in his later years. Subscriptions to new volumes of his poetry and prose were solicited, sometimes at considerably more than the actual price, with the difference going to the poet.

Nobody ever worked harder to further Whitman's literary reputation or to raise money for his aid than the faithful Anne Gilchrist, whose attentions to Walt had not ceased with her return to England. No longer did she feel or express the ardor of the past; their friendship now held the warm, steady, and pervasive glow of late-afternoon sunlight. Anne was a grandmother now— a role she loved to fill. And she had deep cares of her own, such as the sudden death of her daughter Beatrice and her own faltering health. But she had made few complaints to Walt, so her own death, in late November of 1885, was a great shock to him.

Walt had become more dependent on the very fact of Anne Gilchrist's existence than he realized. Writing at once to her son Herbert, he said: "Now nothing remains but a sweet and rich memory—none more beautiful all time, all life all the earth—I cannot write anything of a letter to-day, I must sit alone and think." And to Burroughs he wrote, "Seems to me mortality never enclosed a more beautiful spirit." John agreed, for he too—especially since his sojourn in England, when he had spent many days in her company—had been very fond of Mrs. Gilchrist. "She was the only woman I have ever seen to whose strength of mind and character I humbly bowed," he told her son. "Now she is gone, I see how much she stood to me for all England."

Mrs. Gilchrist's energetic, intelligent optimism—product of the century in which philosophic and scientific thinking endorsed the concept of "progress"—infused her own life and that of her children and friends. It had deeply impressed Walt; and now, remembering Anne vividly and wishing to record something about her to place permanently among his *Leaves,* Walt wrote "Going Somewhere":

My science-friend, my noblest woman-friend,
(Now buried in an English grave—and this a memory-leaf for her
          dear sake,)
Ended our talk—"The sum, concluding all we know of old or
          modern learning, intuitions deep,
"Of all Geologies—Histories—of all Astronomy—of Evolution, Meta-
          physics all,
"Is, that we all are onward, onward, speeding slowly, surely
          bettering,
"Life, life an endless march, an endless army, (no halt, but it is
          duly over,)
"The world, the race, the soul—in space and time the universes,
"All bound as is befitting each—all surely going somewhere."

Anne Gilchrist's children had shared her love for Walt, and
soon after her death Herbert left for America, to stay for some
while with Whitman. Now an established artist—a member of
the Royal Academy of Arts—Herbert Gilchrist made a number of drawings and paintings of the poet in his Mickle Street
home.

Gilchrist was not the only artist who portrayed Whitman. Indeed, he was becoming a popular model for portraitists and
sculptors—and a willing one too, for he apparently often welcomed these chances to record his physical likeness for the benefit of coming generations. Mrs. Davis's tidy housekeeping was
frequently undone because of the easels, paintboxes, sculptors'
tools and chips and half-finished busts which were strewn about
the tiny home—plus the artists themselves, who somehow had to
be accommodated.

Practitioners of the youthful art of photography were also attracted to Walt. During the Civil War the pioneer photographer
Mathew Brady had taken some handsome shots of Whitman; now
other men were eager to capture the poet's white mane and flowing beard upon their plates. Walt seemed to like posing for photographs, and in one famous picture of him a butterfly perched on
his finger. (Some people felt cheated when they learned that the
creature was a fake, made of cardboard.) Usually the camera
proved more honest and successful in catching the real Whitman

than artists' skills. Painters and sculptors invariably made their own interpretations of Walt's essential nature, emphasizing certain features or expressions and ignoring or playing down others which were important too—whereas photography could better record the man as he was.

One of Whitman's best portraits was painted by Thomas Eakins. The artist later explained his special approach toward his subject. He had discovered that in painting Walt "the ordinary methods wouldn't do—that techniques, rules, and traditions would have to be thrown aside; that, before all else, he was to be treated as a *man,* whatever became of what are commonly called the principles of art." Eakins' method coincided with Whitman's own composition of *Leaves of Grass:* perhaps this was why his portrait came out so well.

The New York *Herald's* editor appointed Walt Whitman a "staff poet," paying him a few dollars for every poem he contributed to the paper. Sometimes Walt sent in several a week. The poems Walt wrote these days were usually brief: vignettes of his life or appreciative considerations of such plain yet wonderful things as "The First Dandelion" (published, ironically, on a March day at the start of the terrible Blizzard of '88):

> Simple and fresh and fair from winter's close emerging,
> As if no artifice of fashion, business, politics, had ever been,
> Forth from its sunny nook of shelter'd grass—innocent, golden, calm
> as the dawn,
> The spring's first dandelion shows its trustful face.

Not only did Whitman compose short poems (which were often printed without much ado in magazines and newspapers, earning a welcome pittance); he also worked steadily on prose articles— remembrances, critical commentaries, essays, and biographical sketches. Walt just could not stop writing—his way of talking to other people then and thereafter. This compulsive communicativeness resembled that of the old dinner guest whom Whitman candidly yet sympathetically depicted in "After the Supper and Talk":

After the supper and talk—after the day is done,
As a friend from friends his final withdrawal prolonging,
Good-bye and Good-bye with emotional lips repeating,
(So hard for his hand to release those hands—no more will they
      meet,
No more for communion of sorrow and joy, of old and young,
A far-stretching journey awaits him, to return no more,)
Shunning, postponing severance—seeking to ward off the last word
      ever so little,
E'en at the exit-door turning—charges superfluous calling back—
      e'en as he descends the steps,

      •   •   •

Soon to be lost for aye in the darkness—loth, O so loth to depart!
Garrulous to the very last.

A big one-volume edition of Whitman's *Complete Poems and Prose, 1855-1888* was printed in a limited edition. In the following year, for Walt's seventieth birthday, a small-dimensioned *Leaves of Grass* (in its eighth edition) was published, pleasing him greatly because he had always wanted it to be available in a size easily carried in readers' pockets.

Meanwhile, Walt busily prepared a new collection of prose and poetry, to be called *November Boughs*. It presented a group of new short poems gathered under the title of "Sands at Seventy," eventually to be added as a "first annex" to *Leaves of Grass*. These poems, Whitman knew, were frail offerings compared with the vibrant spirits and lofty themes of the long poems from his younger, highly productive years. But he cherished them nonetheless for what they were—the final leaves clinging to an autumnal tree:

You lingering sparse leaves of me on winter-nearing boughs,
And I some well-shorn tree of field or orchard-row;
You tokens diminute and lorn—(not now the flush of May, or July
      clover-bloom—no grain of August now;)
You pallid banner-staves—you pennants valueness—you overstay'd
      of time,
Yet my soul-dearest leaves confirming, all the rest,
The faithfulest—hardiest—last.

The poems of Walt Whitman's later years are often dismissed as inferior by critics and scholars; in fact, the final two decades of his life, which these poems reflected, have sometimes seemed barely worth mentioning by them. Yet to readers interested in Whitman's entire career, as man and poet, many of these poems have considerable fascination. They demonstrate the genuine success of the huge efforts of his earlier days to search for meanings beneath life's surface and to come to terms with death—involving the construction of his own positive belief-system, which guaranteed the individual's eternal existence. Walt accepted philosophically whatever distresses the realities of old age now inflicted upon him, and calmly, fearlessly, he watched death's approach. And there were certain compensations for a loss of physical vigor and high poetic ambitions: he gained a new perspective on his life and work, release from intense physical and emotional longings, and a sense of real accomplishment of the tasks he had set for himself. Whitman showed his autumnal, harvest-time mood in "Halcyon Days."

> Not from successful love alone,
> Nor wealth, nor honor'd middle age, nor victories of politics or war;
> But as life wanes, and all the turbulent passions calm,
> As gorgeous, vapory, silent hues cover the evening sky,
> As softness, fullness, rest, suffuse the frame, like fresher, balmier
> air,
> As the days take on a mellower light, and the apple at last hangs
> really finish'd and indolent-ripe on the tree,
> Then for the teeming quietest, happiest days of all!
> The brooding and blissful halcyon days!

Whitman's most ambitious offering in *November Boughs* was the essay "A Backward Glance O'er Traveled Roads," which he fashioned out of several articles previously written for magazine publication. Again he summarized his intentions in writing *Leaves of Grass,* and pondered his actual accomplishments, viewed some thirty years after the appearance of the book's first edition. "So here I sit," he reminisced, "gossiping in the early candlelight of old-age—I and my book—casting backward glances over our travel'd road."

Whitman considered the book that contained his literary immortality—his "carte visite to the coming generations"—finished now. And although *Leaves of Grass* obviously had failed in the usual terms of success the poet did not complain: the difficult route he had taken was his own choice. "I bid neither for soft eulogies, big money returns, nor the approbation of existing schools and conventions," he said. At least he had his "small band of the dearest friends and upholders ever vouchsafed to man or cause"; and he could feel satisfied that "unstopp'd and unwarp'd by any influence outside the soul within me, I have had my say entirely my own way, and put it unerringly on record—the value thereof to be decided by time."

Whitman had always allied his book with democracy. Now he ventured to say that both the United States republic and his own poetry were basically experimental: only the test of time could prove or deny the value and endurance of each of them. *Leaves of Grass*, then, was a *"sortie*—whether to prove triumphant, and conquer its field of aim and escape and construction, nothing less than a hundred years from now can fully answer."

In composing his poems, Walt had responded to the challenges to poets being issued by both democracy and modern science: to make a new literary form different from the songs and myths of the past. He now admitted that he had undertaken far more than he had originally intended or envisaged—indeed, he might not have started this long and hard journey at all had he known what it would involve. He realized that the whole endeavor could hardly be fulfilled by any single artist.

But pioneer and revolutionist poet that he was, Walt had staked his claim in the new territory to which other brave spirits, representatives of the "poetic genius," must emigrate after him. The nineteenth century had changed the needs of art; imagination now should give "ultimate vivification to facts, to science, and to common lives."

Whitman acknowledged that his book derived from his own time and place, which had structured him and which he, in turn, reflected in his poems. "I know very well," he said, "that my *Leaves* could not possibly have emerged or been fashion'd or completed, from any other era than the latter half of the Nineteenth Century, nor any other land than democratic America, and from the absolute triumph of the National Union arms."

His project's experimental nature determined his artistic methods. He had put nothing in his poetry, he said, "for beauty's sake" only. Everything had a function, although it might not be obvious. He used "Suggestiveness": "I round and finish little, if anything; and could not, consistently, with my scheme. The reader will always have his or her part to do, just as much as I have had mine. I seek less to state or display any theme or thought, and more to bring you, reader, into the atmosphere of the theme or thought— there to pursue your own flight." And he cautioned would-be readers not to consider or judge his *Leaves* as a specimen of literature: "No one will get at my verses who insists upon viewing them as a literary performance . . . aiming mainly toward art or aestheticism."

Whitman considered the chief trait of any poet might be "the spirit he brings to the observation of Humanity and Nature." He declared that literature should not just "satisfy the intellect, or supply something polish'd and interesting, nor even to depict great passions, or persons or events." Its prime duty, he said, was to fill the reader "with vigorous and clean manliness, religiousness, and give him *good heart* as a radical possession and habit."

Behind all his thinking and writing from the beginning Whitman had a purpose: "To attempt some worthy record of that entire faith and acceptance . . . which is the foundation of moral America." He had wanted to "formulate a poem whose every thought or fact should directly or indirectly be or connive at an implicit belief in the wisdom, health, mystery, beauty of every process, every concrete object, every human or other existence, not only consider'd from the point of view of all, but of each." To describe this religious faith which permeated *Leaves of Grass*, Whitman said: "I fully believe in a clue and purpose in Nature, entire and several; and that invisible spiritual results, just as real and definite as the visible, eventuate all concrete life and all materialism, through Time."

Leaves of Grass, Whitman declared, was "the outcropping of my own emotional and other personal nature—an attempt, from first to last, to put a *Person,* a human being (myself, in the latter half of the Nineteenth Century, in America,) freely, fully and truly on record." His book should "emanate buoyancy and gladness" because it came from them—"and has been the comfort of my life since it was originally commenced."

Whitman finally offered his book as a "candidate for the future," which could fully understand and justify him—and grant him the literary immortality for which he yearned.

Walt Whitman's fairly active life was brought to a sudden halt in 1888, shortly after his sixty-ninth birthday, when he suffered another stroke. For some while Walt's doctors and friends expected his death at any moment; Dr. Bucke even made funeral arrangements. Then Whitman's basic stamina reasserted itself; the poet was to live on for almost four more years, although mostly confined to his upstairs room and in the constant care of a male nurse whose salary was paid by some of Walt's friends.

Whitman often had poetically charged a ship to bear his soul on its passage through space and time. Now he often felt that his own "ship" was not quite up to the awesome task. He certainly portrayed his own near-beached state in "The Dismantled Ship":

In some unused lagoon, some nameless bay,
On sluggish, lonesome waters, anchor'd near the shore,
An old, dismasted, gray and batter'd ship, disabled, done,
After free voyages to all the seas of earth, haul'd up at last and
        hawser'd tight,
Lies rusting, mouldering.

Walt knew he had to guard against allowing his own maladies, grievances, and depressions to enter into his poetry, but he let them in simply by considering them.

As I sit writing here, sick and grown old,
Not the least burden is that dullness of the years, querilities,
Ungracious glooms, aches, lethargy, constipation, whimpering
ennui,
May filter in my daily songs.

Chronic invalid though he was, Whitman still worked on his poems in his room, happy for such visitors as a gentle wind which wafted in to ease his bodily complaints, refresh his spirit, and remind him of the outdoor world he loved—as he told "To the Sun-set Breeze":

Ah, whispering, something again, unseen,
Where late this heated day thou enterest at my window, door,
Thou laving, tempering all, cool-freshing, gently vitalizing
Me, old, alone, sick, weak-down, melted-worn with sweat;
Thou, nestling, folding close and firm yet soft, companion better
than talk, book, art;

$$\bullet \qquad \bullet \qquad \bullet$$

I feel the sky, the prairie vast—I feel the mighty northern lakes,
I feel the ocean and the forest—somehow I feel the globe itself
swift-swimming in space . . .

Whitman was now aided in all matters by his young friend Horace Traubel, a bank clerk who became Whitman's volunteer secretary and reliable factotum. Traubel, an enthusiastic socialist who especially liked Walt's praises of the common man, helped Whitman complete *November Boughs* for its publication in late 1888. He ran errands, proofread, saw to details, and handled much of the poet's private and business correspondence. And without Traubel's invaluable assistance, Walt could never have put together the second volume of his old age's poetry and prose, *Good-Bye My Fancy,* published in 1891.

In his introduction to the new book, Walt frankly but facetiously wondered whether he might do better to "withhold (in this old age and paralysis of me) such little tags and fringe-dots (maybe specks, stains,) as follow a long dusty journey." And he freely and ingenuously admitted—agreeing with the critics of his time and afterwards—that he had probably "not been enough afraid of careless touches, from the first—and am not now—nor of parrot-like repetitions—nor platitudes and the commonplace." But maybe he was just "too democratic": each thought, each word, however insignificant or imperfect, somehow seemed to have its own right to exist in his pages.

Whitman knew that it was time for him "to silently retire." Indeed, there had never been a "loud call or market for my sort of poetic utterance." And he felt like "some hard-cased dilapidated grim ancient shell-fish or time-bang'd conch (no legs, utterly non-locomotive) cast up high and dry on the shore-sands, helpless to move anywhere—nothing left but behave myself quiet, and while away the days yet assign'd. . . ."

But for Walt, to live was to sing, to write—and certainly to publish too, whenever he could. And so he kept on with his small poems, the very activity of composing them helping to pass the time and to record the concluding years of the body and spirit which had created *Leaves of Grass*.

"L. of G.'s Purport," which appeared in *Good-Bye My Fancy*, now summed up what Whitman's big book had been about.

> Not to exclude or demarcate, or pick out evils from their formidable
>   masses (even to expose them,)
> But add, fuse, complete, extend—and celebrate the immortal and
>   the good.
>
> Haughty this song, its words and scope,
> To span vast realms of space and time,
> Evolution—the cumulative—growths and generations.
>
> Begun in ripen'd youth and steadily pursued,
> Wandering, peering, dallying with all—war, peace, day and night
>   absorbing,
> Never even for one brief hour abandoning my task,
> I end it here in sickness, poverty, and old age.
>
> I sing of life, yet mind me well of death:
> To-day shadowy Death dogs my steps, my seated shape, and has
>   for years—
> Draws sometimes close to me, as face to face.

In recent years death had already taken people close to Walt. Anne Gilchrist had preceded him to join with death's mystic ocean. Jeff's daughter Mannahatta had died in 1888, Jeff himself three years later. And in 1891 Walt's fierce defender, William D. O'Connor, had been removed from the ranks of the Whitmanites. No wonder, then, that Walt felt death's presence nearby, especially since his health had deteriorated. Needing to confront closely his own impending mortality, Walt wrote the poem, "Good-Bye My Fancy!"

> Good-bye my Fancy!
> Farewell dear mate, dear love!
> I'm going away, I know not where,
> Or to what fortune, or whether I may ever see you again,
> So Good-bye my Fancy.
>
> Now for my last—let me look back a moment;
> The slower fainter ticking of the clock is in me,
> Exit, nightfall, and soon the heart-thud stopping.
>
> Long have we liv'd, joy'd, caress'd together;
> Delightful!—now separation—Good-bye my Fancy.

At first the poet had thought that death would separate him forever from his "Fancy"—the poetic muse or inspiration inseparable from his soul, who had been his lifetime companion, closer to him than any living person. But while bidding adieu, he realized that death would not take him away from that inner voice which had urged him, through long and trying years, to see visions, hear songs, and compose the poems of *Leaves of Grass*. The poet and his Fancy together would journey into the unknown place:

> Yet let me not be too hasty,
> Long indeed have we lived, slept, filter'd, become really blended
>   into one;
> Then if we die together, (yes, we'll remain one,)
> If we go anywhere we'll go together to meet what happens,
> May-be we'll be better off and blither, and learn something,

May-be it is yourself now really ushering me to the true songs,
(who knows?)
May-be it is you the mortal knob really undoing, turning—so now
finally,
Good-bye—and hail! my Fancy.

All the while Horace Traubel visited Walt, sometimes several
times a day, he was recording his conversations with him, duti-
fully noting his every mood or physical condition. Horace became
a Boswell to Whitman's Dr. Johnson; his literary labors have appeared at intervals in five large volumes called *With Walt Whitman in Camden* (with material enough left for perhaps three
more volumes).

In his long, diary-type accounts of Whitman's twilight years
Traubel quoted the poet's rambling talks, pithy or cranky remarks, and reminiscences; told innumerable anecdotes; gave
verbatim records of visits from other Whitman friends. And he
reproduced many letters which the old poet, after poking around
with his cane at the loose piles of papers scattered about the
floor, would finally locate and then present to him, apparently
knowing that the busy disciple would do something with them
someday.

This was miscellaneous stuff, sandwiched all together into what
might be called "Portrait of the Poet as a Sick Old Man." Whitman scholars frequently draw upon Traubel's tomes for information about Walt's last years and for his opinions (often deliberately
sought by Traubel) on a variety of matters current or in the past.

Horace Traubel was among the small but growing band of
Whitman devotees who gathered around him, tending to treat
him like an oracle or sage. They revered his *Leaves of Grass* as
the modern Bible; one man even showed Walt how he could
quote outright any passage or poem in it.

In his poems Whitman had sometimes cautioned his readers
against hero-worshipping him; he apprised them of his faults,
encouraged "straying" from him, and even warned that evil might
result from contact with him. As if to gain some good from the
savage criticism which had always accompanied the publication

of his poetry, he seemed to welcome foes and adverse opinions more than adulatory followers—as he had expressed in "Stronger Lessons":

> Have you learn'd lessons only of those who admired you, and were
> tender with you, and stood aside for you?
> Have you not learn'd great lessons from those who reject you, and
> brace themselves against you? or who treat you
> with contempt, or dispute the passage with you?

Understandably, however, in Walt's final years—when he was confined, weak, and often in pain—he needed and appreciated the reverential attentions of his friends. On his best sociable days he felt confident at last that his lifework would endure. Relaxed, radiating his special "magnetism" upon the assemblage of disciples and surrogate-sons, Walt truly seemed to have become the mythical poet he had set out to be four decades earlier. He also resembled the picture of himself as a venerable and beloved patriarch projected years before in "A Song of Joys":

> O the old manhood of me, my noblest joy of all!
> My children and grand-children, my white hair and beard,
> My largeness, calmness, majesty, out of the long stretch of my life.

Whitman's work was not quite over yet. Again, with Horace Traubel's help, he prepared a new edition of *Leaves of Grass*— the ninth and final one, still following the plan of the 1881 edition and adding on the "Good-Bye My Fancy!" poems in a second annex. This "deathbed" edition, as it is often called, is usually considered the "official" version because the author sanctioned it. "In the long run the world will do as it pleases with the book," Whitman wrote at the time. "I am determined to have the world know what I was pleased to do." (Thirteen poems composed afterwards, gathered under the title of "Old Age Echoes," are sometimes added in a supplementary section as a third "annex.")

In the prime of his manhood a quarter-century before, Walt Whitman had written his own "Last Invocation," indicating the way in which he hoped his death would come.

At the last, tenderly,
From the walls of the powerful fortress'd house,
From the clasp of the knitted locks, from the keep of the well-
                    closed doors,
Let me be wafted.

Let me glide noiselessly forth;
With the key of softness unlock the locks—with a whisper,
Set ope the doors O soul.

Tenderly—be not impatient,
(Strong is your hold O mortal flesh,
Strong is your hold O love.)

Although Whitman's death was longer and harder, something of this gentle passing did happen. In December of 1891, pneumonia collapsed one of Walt's lungs and left the other scarcely functioning. Other bodily functions too barely operated; yet the poet's stout heart beat on. Totally bedridden, expected to depart momentarily, Walt still grasped life, tenuously but tenaciously. His body seemed to possess a fierce, unconscious will all its own, amazing friends and doctors alike. But at dusk on March 26, 1892, as a light rain pattered down on Camden's rooftops, Walt Whitman died, at the age of seventy-two. His soul was off at long last on that long-anticipated outward-bound journey.

At the news of Whitman's death, newspapers around the nation printed sober and searching appraisals of his life and poetry. As never before, Whitman was publicly acknowledged as a person and poet of a definite and meritorious character—someone uniquely and proudly American, the like of whom would never again be seen. Ironically—as often happens to persons who offer themselves or their works to the public—only death brought Walt the beginning of a popular recognition which he had longed to gain during his own lifetime.

From near and far, people who had known the poet personally or through his poems, or those who were simply curious, gathered in a large crowd in front of his little house on Mickle Street. Several thousand were admitted to view the body of the white-bearded old man who would one day be known as America's greatest poet.

Whitman's friends arranged for a simple funeral ceremony at the nearby Harleigh Cemetery. (Several years before, a friend discovered that Walt had secretly ordered a vault of his own design to be erected on a hillside there, intending it to enclose not only his own mortal remains but those of his family too. He was satisfied with *Leaves of Grass* as a fitting repository for his spirit; apparently he also wanted to guarantee a handsome, lasting interment for his body.)

No minister delivered the customary eulogy to the deceased. Instead, a few of Whitman's friends recited passages from some of the world's great literature—and among them were lines from "Out of the Cradle Endlessly Rocking."

At the ceremony's close, the renowned free-thinking orator Robert Ingersoll, who had known and admired Walt Whitman in his last years, summed up the feelings of those who felt the peculiar power and fascination of *Leaves of Grass*. "He has lived, he has died," said Ingersoll, "and death is less terrible than it was before. Thousands and millions will walk down into the 'dark valley of the shadow' holding Walt Whitman by the hand. Long after we are dead the brave words he has spoken will sound like trumpets to the dying."

But most of all it was to the living that Walt Whitman had sung his wondrous songs. Through them—generation following generation upon life's open road—Walt would live anew, again and again, as each discovered his chants, jubilant or melancholy for the prevailing mood.

A bird's songs cease when it dies, but a man's may endure for as long as people have eyes for reading and ears for listening.

Strong and sweet shall their tongues be,
poems and materials of poems shall come
from their lives, they shall be makers
and finders . . .

XII

STRONG AND SWEET SHALL THEIR

TONGUES BE

(An Epilogue)

After his death, Walt Whitman's fame continued to grow, partly because his poetry proved remarkably adaptable to the different social environments and preoccupying interests of succeeding generations. However, the people who are merely acquainted with his name or can recognize his picture far outnumber those who actually know and read his poems. Whitman never became a "popular" poet, as his contemporary Longfellow was; he has the reputation of being difficult.

Whitman probably has been primarily a "writer's writer." His great influence upon other authors, either stylistically or through sheer inspiration, has gained him some of the immortality he coveted. It is difficult to imagine modern American Literature without Walt Whitman's presence: he straddles it like a Paul Bunyan. Indeed, if Whitman had not existed, it might have been necessary to invent him—which seems to be exactly what Walter Whitman, Jr. did. He has gone unrivaled in what he tried to do and in what he actually accomplished. As a poet he was grandly

343

public and yet exquisitely private; his talents were epical, lyric, and philosophical.

Whitman explored the terrain, broke the soil roughly, and planted the first seeds for twentieth-century writing in America. Better than anyone else he considered those who were to come after him, finding a Whitman-altered landscape which they in turn made over for their own needs and uses. In his poem "Mediums," Walt Whitman forecast the American prophets yet to come, among whom would be his ideal writers:

> They shall arise in the States,
> They shall report Nature, laws, physiology, and happiness,
> They shall illustrate Democracy and the kosmos.
>
> •   •   •
>
> Strong and sweet shall their tongues be, poems and materials of
>   poems shall come from their lives, they shall be
>   makers and finders,
> Of them and of their works shall emerge divine conveyers, to
>   convey gospels,
> Characters, events, retrospections, shall be convey'd in gospels,
>   trees, animals, waters, shall be convey'd,
> Death, the future, the invisible faith, shall all be convey'd.

Writers following Whitman into new territories he had partly cleared for them planted their own seeds, which sprouted new kinds of foliage—but usually acknowledged their debt to *Leaves of Grass*. (Sometimes they addressed poems to him as if to invoke his muse and then show the changes in his beloved land.) Whitman's influence—whether on ideas or feelings or free-verse style—worked directly upon such American poets as Edgar Lee Masters, Carl Sandburg, Hart Crane, Vachel Lindsay, Robinson Jeffers, Stephen Vincent Benét, and William Carlos Williams. The latter generously called *Leaves of Grass* "a book as important as we are likely to see in the next thousand years, especially a book written by an American." In recent years, Whitman has been taken up by various writers in the "Beat" and "Hippie" coteries.

Whitman's effect on writers has also been noticed in prose, detectable in such diverse novelists as Theodore Dreiser, Thomas

Wolfe, John Steinbeck, D. H. Lawrence, and Jack Kerouac. Certainly, too, Whitman has kept several generations of scholars busy with doctoral dissertations or lifetime research into every conceivable aspect of his life and writings. The entries on "Whitman, Walt" in the card catalogue of any large university library may run into the hundreds and occupy several trays.

For a long while Whitman was esteemed abroad more than at home. To foreigners he seemed the veritable voice of American democracy, and through the years his poems have appeared in many translations. What discriminating and self-conscious Americans considered bombastic, repulsive, embarrassing, egotistical, or crude in Whitman's poetry (and sometimes about their own nationality as well) the Europeans of liberal cast tended to find resolute, refreshing, honest, vital, intriguing, inspirational. They were attracted to Whitman because he fleshed out their own idealized conceptions of democracy, conceived in Europe but given birth in America.

As with many artists with distinct characteristics, Whitman's reputation has fluctuated. Sometimes he has been the center of adulation; at other times he is ignored or rudely pushed to the perimeter of critical recognition. Those who adhere to Whitman, fond even of his faults, perennially squabble with those who disdainfully deny that his prosody made valid poetry. Formalistic poets and the "New Critics" of the twenties and thirties formulated a modern, intellectual, finely wrought aestheticism; naturally they discredited Whitman. Actually, they owed him a debt of gratitude if just for giving them somebody and something to react against—as, seemingly, every new generation of creators must do.

Ezra Pound and T. S. Eliot disclaimed any connection at all with Whitman (both becoming expatriates, as if wishing to put greater distance still between them); they and their supporters attacked him as a bad poet who had a severely detrimental influence upon poetry by encouraging others to forsake all attention to form. Yet Whitman had prepared English-language poetry for their own experimental versifying by diminishing the usual expectation of rhymes and set rhythms, by using vernacular words, by composing poems with complex background sources, and by suggesting that in understanding poetry the reader had his own work to do too.

Ezra Pound eventually admitted Walt Whitman's importance and usefulness. "He *is* America," Pound declared—tempering all praises with insults. "His crudity is an exceedingly great stench, but it *is* America. He is the hollow place in the rock that echoes with his time. . . . He is a genius because he has vision of what he is and of his function. He knows that he is a beginning and not a classically finished work." Pound also called Whitman "the first great man to write in the language of his people." And he composed a poem for him:

> I make a pact with you, Walt Whitman—
> I have detested you long enough.
> I come to you as a grown child
> Who has had a pig-headed father;
> I am old enough now to make friends.
>
> •   •   •
>
> We have one sap and one root—
> Let there be commerce between us.

The English novelist D. H. Lawrence, the major proponent of expressing sexuality in literature, recognized his personal debt to the pioneering Whitman in "Studies in Classic American Literature." He judged Whitman "the greatest and the first and the only American teacher." Although he found fault with aspects of Whitman's poetry, Lawrence acclaimed his courage and forcefulness. He especially valued Whitman's insight that art's essential function was moral—not aesthetic, decorative, or recreational—"A passionate, implicit morality . . . which changes the blood, rather than the mind." "Changes the blood first," Lawrence went on; "the mind follows later, in the wake." (Like Whitman, Lawrence linked sex with morality, not immorality.)

The disciples who had begun to gather around Walt in his old age multiplied and spread out in diverse directions after he died. These ardent followers did not heed Whitman's request in "Myself and Mine":

> I call to the world to distrust the accounts of my friends, but listen
>   to my enemies, as I myself do,
> I charge you forever reject those who would expound me, for I
>   cannot expound myself,
> I charge that there be no theory or school founded out of me,
> I charge you to leave all free, as I have left all free.

In the early part of this century, those who were overthrowing the traditional restrictive standards of heterosexual behavior and its expression in art took the Whitman of "Song of Myself" and "Children of Adam" as their eloquent spokesman. Then, advocates of a new "third sex" hailed the poet of "Calamus" as a prime sponsor. Meanwhile, Whitman's quasi-religious philosophy appealed to people who had left the conventional churches yet still wanted to consider ethics, celebrate life's myriad miracles, and find reassuring explanations for death. And national expansionists, harking back to America's great past and urging conquests of new lands to lie beneath Old Glory's sway, easily found jingoistic passages in Whitman's poetry that approvingly echoed their territorial imperatives. On the other hand, those who hoped all the world's peoples could unite and live together harmoniously and peaceably could use Whitman's words in their humanistic slogans. At the same time, "Comrade" Whitman had become an international "patron-poet" of all kinds of political radicals advocating revolutions to improve the status of the common workingmen; they invoked Walt's inflammatory lines to endorse their activistic programs and found a practical application for his mystical concept of the "adhesive" bonds uniting man and man in society.

Altogether, these and other alliances, each claiming Whitman as its own, assembled a bewildering portrait of the poet: a cubistic personality divided into at least a dozen different facets. Whitman thought he had taken care of all accusations of inconsistency by saying—

> Do I contradict myself?
> Very well then I contradict myself,
> (I am large, I contain multitudes.)

But he could hardly halt the confusion over his intentions and meanings. And so, as Stephen Vincent Benét described the scene in "Ode to Walt Whitman"—

> ... each disciple
> Jealously guards his own particular store
> Of acorns fallen from the oak's abundance
> And spits and scratches at the other gatherers.

Still, there are plenty of acorns left on that great oak tree for those who will climb to get them.

The United States has changed considerably since Whitman knew it, both physically and spiritually; yet he would find it recognizable for its virtues as well as its defects. All his life, Whitman worked to make his nation's future good. If the present time is less than perfect, he is not to blame: he issued warnings often enough. Setbacks and failings he expected in democracy's progression, but he knew they would be temporary and remediable as long as the American people kept faith in their cherished dreams of humanity's destiny.

In our own time, Whitman can offer much by way of guidelines and inspiration to the new generation, who seem more like Walt Whitman's own progeny than any others that have come after him. Like him, they combine and somehow assimilate many contradictory inclinations and attitudes. In Whitman they will often find anticipations and fascinating reflections of their own searchings, responses, concerns, and commitments. He may convince some of them that he had them particularly in mind when he wrote "Full of Life Now" for his *Leaves of Grass:*

> Full of life now, compact, visible,
> I, forty years old the eighty-third year of the States,
> To one a century hence or any number of centuries hence,
> To you yet unborn these, seeking you.
>
> When you read these I that was visible am become invisible,
> Now it is you, compact, visible, realizing my poems, seeking me,
> Fancying how happy you were if I could be with you and become
> your comrade;

Be it as if I were with you. (Be not too certain but I am now with
you.)

Those who look for further tangible locations for Walt Whitman's vital and pervasive presence in America may visit his birthplace house on Long Island, his own little home on Mickle Street
in Camden, and his burial vault. But above all, Whitman's enduring spirit walks robustly among the crowds in cities, sings and
soars with the birds, hears the fall of surf upon the sand—and
rejoices in the eternally sprouting grass.

SELECTED BIBLIOGRAPHY

I. Walt Whitman's Own Writings

Calamus, ed. R. M. Bucke. Boston, 1897. (Whitman's letters to Peter Doyle.)

The Complete Poetry and Prose of Walt Whitman, ed. Malcolm Cowley. (2 vols.) Garden City, New York, 1954.

The Correspondence of Walt Whitman, ed. Edwin H. Miller. (5 vols.) New York, 1961-1969.

Faint Clews & Indirections, ed. Clarence Gohdes and Rollo G. Silver. Durham, N. C., 1949. (Manuscripts of Walt Whitman and his family.)

The Gathering of the Forces, ed. Cleveland Rodgers and John Black. (2 vols.) New York, 1920. (Material written by Whitman as editor of the *Brooklyn Daily Eagle*.)

I Sit and Look Out, ed. Emory Holloway and Vernolian Schwarz. New York, 1932. (Material written by Whitman as editor of the *Brooklyn Daily Times*.)

Leaves of Grass: Comprehensive Reader's Edition, ed. Harold Blodgett and Sculley Bradley. New York, 1965. (Provides many footnotes helpful in reading the poems.)

Leaves of Grass: Inclusive Edition, ed. Emory Holloway. New York, 1924. (Gives all versions of the poems, with dates of alterations.)

The Letters of Anne Gilchrist and Walt Whitman, ed. Thomas B. Harned. New York, 1918.

Memoranda During the War and Death of Abraham Lincoln, ed. Roy P. Basler. Indiana, 1962.

New York Dissected: A Sheaf of Recently Discovered Newspaper Articles by the Author of Leaves of Grass, ed. Emory Holloway and Ralph Adimari. New York, 1936.

The Portable Walt Whitman, ed. Mark Van Doren. New York, 1945. (Includes selections from *Leaves of Grass* and *Specimen Days*, and the 1855 Preface, *Democratic Vistas*, and "A Backward Glance O'er Travel'd Roads.")

Walt Whitman of the New York Aurora: Editor at Twenty-two, ed. Joseph J. Rubin and C. H. Brown. State College, Pa., 1950. (Material written by Whitman as editor of the *Aurora*.)

Walt Whitman's Civil War, ed. Walter Lowenfels. New York, 1960. (Poems, letters, and descriptions bearing on the Civil War.)

Walt Whitman's Workshop, ed. Clifton J. Furness. Cambridge, Mass., 1928. (Shows the evolution of a number of poems.)

Whitman's "Song of Myself"—Origin, Growth, Meaning, ed. James E. Miller, Jr. New York, 1964.

The Wound Dresser, ed. R. M. Bucke. Boston, 1898. (Whitman's letters to his mother during the Civil War.)

II. Biographies, Reminiscences, and Critical Studies

Allen, Gay Wilson. *The Solitary Singer: A Critical Biography of Walt Whitman*. New York, 1955.

——. *Walt Whitman Abroad*. Syracuse, N. Y., 1955.

——. *Walt Whitman as Man, Poet, and Legend*. Illinois, 1961.

——. *Walt Whitman Handbook*. Chicago, 1946.

Arvin, Newton. *Whitman*. New York, 1938.

Asselineau, Roger. *The Evolution of Walt Whitman*. (2 vols.) Cambridge, Mass., 1961.

Barrus, Clara. *Whitman and Burroughs, Comrades*. Boston, 1931.

Benét, Stephen Vincent. "Ode to Walt Whitman." *New Poems*. New York, 1936.

Brooks, Van Wyck. *The Times of Melville and Whitman*. New York, 1953.

Bucke, R. M. *Walt Whitman*. Philadelphia, 1883.

Burroughs, John. *Whitman: A Study*. Boston, 1896.

Canby, Henry Seidel. *Walt Whitman, An American*. Boston, 1943.

Carpenter, Edward. *Days with Walt Whitman*. London, 1906.

Chase, Richard. *Walt Whitman*. Minnesota, 1961.

——. *Walt Whitman Reconsidered*. New York, 1955.

Deutsch, Babette. *Walt Whitman: Builder for America*. New York, 1941.

Dutton, Geoffrey. *Whitman*. New York, 1961.

Ghiselin, Brewster (ed.). *The Creative Process*. Berkeley, Calif., 1952.

Hindus, Milton (ed.). *Leaves of Grass, One Hundred Years After*. Stanford, Calif., 1955.

Holloway, Emory. *Free and Lonesome Heart*. New York, 1960.

——. *Whitman: An Interpretation in Narrative*. New York, 1926.

Jackson, Holbrook. *Dreamers of Dreams*. London, 1948.

Kennedy, W. S. *The Fight of a Book for the World*. Massachusetts, 1926.

Masters, Edgar Lee. *Whitman*. New York, 1937.

Mathiessen, Francis O. *American Renaissance*. New York, 1941.

Miller, Edwin Haviland. *Walt Whitman's Poetry: A Psychological Journey*. New York, 1968.

Miller, Jr., James E. *A Critical Guide to Leaves of Grass*. Chicago, 1957.

Molinoff, Katherine. *Some Notes on Whitman's Family*. Brooklyn, 1941.

Pearce, Roy H. (ed.). *Whitman: A Collection of Critical Essays*. New Jersey, 1962.

Perry, Bliss. *Walt Whitman, His Life and Work*. Boston, 1906.

Shephard, Esther. *Walt Whitman's Pose*. New York, 1938.

Stoutenberg, Adrien, and Baker, Laura Nelson. *Listen America: A Life of Walt Whitman*. New York, 1968.

Traubel, Horace L. *With Walt Whitman in Camden*. (Vol. I, Boston, 1906; Vol. II, New York, 1908; Vol. III, New York, 1914; Vol. IV., Philadelphia, 1953; Vol. V, Illinois, 1963.)

Traubel, Horace L., *et al*. *In Re Walt Whitman*. Philadelphia, 1893.

Winwar, Frances. *American Giant: Walt Whitman and His Times*. New York, 1941.

SOURCES OF POETRY QUOTATIONS

INDEX